NOTES ON THE METHODOLOGY OF SCIENTIFIC RESEARCH

NOTES ON THE METHODOLOGY OF SCIENTIFIC RESEARCH

Walter B. Weimer
The Pennsylvania State University

 LAWRENCE ERLBAUM ASSOCIATES, PUBLISHERS
1979   Hillsdale, New Jersey

DISTRIBUTED BY THE HALSTED PRESS DIVISION OF
JOHN WILEY & SONS
New York   Toronto   London   Sydney

Lawrence Erlbaum Associates, Inc., Publishers
62 Maria Drive
Hillsdale, New Jersey 07642

Distributed solely by Halsted Press Division
John Wiley & Sons, Inc., New York

Library of Congress Cataloging in Publication Data

Weimer, Walter B
  Notes on the methodology of scientific research.

  Includes bibliographical references and indexes.
  1. Research—Methodology. 2. Science—Philosophy.
3. Knowledge, Theory of. I. Title.
Q180.55.M4W44   507'.2   78-31093
ISBN 0-470-26650-3

Printed in the United States of America

Contents

Preface

This essay is an elaboration and a considerable expansion upon outline notes prepared for distribution to participants of the Summer Institute program of the Center for Research in Human Learning of the University of Minnesota during 1970. Its purpose is to provide an overview of the major parts of epistemology, philosophy and sociology of science, psychology, and rhetoric that address the methodology of scientific research. Our knowledge of the nature of science and its growth has increased greatly in recent years, and traditional conceptions of science and its methodology have been examined, found wanting, and are in large part being abandoned. New conceptions of the nature of knowledge and the means of its acquisition, even of rationality itself, are emerging. When viewed from the proper perspective, they provide a novel and informative framework from which to view both science and philosophy. The chapters that follow attempt to characterize the heretofore dominant metatheory of science, a position I call *justificationism,* and then concentrate on its inadequacies both by exhibiting criticisms that arise within the justificationist metatheory and also criticisms from outside the received view. Further, these chapters single out strong and weak points in metatheoretical alternatives to the received view to indicate in what directions future research into the methodology of scientific research must lead. With this as background, we briefly examine the justificationist nature of "philosophical" positions within the psychological sciences, especially with regard to statistics in research. Finally, there are some indications as to how it will be necessary to reformulate methodology in the psychological sciences to bring it in line with nonjustificational approaches.

This essay is an argument: Its fundamental objective is to urge considerable change in our perception of a seemingly familiar phenomenon, the nature of science. What it argues is that the vast majority of contemporary as well as historical thinkers have pictured the nature of science (and, indeed, all rational inquiry) in a manner that is fundamentally incorrect. Because of the tremendous power of the tacit conceptual framework from which such theorists operate, they are constrained to conceive of science in such a manner that its practice cannot be explained in (what they accept as) a rational manner. Justificationism is a self-stultifying metatheory—successful application of its tenets guarantees that even its most brilliant practitioners will succeed only in exhibiting the impossibility of success in their self-appointed tasks. Skepticism and conventionalism are the only ends available within justificationism. Existentialism is thus a paradigmatic justificational philosophy, as are the continental hermeneutic approaches now becoming popular in America.

What may be surprising is that other approaches—to all intents, polar opposites to the torpor of existentialism and the tedium of hermeneutic analysis—are in the same boat. Logical Positivism and logical empiricism are perhaps the most self-consciously "positive" philosophies ever to pretend to explicate the essential nature of rational inquiry, and their impact upon the budding "soft" sciences has been pervasive enough to ensure that no alternatives are taken seriously (at least in the English-speaking world). But the logical "-isms" are equally paradigm exemplars of justificationism, and the only thing that staves off skepticism in that tradition is the proliferation of technical puzzles that allow its practitioners to hop from tangent to tangent without ever addressing a genuine issue. Because of the virtual synonymity of logical empiricism with "philosophy of science" to researchers in the psychological sciences, I have chosen to examine recent empiricist philosophies in explicating and criticizing justificationism. Were they more representative of common sentiment within the research communities to which this essay is primarily addressed, we could just as easily have examined phenomenological traditions, the so-called hermeneutic–dialectic philosophies, conventionalist strategisms such as pragmatism, even the "new" experientialism that attempts to revivify the oriental "ways of life" as epistemology and philosophy of science. All these positions (and more), instead of being alternatives, are actually variants of the same metatheory; and once it is understood why justificationism is to be rejected, it is easy to see the inadequacies of these approaches. Due to the schematic nature of the essay that follows, I can do no more than state that as a claim and as food for thought for the interested reader to pursue. Nonetheless, it is obvious that the chapters that follow must ignore numerous important problems—and that requires no apology but does require acknowledgment. The easiest way to dismiss a challenge to one's presuppositions is to assume that it is directed toward someone else's position and then to ignore it as inapplicable. I hope to undermine that strategy at the outset by calling attention to it and stating explicitly that it does not apply.

Some brief historical and autobiographical remarks may set the stage for a better understanding of this essay and may prevent one possible misunderstanding of its nature and scope. The two greatest influences upon both this essay and contemporary philosophy of science are the works of Thomas Kuhn and of Karl Popper and his students. Much contemporary literature is only intelligible in terms of its violent reaction, either pro or con, toward positions associated with these theorists. As a student reading *The logic of scientific discovery, Conjectures and refutations,* and *The structure of scientific revolutions* roughly 15 years ago, I was puzzled about why there should be so much furor raised by what seemed to me to be statements of the obvious. To me it was intuitively obvious that Kuhn's account of science as alternating periods of normal and revolutionary activity was extremely informative, and Popper's arguments against "inductivism" were devastating. What struck me was the degree to which these (and other) views were systematically misunderstood, by both protagonist and antagonist alike. It became clear to me that there was a "paradigm clash" of philosophical frameworks involved; and this essay is in part the result of my attempt to understand how Kuhn and Popper could be so consonant on some points, dissonant on others, and nonetheless remain diametrically opposed to the vast majority of other philosophers and methodologists.

This task, although easily stated, becomes formidable upon application: Like Plato's paradox in the *Meno,* it seemingly requires one to know everything before one can know anything. An immediate complication arose when I studied what I have come to call the Popperian church—instead of a coherent philosophical position, one finds a lightly disguised squabble of alley cats. Popper's students, taught to be critical, search for something worthy of criticism and find Popper's philosophy their best target. Not surprisingly, their reward for challenging Popper is excommunication— witness Feyerabend, Bartley, and Lakatos. Paradoxically, the only remaining Popperians are the uncritical ones content to preach the orthodox line.

Gradually I learned that examination of detail was not the answer and returned to my initial attempts to overview the framework behind the surface clashes. Things began to fall into place as a result of Imre Lakatos's lectures defending his revised version of Popperian philosophy against Kuhn. I began to see that what Lakatos called justificationism was not just a synonym for inductivism (as he was then using the term). Then I realized that W. W. Bartley III was light years ahead of the other Popperians and that *The retreat to commitment* contained the most defensible Popperian philosophy available. What I have finally done is to elevate justificationism from Bartley's initial usage (referring to a conception of criticism) to the status of a metatheory of rational inquiry. To understand a phenomenon we must first do something that appears paradoxical—turn our backs upon it, to distantiate it from our experience in order to make it amenable to understanding in abstract conceptual thought. Bartley and Lakatos had grasped different surface structure manifestations of justificationism; but perhaps because it was not required for their purposes, they did not see beyond the surface to the essential unity of the metatheoretical position underlying it. In one sense, all I have done is take Bartley's insight to a more inclusive level of analysis.

From this point of view, the reason why Kuhn and Popper agree was obvious: Both represent nonjustificational positions in opposition to the received view. It is equally clear why they disagree and why the disagreement is perceived by all concerned as so important: The clash is between alternative nonjustificational philosophies that have little in common beyond their opposition to justificationism.

Now we are in a position to see how this essay differs from being just one more instance of the new pastime of "correcting" or "improving" upon Popper's and Kuhn's views. There are many criticisms of both theorists in the pages that follow, as well as considerable utilization (or presupposition) of their contributions. But the important clash that presages understanding of particular nonjustificational philosophies is the metatheoretical one between justificationism and nonjustificationism. Without an understanding of what the essential unity of justificational thought consists of, and of the self-stultifying nature of that metatheoretical framework, little progress is likely to be forthcoming in our understanding of the import of the controversy between Popperians, Kuhn, and the few other nonjustificational theorists. If this essay succeeds, it will provide one framework from which to understand both.

One thing that this essay must not be considered is an exhaustive summary of all relevant research. Like most fields the philosophy and methodology of science is suffering from severe information overload, occasioned not only by renewed interest in the area but also by a publication explosion (chiefly consisting, in my opinion, of juvenilia and trivia) that appears to be due to the prevailing publish or perish atmosphere in academia. What I have found that I need as a professional, and my students are most aided by as apprentices, is a way of organizing and conceptualizing the field so that one need not be overwhelmed by the literature. Rather than be buried in detail I have attempted to overview and organize so as not to be caught up in the impossible task of exhaustive summarization. Thus I cite, and sometimes quote extensively from, a restricted set of sources that I regard as the most important to that task.

Two dangers are inherent in any attempt to conceptualize a large domain in this fashion, and they must be acknowledged at the outset. First, such a conceptual overview may be wrong, in that it simply does not adequately explain the field in question. Second, even if adequate in an abstract conceptual sense it may be useless practically because it does not apply to the literature. What is required to assess both conceptual adequacy and practical utility is an examination of detail, at least in selected areas. The material in the Appendix (Chapters 9–12) attempts to examine enough detail in certain areas to indicate the merit and utility of the analysis presented in the first eight chapters. While this style of presentation is far from ideal, it appears to be the least objectionable compromise. Like Kuhn, I see minimal utility in either data or theory alone; one must instead learn from their admixture in exemplary puzzles and their solutions.

Walter B. Weimer

1 A Framework for the Understanding of Science

The vast majority of contemporary and historical thinkers—whether philosophers, scientists, theologians, artists, or whatever—share the essentials of a metatheory of rational inquiry and behavior that, elaborating ideas in Bartley (1962), I call justificationism. We must characterize this metatheory and its implications to show the underlying unity of countless otherwise apparently different positions; that is, we must exhibit the *common deep structure* of justificationism underlying the chaotic diversity of "received view" positions in philosophy, theology, art, even the theory of rationality and rational inquiry itself.

First the concept of a "metatheory" must be defined and clarified. A metatheory is a *generative* conceptual scheme that enables one to deal with *any conceivable instance* of phenomena falling within its domain. It is a "productive" or "creative" schema that provides an explanation for or a perspective from which to view the occurrence of anything within its domain. It is a framework to which anything that can be conceived or discovered in phenomena can be assimilated. It is thus the ultimate framework that renders intelligible past and present knowledge and provides a rationale for future inquiry. It is the ultimate point of view from which inquiry originates and to which conceptualization returns. Metatheories are background conceptual frameworks from which particular substantive theories originate and develop, but they do not lead to the "deduction" of substantive theories. Particular substantive theories are *consonant* with the metatheoretical framework in which they are embedded rather than being (deductive) *consequences* of it. Thus metatheories may provide a rationale for conflicting substantive theories—they rationalize many disparate surface-structure phenomena by being the common deep structure underlying them.

1

A central thesis of this book is that it is more profitable to examine alternative metatheories of a domain (such as our chief concern—science), their presuppositions and ramifications, than to examine traditional philosophical theories or "world views" such as empiricism, rationalism, or idealism. This is because *all such traditional positions*—philosophical world views, world hypotheses, religions, and more—*are variations of one and the same metatheory*. In short, the traditional distinctions between "philosophies" are largely epiphenomenal: They are surface-level differences between essentially similar positions that share a common deep conceptual structure. All traditional philosophies are *generically related* in the sense that they are variants of the same metatheory.

FOUR PROBLEMS CENTRAL TO THE UNDERSTANDING OF SCIENCE

Granted that we are attempting to understand conceptions of science as they reflect metatheoretical principles, it is convenient to examine, in order to attempt to reconstruct philosophical thought upon the scientific endeavor, four problematic areas essential to understanding the nature of science. These problems are:

1. *The quest for a theory of rational inference.*   The key feature of science is that its propositions are meant to apply to cases that have not been examined in the formulation of its generalizations. Science attempts to formulate propositions that apply every-where, every-when. Thus, in formulating laws of nature, universal quantification is the rule: Laws are meant to apply anywhere and everywhere in the universe, without exception (unless they are specifically about particular spatial and temporal domains). Thus the problem of *inductive inference*, its nature and its justification, is at the heart of problem 1.

2. *The theory and criteria of scientific growth or progress.*   We *all* "know" that Einstein's theory of dynamics is superior to Newton's theory, which is in turn (vastly) superior to nonscientific accounts such as astrology. But what are the criteria by which we judge one theory, such as Einstein's, to be more successful than its rivals and predecessors? The problem of the growth of scientific knowledge and its adequate characterization and explanation is at the heart of problem 2.

3. *The quest for a theory of pragmatic action.*   We know, from considerations of the finitude of the human situation, that *none* of our theories is actually "true." So if we grant that "all theories are lies but some are blacker than others," *how are we to go about ascertaining which of our a priori false theories is the least "black" of any given set of alternatives*? In

short, if everyone's theory is equally wrong (in the sense that all theories are known in advance to be false in the sense of being factually incorrect), why should I apprentice myself to Professor X's laboratory and research program rather than Professor Y's? The problem of *rational* action in scientific *practice* is at the heart of problem 3.

4. *The problem of intellectual honesty.* In order to practice science, to participate in ongoing research, we must suspend our doubts and questions concerning an (indefinitely large) number of things that constitute the "background knowledge" or presuppositions of the research we are undertaking. Thus, astronomy takes for granted the theories of optics underlying its lens telescopes and even more "abstruse" theories underlying radiotelemetry. But we can always ask: "When am I kidding myself in taking such and such proposition, theory, research program, etc. for granted?" Taking particular theories of rational inference and pragmatic action for granted, the problem of intellectual honesty becomes one of squaring the actual behavior of scientists with the theories to which they pledge allegiance. The heart of problem 4 is thus to square the practice of science by scientists with their theories of rational inference, growth, and pragmatic action.

Metatheories characteristically take stances on these four issues (and obviously, because they are generative systems, on an infinitude of others) that enable one to "evaluate" them. Now we must sketch the essentials of the received view position in order to understand how and why it must be rejected when we assess its answers to these four problem issues. To begin this task let us consider the first problem area in more depth.

THE QUEST FOR A THEORY OF RATIONALITY TO SUPPORT THE SCIENTIFIC ENTERPRISE

One enlightening perspective from which to view historical development of the philosophy of science is obtained by viewing the philosophy developed for science as a *quest for a theory of rationality* (or rational inquiry) that would render the practice of science both a rational form of inquiry and, hence, a legitimate source of knowledge. Classical epistemologies (literally—theories of knowledge) developed by philosophers concerned with the scientific endeavor have all been in response to one fundamental question: What is the nature and source of the rational authority or criterion to which appeal is addressed to justify scientific inference as a source of knowledge?

The quest for a theory of rationality, applied to the scientific endeavor, becomes the quest for an authoritative source of knowledge *that will justify science as a method* for the attainment of genuine knowledge. The specific question becomes: What is the nature of the rational authority that will justify scientific claims *as* knowledge claims? Historically, the two major classes of answers have been: (a) the rationalist (or intellectualist) answer: Rational authority lies in the intellect, and the justification of all knowledge claims (including those of science) lies in intellectual intuition; and (b) the empiricist answer: The rational authority that justifies all knowledge claims lies in the deliverances of sense. Thus empiricists justify their beliefs by appealing to sense observations and rationalists by appealing to intuition, but knowledge (as opposed to mere opinion) is dependent on justification in either philosophical position.

Both positions share crucial features in common: They assume implicitly that the only possible choice is between their source of intellectual authority as a guarantor of the knowledge disclosed by whatever sources (not just science) that are admissible on one hand and an inherently irrational picture of knowledge (and hence of science) on the other hand. A second feature that both approaches have in common is their attempt to avoid *what they perceive to be the limits of rationality* by establishing a *foundation for knowledge*. Both major brands of classic justificationism, and in modified form their contemporary or neojustificationist descendants, attempt to circumvent the alleged limits of rationality by establishing an authority as a foundation of knowledge. This enshrined authority then turns out to be the only reliable source of knowledge and the only means of avoiding the specter of irrationalism.

The problem that classic justificationist thinkers have perceived has to do with the possibility of an infinite regress in the justification of ultimate standards of rationality and hence of the ultimate source of knowledge. The problem is this: How can one justify knowledge claims, and indeed the rational way of life itself, without avoiding an infinite regress of justifications on one hand and a fideistic or dogmatic, irrational acceptance of whatever rational standard is accepted on the other hand? Seemingly the only alternative left, should one not embrace one or another horn of this dilemma, is skepticism: the view that no genuine knowledge at all is (rationally) possible. (It is in this context that justificationism proposes a two-cornered choice between its rational authority with respect to knowledge as one corner and an irrational conception of knowledge and its acquisition as the other corner.) Thus the basic epistemological problem faced by classical philosophers can be characterized as the dilemma of ultimate commitment. We must either succeed in justifying our ultimate rational authority, or we shall be forced to conclude that not only science but even the rational way of life in general cannot be shown to be rationally superior to its alternatives. Either we succeed in justifying commitment to the rational, scientific way of life, or intellectual honesty demands that we embrace an irrational way of life. In either case, an ultimate commitment is called for: We must rationally justify rational ways of life (such as science), or we will be forced to acknowledge that irrationalism is *rationally* justifiable.

THE DILEMMA OF ULTIMATE COMMITMENT AND
THE SPECTER OF IRRATIONALISM

Let us be sure that the full impact of the dilemma of ultimate commitment is understood. An alternative name for the dilemma, as Bartley notes, is the problem of the limits of rationality, specifically with regard to making a decision concerning a way of life—the rational way of life (or the scientific way of life). We are apparently faced with a forced choice between two allegedly exhaustive and exclusive alternatives: rationally proving the *rationality* of the rational way of life on one hand and rationally showing the *irrationality* of the rational way of life on the other.

But can we rationally defend the superiority of the rational way of life, of such rational procedures as the employment of scientific reasoning to disclose knowledge about ourselves and our world? According to an extremely powerful argument, the answer is "no," because of the limits of rationality *per se*. Bartley (1962) develops the argument this way:

> No matter what belief is advanced, someone can always challenge it with: "How do you know?" and "Give me a reason." Unless this procedure is to go on forever, it must be halted at a "standard," "criterion," "ultimate presupposition," "end," or "goal" whose authority is simply accepted. If all men do not cease their questioning at the same point, however, "ultimate relativism" results. For there is no Archimedes' lever with which to decide among competing sets of ultimate standards. Even if everyone did happen to stop at the same place, there would be no way to determine whether this universal subjective standard led to objectively true statements about the world. Obviously, a man cannot, without arguing in a circle, justify the rationality of his standard of rationality by appealing to that standard. Yet, if he holds certain beliefs—for example, the standard itself—to be immune from the demand for rational justification and from the question "How do you know?" he can be said to hold them irrationally or dogmatically. And, so it is claimed, argument among men about the radically different beliefs they hold in this way is pointless. For rational argument consists in mutual criticism, with each man supporting all his beliefs with good reasons. The limits of rational argument within any particular way of life, then, seem to be defined by reference to that object or belief in respect to which commitment is made or imposed, in respect to which argument is called to a halt [pp. 90–92].

The skeptical critic of rationalism has a *tu quoque* argument to *rationally justify* his or her commitment to irrationality. If this argument form is valid, then one has, so to speak, a "scientific" excuse for being unscientific! The mystic, theologian, existentialist, etc. who does not accept the validity of scientific reasoning is now provided with a "scientifically valid" justification for saying: "I do not accept the findings of science"! If this argument were valid, there would be no way to justify science as a means to knowledge and hence no rational reason whatsoever to prefer it to other putative sources of knowledge, including the most irrational ones! Scientific knowledge would thus be irrational, that is, *without foundations* in the traditional rational sense.

And what is this *tu quoque* argument? It is the combination of these three premises:

1. For certain logical reasons (discussed in the prior quotation from Bartley), rationality is limited such that *everyone must* make a dogmatic, irrational commitment.
2. Therefore, one has a right to make whatever commitment one pleases: the scientist to science, mystics to mystical relevation, etc.
3. Therefore, no one may criticize anyone else's commitment, nor can anyone be criticized for making that commitment.

The devastating implications of the *tu quoque* are so obvious, once the argument is understood, that Bartley makes a convincing case that the problem of defeating it is "the fundamental problem of modern philosophy." Regardless of whether or not anything is the "fundamental" problem, it is obvious that tremendous effort has been expended in an attempt, either explicitly or implicitly, to evade the force of the *tu quoque*. In one form or another, defeating the specter of irrationalism has been, historically, the prime task of scientific methodology and epistemology. In this framework the quest for a theory of rationality for the scientific endeavor may be discerned as the central preoccupation of the philosophy of science since its inception. The implicit reasoning has been that only if science as a method—i.e., as a source for knowlege—can be rationally justified, can the devastating force of the *tu quoque* be avoided.

But how can one rationally justify scientific knowledge claims? One must first characterize what would count as knowledge and justification. By supplying ready-made answers to these and other questions, justificationism came to dominate and direct all brands of philosophical thought on these matters. For classic justificationism, *no claim may be considered to constitute knowledge unless it can be proved or shown to be certain.* All genuine knowledge is thus *proven* knowledge. The epitome of justificationist knowledge is that provided by the formal "sciences" of mathematics and logic. One need only recall the desire of classic rationalist and empiricist alike, that their philosophical pronouncements be certified as true "*in more geometrico*" to see the influence of the equation of knowledge with proof or, what is to say the same thing, of knowledge with certainty.

Within the justificationist metatheory, justification of a knowledge claim can mean only one thing: that it can be shown to follow from a supreme epistemological *authority*. *In order to justify a knowledge claim, it must be proven to follow from a genuine epistemological authority*. On this point there was conflicting opinion, and from this conflict the traditional philosophical "world views" and their respective "schools" devolved. But the key feature to note is that in its traditional forms, western epistemology is inherently authoritarian in character.

At this point the dilemma of ultimate commitment with regard to the rationality of science becomes clear. Traditional epistemology may be viewed as a succession of proposals of rational authorities or criteria that were candidates for being the necessary and sufficient *justification* of scientific "inference" as a legitimate source of knowledge—to avoid the specter of an irrational picture of science. In order to avoid skepticism (which for the justificationist means that science is not rational), one must embrace fideism of one or another form. This commitment to a rational account of scientific procedure forced traditional epistemologists to provide answers to two questions: What is the source of our knowledge, and what is the authority that justifies it as a source of knowledge?

The philosophies of rationalism and empiricism have constantly attempted to provide satisfactory answers within this framework. And yet the history of both answers is one of constant failure, for neither rationalism nor empiricism has produced any rational authority capable of justifying scientific practice or "method" as a source of knowledge. When one understands the reasons for this persistent failure, one also understands the failure of justificationism as a metatheory of the scientific endeavor. But before examining why justificationist conceptions of scientific method are self-stultifying, we must overview the position in more detail.

2 The Received View Metatheory and Its Variations: Justificationism and Neojustificationism

Justificationism is a "rule system" or "grammar" of concept formation (comparable to the way transformational grammar is a grammar of language), and one must be content with "listing" its most salient rules *while taking care not to talk as if any one "rule" or set of them were "the" definition* of justificationism. Thus highly divergent positions may share little in common other than their endorsement of one or more of these "rules" or "maxims" or "manifestos."

Justificationism enshrines a number of definitional fusions and confusions that are characteristic of its outlook. By fusing certain concepts together, it defines *in advance* what can be taken as appropriate answers to questions concerning the nature of science and of rationality itself. By listing some of these major fusions and confusions, this chapter sketches how a justificationist *must* approach the questions and issues concerned with science and its growth.

THE CLASSIC FORM OF JUSTIFICATIONISM

Justificationism's two cardinal traits are the identification of knowledge with *proof* and the identification of knowledge with *authority*. Historically this is the central unity in Western philosophy. In Bartley (1962):

> *The Western philosophical tradition is authoritarian in structure, even in its most liberal forms.* This structure has been concealed by oversimplified traditional presentations of the rise of modern philosophy as part of a *rebellion*

against authority. In fact, modern philosophy is the story of the rebellion of one authority against another authority, and the clash between competing authorities. Far from repudiating the appeal to authority as such, modern philosophy has entertained only one alternative to the practice of basing opinions on traditional and perhaps *irrational* authority: namely, that of basing them on a rational authority.

This may be seen by examining the main questions asked in these philosophies. Questions like: How do you know? How do you justify your beliefs? With what do you guarantee your opinions?—*all beg authoritarian answers*—whether those answers be: the Bible, the leader, the social class, the nation, the fortune teller, the Word of God, the intellect, or sense experience. And Western philosophies have long been engaged in getting these supposedly infallible epistemological authorities out of trouble [pp. 134–135].

A putative knowledge claim cannot be accepted as genuine knowledge unless it can be proven, and it cannot be proven except by submission to the appropriate epistemological authority. For the empiricist such as Locke, *the* epistemological authority is sense experience. For the intellectualist such as Descartes, *the* supreme epistemological authority needed to certify a knowledge claim is rational intuition. Regardless of the particular philosophy endorsed, the justificationist philosopher will not accept as genuine knowledge any claim that cannot be validated by whatever ultimate epistemological authority that philosopher accepts. This is the problem situation that leads to the dilemma of commitment. But to repeat: Justificationism fuses and confuses knowledge with proof and with authority.

A third confusion also stems from the identification of knowledge with proven assertion: the indistinguishability of truth and knowledge. Because truth for the justificationist *is* proof and knowledge *is* proof, it follows that *knowledge is truth is proof.* That is, knowledge must be possession of the truth: *To know is to be in possession of the truth.* As A. J. Ayer (1956) stated, "to say that one knows a fact is to claim the right to be sure of it [p. 6]"; and as he makes clear in a section entitled, "Knowing as having the right to be sure [31 *ff.*]," that means to know *for certain.*

From this third fusion follows a fourth: the conception of eternally valid knowledge inductively accumulating into the growth of science. If knowledge if proven, then once certified, it remains so forever. And if the progress of science is the growth of knowledge, then scientific progress must be the accumulation of more and more eternally valid truths. The "cummulative record" or continuity model of scientific growth is the result: All successor theories are merely enlargements upon their predecessors—they can *never* contradict their predecessors. There can be no scientific revolutions within the justificationist conception of scientific history; only what Thomas Kuhn (1970c) terms *normal science growth* is permitted.

The goal of science for classic justificationism was to establish that all the propositions of science have the same probability of being true: the probability value 1 or certainty. For every proposition *h* of science, given relevant evidence *e*, the probability *p* of that proposition must, according to the demands of justificationist intellectual honesty, be expressed as : $P(h,e)$ =1. One reads this formula as: The probability of hypothesis *h being true* on the basis of evidence *e* is 1 (or certain, or proven true). To establish this, justificationism *had* to develop a valid logic of scientific assessment—an inductive logic—as the methodology of scientific inference.

FROM CERTAINTY TO PROBABILITY:
THE GENESIS OF NEOJUSTIFICATIONISM

Classic justificationism gave way to *neojustificationism* when it was gradually realized that *no* scientific proposition is provable, or can be "known for certain." (Fries showed this in 1828, as a special case of the logical thesis that the logical relations such as provability, consistency, etc. can refer only to propositions. And propositions can be derived *only* from other propositions, never from "facts.") Thus *all theories are equally unprovable*, and it is always the case that $P(h,e) = 0$. Thus failed the method of justification, and hence the theory of scientific inference in classic justificationism. The eternal factual basis failed also, when in 1906 Duhem (1954) noted that science is fact correcting in its nature rather than fact preserving. New theories often refute the facts of older ones. There is no eternally valid "factual basis," and genuine revolutions of both theoretical and factual import do occur in science.

Neojustificationism watered down "proof" to "probable"; intellectual honesty now requires only the selection of the most highly *probable* propositions. Thus has developed (from W. E. Johnson at Cambridge in the late 19th century) *probabilistic inductive logic.* Contemporary inductive logicians and mathematical statisticians are hard at work refining it, with the goal of a "confirmation theory" that will assign a probability ranging from 0 $< p <$ 1 in the new formula $P(h,e) = C$ (C = degree of confirmation). Nothing else has changed in the switch from classic to neojustificationism; instead of $P(h,e) = 1$, it now assumed that $P(h,e) = 0 < p < 1$. That is, the body of accepted scientific propositions is no longer composed of certain indubitable factual propositions; rather, it contains highly probable (exactly *how* highly probable is never quite clear) propositions. If science cannot be certain, as there is no firm foundation of objective fact, then it must be the next best thing—which everyone assumed is (highly) probable. To put it in Reichenbach's (1938) terminology, the sole predicate of scientific propositions is their weight (conceived as a probability) of evidential support:

> Thus there are left no propositions at all which can be absolutely verified. The predicate of truth-value of a proposition, therefore, is a mere fictive quality; its

place is in an ideal world of science only, whereas actual science cannot make use of it. Actual science instead employs throughout the predicate of weight. We regard a high weight as equivalent to truth, and a low weight as equivalent to falsehood; the intermediate domain is called "indeterminat. ." The conception of science as a system of true proposition is therefore nothing but a schematization [p. 188].

Thus, it is easy to see that a fusion of concepts introduced by *neo*justificationism is that of induction and probability. Having dropped the admittedly impossible quest for certainty, the neojustificationist aims at the next best thing: near certainty. And the "near certain" has been identified with the "probable." Probabilistic inductive logic is the result: It is to be an algorithmic assessment procedure for probable knowledge claims instead of certain knowledge claims.

The chief problem for neojustificationism is to *justify* probable knowledge. Induction, as the means to empirical or nondemonstrative knowledge, must be rescued from the skeptical doubts so clearly voiced by David Hume. The *authority* of knowledge must be relocated in the probabilistic inductive procedure. Otherwise, there is no authority, no "proof," and therefore no rationality to science; it is irrational, psychological perhaps, but not logical— which is exactly where Hume left it two centuries ago.

All this arises from another fusion of concepts within both classic and neojustificationism—the tacit assumption that *inference requires validation*. The ideal model of a knowledge system for the justificationist is the purely formal system of Euclidean geometry. In such a system, deduction—as the only possible form of inference—is truth or proof preserving. But deductive inference is not a source of new knowledge; nothing that is not already contained in the premises can be deduced. But science gains *new* knowledge, as we all admit. According to the justificationist, science gains its new knowledge by *inductive inference*, that form of inference in which the conclusion goes beyond the premises (in science, perceptual experience). But now the problem arises: How can inductive inference be validated? The only concepts and criteria of validation or justification that are available apply to certain or formal systems, which are deductive systems. Hence the perennially unsolved problem of the justification of induction arises. This problem of instant rational assessment is so acute within the justificationist framework that these theorists never get beyond it at all. In Lakatos (1968a):

Neojustificationists thought that even if science does not produce certainty, it produces near-certainty. Ignoring Duhem's master-argument against induction, they insisted that the main pattern of scientific progress is 'nondemonstrative inference' from factual premises to theoretical conclusions. According to Broad the unsolved problem of *justification of induction* was a 'scandal of philosophy' *because* inductive method was the 'glory of science': scientists proceeded successfully from truths to richer truths (or, at least, to very probable truths) while philosophers toiled unsuccessfully to justify this procedure [p. 322].

Logical positivism and empiricism, as dominant received view philosophies of science, are easily shown to be justificationist at heart. All the "theories" of cognitive significance (principles of verifiability, etc.) are explicit statements of the equation of knowledge with proof (or probability). For all these philosophers *meaning* is assimilated to proof. The appeal is to a rational authority to say "What do you mean?" and "How do you know?"; and science, which is the meaningful and the sensible, is demarcated from nonscience by the fact that the latter is unverifiable, i.e., meaningless and nonsense. The entire unity of science movement stems from the notion of a common, intersubjective, fixed-for-certain-for-all-time basis of "facts." All science must be Kuhnian normal science "fact accumulation." There can be no revolutionary science, because science never overturns prior certified facts. There is no real problem of growth, nor of pragmatic action, nor of intellectual honesty. There remains only the task of justifying induction as the theory of instant rational assessment (i.e., of *proving* that induction yields *valid* knowledge).

Because of the manner in which it fuses concepts together, the justificationist approach *demands* that certain things obtain in science and its methodology. First, there must be an "empirical basis" of facts that are *known for certain*. This is the *foundation of empirical knowledge* (the basis for inductive inference). Second, theories are second-class citizens, being "derivative" from facts and accumulated generalizations (i.e., they are inductions based upon inductions). Third, science must be cumulative and gradual; facts must be piled upon facts to construct the edifice of scientific knowledge. Fourth, factual *meaning* must be fixed for once and for all *independently* of theory, and must remain invariant. Fifth, explanation consists in showing that a "proven" factual proposition follows logically from a theoretical proposition. Sixth, science evaluates *one* theory at a time, never two or more. Justificationism enshrines what may be called a *monotheoretical* model of assessment.

THE JUSTIFICATIONIST CONCEPTION OF THE NATURE AND DIRECTION OF RESEARCH IN THE PHILOSOPHY OF SCIENCE

As the dominant metatheoretical approach, neojustificationism determines the nature and course of the majority of ongoing research in philosophy and methodology of science. The literature in the philosophy of science may be organized and understood in terms of its reflection of the justificationist conception of science and its rationality. The justificationist philosopher will strive to articulate conceptions of philosophy and science that instantiate ideal realizations of justificationist principles. Once having formulated an ideal of some problematic area (say, explanation) and developed research tools within that area (such as symbolic logic), such a philosopher will attempt to assimilate new problems to the ideal model and research tools aready available. The justificationist metatheory in that sense provides what Kuhn (in 1962) had referred to as a 'metaphysical paradigm,' which—when taken for granted as background knowledge in the philosophical community —allows ongoing research in philosophy of science to take on a 'normal science' *puzzle-solving* air. That is, such philosophers, like normal science researchers, conceive their problems in terms of being at a reasonably defined initial point *A* and wishing to reach a clearly defined goal, point *B*, by the most efficacious route, given the research tools available. For example, if the ideal of justificationist explanation is instantiated in the model called the *hypothetico–deductive* (H–D) method, then when a problematic area is encountered (e.g., statistical explanations, or explanation in history or the social sciences), the normal science puzzle-solving approach the neojustificationist philosopher adopts will subsume these problematic cases to the H–D model initially developed as an ideal of the physical sciences. Ongoing work in the philosophy of science may thus be construed as a normal science puzzle-solving attempt to secure the justificationist conception of the rationality of the scientific endeavor by extending its ideal type account to the problematic issues that invariably arise.

This section overviews some major justificationist research programs as they occur in logical positivism and its successor, logical empiricism, to see what constitutes the starting points (point *A*) and the desired goals (point *B*) that the metatheory specifies, as well as what appears to be the most efficacious routes from *A* to *B*. The programs we sketch are those of the logical "-isms" and are only *illustrative* of those of neojustificationism rather than *definitive* of them.

The ideal of knowledge for these philosophers is a unified deductive system consisting of a few essential postulates together with the theorems that can be derived from them. Euclidean geometry provided the first *realization* of a knowledge system that fit the justificationist ideal, and it has remained the paragon exemplar, to which it is assumed that all of science should properly aspire, ever since. The logical "-isms" attempt to articulate an *ideal* form of science on the basis of Euclidean gometry. The goal of the entire philosophical endeavor is to provide a unified science into which all the individual disciplines can be integrated. According to Radnitzky (1970):

> In linea massima this ideal of science is monistic, reductionistic and "physicalistic": All "scientific" disciplines should form part of one basic

discipline (monism). Among the scientific disciplines now in existence physisc [sic] approximates the ideal best ("physicalism"). Other disciplines may be reduced to physics by making a language that has been designed for an idealized physical science the common language of all "science-like" disciplines, and by making physical concepts the fundamental concepts of the ideal unified science (reductionism). The ideal physics is conceived as a deductive system [p. xvi].

The task of philosophy for the logical "-isms" is the spelling out of the language system and theoretical form (syntactic structure) of the ideal unified science. This is the point *B* to which research is directed. The key research traditions of philosophical inquiry may all be seen as subtasks of the major project of articulating the ideal of a unified science. Philosophy is thus *re*constructive and deals not with actual growing science but rather with finished theories or knowledge systems. These finished systems are studied with the idea of improving their explicitness, precision, etc., to make them fit the integrated, ideal, unified picture. Thus the *products* of scientific inquiry are scrutinized rather than the *ongoing process* of inquiry, and the aim of such investigation is to perfect our accumulated knowledge within the conception of an ideal, unified, scientific world picture.

Radnitzky (1970) put this approach to philosophy in clear perspective:

> When Neoclassical Empiricists "look at science," they are looking for problems that can be tackled by the techniques to which they are committed. Otherwise they process the problems they find in such a way that these become problems in applied logic. Their work on such problems ultimately serves to spell out various of the features of their ideal of science. For instance LE's [Logical Empiricism's] theory of scientific explanation may be viewed as the spelling out of what explanations in Ideal-Unified-Science look like. Thus, once the logical empiricists' *program* has been reconstructed from their deeds, *one can depict the key themes of LE as subtasks of the global theme of spelling out the ideal of science* [p. xvi].

The ideal science is physics when physics is construed as applied mathematics—as a mathematical formalism plus correspondence rules telling how the formalism is to be interpreted or tied to experience. All other sciences are to be both *modeled* after physics (in the pattern of their language, method of explanation, etc.) and also *reduced* to physics (in the sense that the theories and entities of other disciplines must be built up from the basics provided by physics). Thus *the major tasks of the philosophy of science consist of modeling all sciences upon* (idealized) *physics and ontologically and epistemologically reducing all science to physics.*

The Unity of Science program is the result of this conception of philosophy. The Unity of Science movement has both ontological and linguistic components. Linguistically, it results in the thesis that the language of idealized physics is the necessary and sufficient language for *all* sciences; the philosopher is thus provided with a research program whose task is to *reduce* the "languages" of other sciences (especially the problematic behavioral sciences) to the physicalistic language (the language of ideal physics). Ontologically, the thesis of reductionism (which states that the theoretical entities and concepts of other sciences are reducible to those of physics) results, and a similar research program—to reduce all sciences to the idealized physics—is engendered. The drive toward unification within one language framework and one ontology is so strong that some (e.g., Turner, 1967) have made reducibility a criterion of acceptability for scientific theories, especially in psychology.

Modeling other sciences upon physics leads to the major programs envisaged by the logical "-isms." Three that are of central importance are based upon the problems of : (a) empirical significance; (b) confirmation or assessment: and (c) explanation. These problem areas center around *semantic* issues in applying theories-as-uninterpreted-formal-calculi to specific applications. That is, they are problems in explicating the meaning and use of concepts originally pertaining only to formal systems when those concepts are used for describing science.

The problems of empirical significance center around how the nonlogical (i.e., empirical) concepts should be introduced into the language system of the ideal unified science. These are demarcation problems of meaning, and the goal is to distinguish scientifically significant or 'meaningful' terms; empirical and 'meaningful' science must be sharply distinguished from transcendental and 'meaningless' metaphysics. Within logical positivism, the research program centered around developing an adequate verifiability theory of meaning, where 'adequate' required the theory should succeed in separating good science from bad metaphysics without losing anything essential to science in the process. This has proved to be a degenerating research program, for it has become obvious that no such demarcation is possible. Regardless of whether meaning is presumed to attach to verifiability (the usual interpretation) or falsifiability, the same result obtains: Too much essential to science is deemed meaningless, i.e., *un*verifiable or *un*falsifiable. The verifiability theory leads to the same skeptical doubts that Hume himself was confronted with: Throw metaphysics into the Humean fireplace, and science burns with it; preserve science by pulling it out of the fire, and metaphysics always comes creeping back. And indeed, the dilemma is insoluable, as a look at the "nonsensical" status of the principle of verifiability *itself* indicates. The principle of verifiability cannot be verified; thus, it is, by its own criterion, nonsensical. Indeed, *all* such methodological directives and prescriptions for scientific methodology and rationality are equally nonsensical on this view. And certainly no rational scientist or philosopher would say that it was sensible to heed directives that were themselves nonsense. And yet, despite its absurdity, this is precisely what a most venerated founder of logical positivism seriously recommended; Ludwig Wittgenstein put the matter thusly in 1922: "My propositions are elucidatory in this way: he who understands me finally recognizes them as senseless when he has climbed out through them, on them, over them [p. 151]." This position, aptly called "hayloft metaphysics," recommends that the ladder be kicked away once one has used it to climb up (to enlightenment). That is, once having ascertained that my directives are metaphysical, says Wittgenstein, one must throw them away. Unfortunately for the justificationist who confuses meaning with verifiability (and sense with meaning and nonsense with 'metaphysics' and unverifiability), Wittgenstein's directive to throw the ladder away is also unverifiable and must accordingly be thrown away.

The problems of confirmation are problems of the theory of instant rational assessment. The method of inference that science is to employ, inductive logic, must have criteria of adequacy clearly specified or its use will not be legitimate. More important, the method must be justified as a valid source of knowledge and the relationships of hypotheses to their evidential basis clearly spelled out. These and similar problems serve to mark out a research program in confirmation theory, where all the esoteric tools of formal logic and statistical inference theory can be used to generate and solve technical puzzles. This line of research is self-perpetuating, for it turns out that each technical puzzle leads in its solution or dissolution to either a paradox or another puzzle. The inductive logician may profitably pursue these technical puzzles *forever* and need never return to the original problems that motivated the confirmation theory research program. That is, instead of explicating the manner in which inductive logic as a language system is related to empirical science, the confirmation theorist winds up refining the language system *per se*, with no regard for the original problem of application. (Confirmation theory is examined in detail in the Appendix, Chapter 9.)

The problems of explanation stem largely from the equation of knowledge with proof. The ideal explanation for the logical "-isms" is a proof, which is to say, a logical deduction. Thus ideal science explanation must be deduction; a scientific theory should be a system in and from which deductions are made. In this manner, from a cursory study of mathematics and physics, the hypothetico–deductive model of explanation is enshrined as the ideal of scientific explanation. The technical puzzles that constitute the research program surrounding explanation center around explicating key terms—e.g., law and truth—such that the H–D schema can be maintained. Problems arise in these concepts when the model is applied to situations other than the deterministic physical science ideal, such as historical explanations, statistical laws and explanations, etc. But the extension of the model to *concrete* cases is never of primary concern; rather than attempting to deal with actual scientific practice, the logical empiricist is more concerned to articulate an ideal schema of explanation. Thus the tools are sharpened and polished in conceptual isolation, and it does not seem to matter that they are never used by the working scientist. Actual scientific practice is really of only passing interest to these reconstructive philosophers. The philosophical research program thus becomes simultaneously self-supporting and completely detached from its original source—actual scientific practice (see Chapter 10).

In a similar vein, something worth noting is the *lack* of a role for historical inquiry within the logical "-isms." For the justificationist, history must be the gradual accumulation of propositions or "facts" that have been certified by *the* method, i.e., inductive inference. A "building block" conception of history results, which both stems from and reinforces the unitary science conception sketched earlier. Within this framework, there is only one reason to study history: to get the "facts" in proper chronological order and to assign praise to researchers who followed *the* method (and hence advanced science) and to assign blame to those who did not (and hence retarded progress). There is no problem for historiography, for there is no *theory* of history other than one that says "interpret history as a series of successful applications of scientific method." Futhermore, philosophers confronted with the fact that virtually *no* instances in the history of science reflect the methodology developed from idealized unified science will not be disturbed; they will retort that they are articulating an ideal of science and that it is not surprising that past researchers were less than ideal in their methodology. Thus there are very few historical case studies within the literature of the logical "-isms"; they are really *irrelevant* to understanding science, and those few philosophers (e.g., Reichenbach) who undertook them did so to make philosophical rather than historical mileage. The conception of science and its philosophy developed by the logical "-isms" is thus *internally immune to historical criticism*, and the only theorists who employ historical case studies (or studies of historiography) are *external* critics of the logical "-isms." But within their framework this immunity to criticism is not a drawback, and many such theorists cannot understand why other philosophers (such as Popper, especially 1963) constantly employ "stuffy" historical themes. For them, intellectual enlightenment lies in articulating the eternalized ideal rather than in studying actual practice. The distance from which logical empiricists view science is enormous, and their program alienates them from the problems of the actual researcher—whether scientist or historian. No wonder the irony of the logical "-isms" is that despite the fact that they have more thoroughly articulated a picture of science and its nature than any other group of philosophers in history, their program is virtually useless to the practicing scientist. Logical empiricists can speak only to themselves at this point.

This is not a terribly optimistic conception of science and its philosophy. To close this section, note another factor—the security mindedness—characteristic of the logical "-isms." In Radnitzky (1970):

As with people who grow old, so with logical empiricism when it grew older, there has occurred a general increase in the disutility of failure—the loss of "respectability"—over the utility of success, such as new vistas, intellectual adventures, etc. Hence logical empiricists are cautious; they try to eliminate errors before they make them. They are method-centered: they fix themselves to methods that give prestige and are assumed to be safe, and they even go so far as to let the methods decide which problems they will deal with. The only "respectable" tends, sure enough, to be the problems to which they can apply their own methods. On several occasions we have hinted at this syndrome of security-minded-ness—they are like gardeners who for fear of the sot-weed factor do not dare to allow flowers to grow in their garden [pp. 188–189].

JUSTIFICATIONISM AND THE FOUR PROBLEMS OUTLINED IN CHAPTER 1

Now one can understand that justificationism takes these positions on our four problems. To construct the theory of instant rational assessment is the primary task of philosophy, and that theory is inductive logic or "confirmation theory": The growth of knowledge is the gradual (inductive) accretion of proven, eternal truths (a theory of instant assessment is thus automatically also one of growth); pragmatic action is no problem because inductive method is the *only* rational means of knowledge acquisition and all who are rational will employ it; intellectual honesty demands that one accept into the body of knowledge claims constituting science only *proven* assertions (or probable assertions that are *proven* to be probable) and reject all others as unscientific, no matter how plausible or necessary they may seem. The methodology of scientific research within justificationism consists of cookbooks and recipes for inculcating this program, and it is these recipes that must be memorized by apprentice scientists in "experimental method-olgy" or "research techniques" or "experimental design" courses.

Justificationism is a metatheory of, generically construed, rational inquiry. As such, it is the "received view" of every domain of rational inquiry—not just the scientific endeavor. For example, in theology, contemporary protestant irrationalism is based upon a perceived dilemma in justificationism; see Bartley (1962). For justificationism in art, see Gombrich (1960), Goodman (1968), and Cavell (1969). Further, one must not think that it is peculiar to Western, scientifically oriented cultures such as the heritage we now trace to the ancient Greeks. Justificationist thought pervades mythic thinking (as studied by philosophers such as Cassirer [1953, 1955, 1957], so-called primitive cultures, and aspects of Oriental philosophy. Indeed, many of the strong points of Oriental thought that authors familiar with both traditions (e.g., Capra, 1975; Siu, 1957) would introduce to Western science are skeptical justificationist positions. Discussion of justificationism beyond contemporary philosophy of science, however, is beyond our present scope.

There are criticisms that are absolutely devastating to the justificationist approach. Many were developed within that metatheory by arch justificationists; some were not. When taken together they kill the position once and for all. Ultimately, they lead to a nonjustificational philosophy of criticism, as we soon see. However, one must guard against the sophisticated justificationist, who is wont to say: "Since I accept certain criticisms (of justificationism) as valid, I am not a justificationist." This is, of course, then coupled with an affirmation of faith in a particular pet sophisticated justificationist philosophy. Once again, the test of a theorist's position is the *overall*, global position *accepted*, which determines the "transfer" to novel situations and problems, not just the denial of one or another facet of the metatheory. It is the acceptance of that global justificationist position that is central; because all contemporary theorists are sophisticated with regard to one or another criticism, they thus are wont to regard criticism of the metatheory as of historical interest only, as an attack upon straw men rather than upon themselves. Thus, after detailing separate criticisms of essential tenets of the metatheory, it will be necessary to show their essential unity and the inconsistencies that result from acceptance of some and rejection of others.

3 Factual Relativity: A Criticism of the Received View from Within

This chapter outlines a major criticism of the "foundations" of knowledge view that is indispensable to justificationism. It is in one sense an overview of an exercise in futility: Were the criticism understood as a devastating argument against the received view (rather than a refinement within it), justificationists might be led to abandon the metatheory. Instead, the criticism reinforces the switch from classic to neojustificationism; finding no firm foundation for knowledge, these theorists try to establish human knowledge upon probable foundations in order to stave off skepticism. Sadder but "wiser," they admit that there are limitations to scientific rationality and attempt to buttress their philosophies by incorporating an acknowledgment to that effect. The acknowledgment we wish to overview is the incorporation of factual relativity into contemporary empiricism.

EMPIRICISM AND THE FOUNDATIONS OF KNOWLEDGE

First let us review the motivation for assuming there are foundations to empirical science. The reasoning is straightforward: Justificationism requires that knowledge claims be validated, and there must be an authority that confers that validation. When applied to empirical knowledge claims, the authority is the foundation upon which the claim is based. If the statements of science are not to be accepted dogmatically or as conventional agreements, we must be able to justify them (or face infinite regress). But what could count as the justification of an empirical claim? The authority must be both ultimate and noninferential, and it must constitute knowledge. For the empiricist, the perceptual experience of the observer, or better—that which is *given* in experience—is this ultimate foundation of scientific knowledge. It is assumed that the "factual basis" out of which is constituted the "observation language" of science is, in its turn, constituted from perceptual experience. It is what is given in experience that is "taken" as the starting point for empirical knowledge. Epistemically, it is this given that is taken to be self-authenticating and therefore as a foundation that is not in need of further foundation.

The theses of phenomenalism and physicalism are common variants of this foundations theme. Phenomenalism asserts that the irreducible givens are sense data. Physicalism replaces sense data statements by physical object statements and thus builds the factual basis of science out of more familiar objects than the rather elusive, and perhaps only psychologically specifiable, sense data. Carnap was largely responsible for converting the logical positivists to physicalism in the later 1930s after abandoning the naive phenomenalism of his earlier period (see Carnap, 1928, 1937). It is physicalism that is largely responsible for the idea that facts (actually, statements about facts) are independent of theory and that theories are second-class citizens "based upon" facts. Fortunately, it does not take much to destroy that simplistic conception.

FACTUAL RELATIVITY

The doctrine of factual relativity, or the conceptual nature of facts, is the crystallization of the repudiation of "foundations," "certainty," and "objectivity" that is so prominent in classical thought. Its essense is in fact a tautology: One cannot have a fact without having a prior theory. To see this, consider the following bald instruction: Observe carefully and write down every fact you see. It is clear that the instruction cannot be carried out—for one does not know what, if any, "observation" constitutes a "fact." Observation is a *skill* over and above the passive reception of the raw data of sensory experience. Facts are not picturable, observable entities; instead they are *wholly conceptual* in nature. They do not exist apart from a conceptual scheme. Were there no conceptual scheme available to single out recurrent regularities in it, all that "observation" would disclose would be the chaotic flux of phenomenal experience, the "buzzing confusion" attributed to William James. People with different conceptual schemes live in different worlds; the "facts" of one are not those of the other. Hanson (1958) put this very explicitly:

If in the brilliant disc of which he is visually aware Tycho sees only the sun, then he cannot but see that it is a body which will behave in characteristically 'Tychonic' ways. These serve as the foundation for Tycho's general geocentric-geostatic theories about the sun...

> Tycho sees the sun beginning its journey from horizon to horizon. He sees that from some celestial vantage point the sun (carrying with it the moon and planets) could be watched circling our fixed earth. Watching the sun at dawn through Tychonic spectacles would be to see it in something like this way. Kepler's visual field, however, has a different conceptual organization. Yet a drawing of what he sees at dawn could be a drawing of exactly what Tycho saw, and could be recognized as such by Tycho. But Kepler will see the horizon dipping, or turning away, from our fixed local star [p. 23].

Popper, in the *Logik der Forschung*, argued forcefully against the foundations of knowledge notion in discussing the problems involved in understanding the empirical basis of science (see Popper, 1959, Chapter V). Popper's very simple, but quite devastating, argument concerns the dispositional nature of all "observational" or "factual" statements:

> We can utter no scientific statement that does not go far beyond what can be known with certainty 'on the basis of immediate experience'. (This fact may be referred to as the 'transcendence inherent in any description'.) Every description uses *universal* names (or symbols, or ideas); every statement has the character of a theory, of a hypothesis. The statement, 'Here is a glass of water' cannot be verified by any observational experience. The reason is that the *universals* which appear in it cannot be correlated with any specific sense-experience. By the word 'glass', for example, we denote physical bodies which exihibit a certain *law-like behavior*, and the same for the word 'water' [pp. 94–95].

Popper's point is that all "empirical" statements *transcend* experiences and can thus hardly be "constituted" out of them. This same point was made in slightly different fashion by C. I. Lewis (1929) in developing the pragmatic conception of the a priori. Lewis emphasized the futility of conceiving the "given" as ultimate in any epistemic sense:

> The acceptance of such preanalytic data [the given] as an ultimate epistemological category would, if really adhered to, put an end to all worthwhile investigation of the nature of knowledge—or to any other intellectual enterprise. What lies on the surface can be taken as ultimate only so long as there is no problem to be solved, or else no solution to be hoped for. Without analysis, there can be no advance of understanding [p. 54].

Thus although there is something "given" in phenomenal experience, it is not the sort of thing that can be "taken" for the purpose that the empiricist desires—as an authoritative foundation for epistemology.

As an historical aside, note that although it has been known since early in the 19th century, justificationists have not realized that *no factual proposition can be proven from an experiment*. Propositions cannot be *derived* from facts—they can *only be derived from other propositions*. That is, facts are not the sort of "entity" from which one can *derive* propositions—in the same manner, apples cannot be "derived" from oranges. This is just a special case of the general logical thesis, apparently first publicized by J. F. Fries in 1828 (see Popper, 1959), that *logical relations*—such as provability, consistency, derivability, etc.—*can refer only to propositions.* Propositions can only be derived from other propositions, never from "facts." Popper noticed this in 1934, in *The logic of scientific discovery* (1959):

> The problem of the basis of experience has troubled few thinkers so deeply as Fries. He taught that, if the statements of science are not to be accepted *dogmatically,* we must be able to *justify* them. If we demand justification by reasoned argument, in the logical sense, then we are commited to the view that *statements can be justified only by statements* [p. 93].

Later Popper (1959) noted that "Fries in his theory of our 'predilection for proofs' emphasizes that the (logical) relations holding between statements are quite different from the relations between statements and sense experiences... [p. 105]." Factual *propositions*, then, could serve only as a basis from which to "justify" or derive other propositions; but as Fries indicated, we cannot ever get from facts themselves (experiments and their outcomes) to "factual propositions."

It is not surprising that "empiricists" long denied factual relativity. Empiricism says that reality (with a capital *R*) is what is "given" in sense experience and that it is concrete and particular. Factual relativity says neither knowledge nor reality is given at all (instead both are constructed); nor is there anything concrete as the empiricist uses the term; nor can "the particular" (the empirical) be known without prior knowledge of "the general" (the transcendent).

Factual relativity is an a priori constraint upon the nature and products of human knowledge, an *epistemological* a priori constraint. It has (as correlates) a physiological a priori basis (due to our physiological structure and functioning) and the consequence of a conceptual a priori limitation. The limitation is that what we can think about reality is limited by our ability to "see" aspects of it in our experience.

CLASSIFICATION AND THING-KIND
IDENTIFICATION:
THE CONCEPTUAL AND PHYSIOLOGICAL A PRIORI

An alternative approach to the problem of foundations for knowledge results from considering what is involved in the classification of abstract and concrete entities. Empiricists are wont to construct *nominalistic* ontologies. (Nominalism is the thesis that there exist no nonconcrete, nonparticular entities.) For the empiricist, the problem of abstract entities is to account for generalizations that transcend experience in terms of concrete experience plus a theory of how the mind works. And "abstraction" (how the mind works) is usually handled by an inductive, associationistic psychology. What is "real" and "primary" is said (following the "foundations" view) to be particular and concrete; abstract entitites (like theories) are derivative, second class, not really "real." But consider what must occur in order to perceive an event in the phenomenal flux as an instance of kind X: that is, to identify a particular *as a particular* (of kind X). If a "thing" is proffered to me as "an X," how do I know that to be so? I cannot claim to know (or to 'see') that the "thing" is "an X" without presupposing knowledge of generic thing-kinds—namely, of kind X. Consideration of the general phenomenon of classification makes it clear that one cannot know a concrete particular without knowing abstract thing-kinds. As Popper and Lewis observed, in order to gain knowledge of particulars the mind must operate with a conceptual framework of abstract entities.

Thus the problem of factual attribution or construction in scientific theory has a counterpart at the psychological and physiological level of analysis. Just as scientific theory is a matter of conceptual abstraction (see Hanson, 1970) rather than the reception of independently specified facts, our experience itself is the product of the classificatory and abstractive nature of our neural organization. Because empiricist philosophies base so much upon "experience," it is worthwhile pausing to note that experience is quite different in character from what traditional empiricist accounts have portrayed. The conceptual primacy of the abstract underlies the "reception" of sensory information as much as it does factual attribution. F. A. Hayek (1952b, 1969) has shown very clearly why this must be so.

Hayek's thesis is that no sensory input is "perceived" (i.e., inputted through the active central nervous system) at all unless it is perceived as one of the kinds of input accepted by the (innate or learned) classes of sensory order. Sensory perception is always an act of classification; the input signal is "processed" by any member (to which it "keys") of the sensory "orders" that impart to the phenomenal event the properties it has. No sensory input is perceived unless it can be "isomorphically" accepted as a match by the classes of sensory order. No constructions of phenomenal existents are possible except in terms of the (prior) apparatus of classification inherent in the operation of the functional nervous system. Unless an "event" gives rise to the pattern of sensory input that fits an organism's preexisting natural kind classifications, it is not perceived at all. Perception is thus never of the attributes of "objects" in the world at all; instead, phenomenal objects are abstractions of the organization and memory of the central nervous system. According to Hayek (1952b):

> The sensory (or other mental) qualities are not in some manner originally attached to, or an original attribute of, the individual physiological impulses, but. . . the whole of these qualities is determined by the system of connexions by

which the impulses can be transmitted from neuron to neuron;. . . it is thus the position of the individual impulse or group of impulses in the whole system of such connexions which gives it its distinctive quality;. . . this system of connexions is acquired in the course of the development of the species and the individual by a kind of "experience" or "learning"; and. . . it reproduces therefore at every stage of its development certain relationships existing in the physical environment between the stimuli evoking the impulses. . . . This central contention may also be expressed more briefly by saying that "we do not first have sensations which are then preserved by memory, but it is as a result of physiological memory that the physiological impulses are converted into sensations. The connexions between the physiological elements are thus the primary phenomenon which creates the mental phenomena" [p. 53].

Again, Hayek's thesis is that an "event" is not seen at all unless it is assimilated to a classification that already exists in the functioning of the central nervous system. Everything that we know about external stimuli, our entire knowledge of the "external" world, consists in the classifications effected by the action patterns of the functioning nervous system. Human knowledge is a system of rules of determination that indicate equivalences and differences of various combinations of CNS patterns. Hayek elaborated (1969):

This implies that the richness of the sensory world in which we live, and which defies exhaustive analysis by our mind, is not the starting point from which the mind derives abstractions, but the product of a great range of abstractions which the mind must possess in order to be capable of experiencing that richness of the particular [p. 318].

Returning to the level of methodology—if one grants factual relativity, then science can be "fact correcting" or, to say the same thing, fact *refuting*. A theory may *deny the facts* of its predecessor. Indeed this happens with all Kuhnian scientific "revolutions." Einstein's theoretical concepts of "force," "mass," "simultaneity," etc. are literally denials of the validity of the Newtonian "facts" that were called by the same name. And it was once a "fact" (detailed in the first edition of the *Encyclopaedia Britannica*) that phlogiston was given off by burning substances. By the third edition of the *Britannica*, however, this "fact" was nowhere to be found. (Recall that "fact correction" is the basis of Duhem's (1954) argument against induction; one cannot "induce" ever more encompassing and "truly" established theories *if the facts change*. This is explored later.

Kuhn captured this aspect of science in *The structure of scientific revolutions* (1970c):

A new theory, however special its range of application, is seldom or never just an increment to what is already known. Its assimilation requires the reconstruction of prior theory and the re-evaluation of prior fact, an intrinsically revolutionary process that is seldom completed by a single man and never overnight. . . . No natural history can be interpreted in the absence of at least some implicit body of intertwined theoretical and methodological belief that permits selection, evaluation, and criticism. If that body of belief is not already implicit in the collection of facts—in which case more than "mere facts" are at hand—it must be externally supplied, perhaps by a current metaphysic, by another science, or by personal and historical accident [pp. 7, 17].

Kuhn's monograph created a furor within the received view. One reason why is that it documented in the history of science the inadequacy of the foundations approach to empirical knowledge and with it, the futility of the received view of theory construction, assessment, and indeed everything else. Thus it is not surprising that justificationists (e.g., Achinstein, 1968; Shapere, 1966; and Scheffler, 1967) attacked Kuhn as an irrationalist. Because he denied that science was rational according to justificationist criteria, these theorists assumed that he must be arguing that it is irrational (see Laudan, 1976, p. 3 and Chapters 3 and 4 for an example). As he was not a positive justificationist, it was assumed that he was a skeptic, glorying in the irrationality of science: thus the frequent portrait of Kuhn as a darling of the radical left and, by insinuation, an enemy of "freedom and democracy." This is an instance of the tacit assumption that if science is not rational according to the only conception of rationality that a theorist understands, it must be irrational. When others make this claim, justificationists revile them as irrationalists; when they finally come to the same conclusions on their own, justificationists regard themselves as "sophisticated" and as "sadder but wiser."

EXPLANATION AND THE DEDUCTIVE
UNIFICATION OF EXPERIENCE

Although there is increasing acceptance of the theoretical nature of factual attribution by empiricists, there is still almost unanimous assent to the claim that the ultimate "foundation" of science is the perceptual experience of the scientist. This is usually taken to be the "justification" for endorsing empiricism rather than idealism (or some other alternative). But there is no such justification, because *science is not based on perceptual experience at all*. That is, the total *disconnection* of experience from scientific theory is easy to demonstrate, even within the received view account of theoretical explanation. We can see this by asking what must occur to experience before it becomes amenable to hypothetico–deductive "scientific" explanation. The H–D method *idealizes* the entities to which it applies, and that idealization removes all traces of perceptual experience. Körner (1966) examined this issue in asking what deduction requires for the construction of 'empirical' predicates before it may legitimately be applied.

Körner considered two constraints upon empirical predicates. The first requires the elimination of inexactness and indefiniteness from all predicates. The logic of the H–D framework is an unmodified, classical, two-valued (true or false) logic that, strictly speaking, can admit no inexactness whatsoever. Thus it requires that raw perceptual experience be rendered into "concrete" categories. This abstraction distinguishes between the exact and inexact (or relevant and irrelevant) determinable characteristics and discards the latter. It creates new abstract determinables that *replace* the original perceptual ones at the "basis" of science.

But even this is not sufficient to render a so-called empirical predicate fit for inclusion in a deductively unified system. Further idealization removes perceptual experience entirely. Körner (1966) noted:

> The disconnection of the theory from its perceptual subject-matter can now be also expressed by saying that no perceptual proposition and no perceptual predicate occurs in any deductive sequence. That this must be so is clear. All inexact perceptual predicates are precluded from occurring in any sequence, and the exact—though internally inexact—determinables have been replaced by nonperceptual predicates through abstraction—to say nothing of the further replacements due to the conditions of measurement, general and special.
>
> No perceptual proposition will be a last term in a deductive sequence. The theory will be linked to perception not by deduction but by identification. [pp. 168–169].

Thus the *reference* of the empirical terms of science ("facts") *cannot be given* in our acquaintance but is rather idealized, i.e., *constructed*, by our conceptual schemes. Not only are there "correspondence rules" between theory and empirical predicate (fact), but there are similar linkages needed to identify facts in the flux of experience. This has disastrous consequences for the received view account of theory construction and verification. According to Körner (1966):

> Since the lowest-level propositions of a hypothetico–deductive system are not identical with resemblance-propositions or perceptual ones, the orthodox views about their verification, falsification or confirmation cannot be accepted without serious qualifications. *All* these views imply that a hypothetico–deductive system permits us by itself or in conjuction with empirical propositions (stating so called initial conditions) to deduce empirical conclusions. But this is made impossible by the formal framework of any such theory [p. 90].

Thus even on the empiricist account, theoretical knowledge is nonperceptual and nonempirical, because its reference is to ideal, nonperceptual entities rather than to concrete, physical ones. The "foundation" for empirical knowledge thus becomes abstract, theoretical, and nonperceptual. An empiricism based upon such a foundation is a contradiction in terms much like "square circle." Nevertheless, the committed faithful regard the arguments against foundations and in favor of factual relativity as strong points in their sophisticated empiricism. Consider some illustrative cases.

THE RETREAT TO SOPHISTICATION

The arguments in favor of factual relativity can be extended and strengthened almost indefinitely. But there is little need to do so; even the staunchest justificationists now admit the conceptual nature of facts. Yet none go on to draw comparable conclusions about other justificationist tenets that the denial of a "foundation" entails. Two classic examples of the strength of justificationism as an unconscious influence constraining thought are the positions of Carl Hempel (1965, 1970, 1974) and Merle B. Turner (1967, 1971). Both accept and endorse the doctrine of factual relativity. Both feel it is a strong point of their "enlightened" empiricism and an admission that the nice, pat picture of logical positivism was wrong. But both defend other justificationist principles (to the *n*th degree) that should be abandoned *if the implications of factual relativity were actually understood.*

Turner defends factual relativity and also reductionism and the unity of science movement. Yet *if* there is no common foundation of fact, there is no defense of reductionism or unitary science. There can be no unity without a common basis, and there can be no sense to reductionism unless the meanings of the terms in the theories involved remain constant. And yet factual relativity entails that neither a common basis nor meaning invariance obtains.

The given in experience, as a "neutral" or independent foundation for knowledge, as a "basis" of firm and invariant facts, is a myth (Sellars, 1963). There is nothing given in experience *that can be so taken* (there *is* a given, clearly; it is what Russell called *acquaintance*, and it stands in contrast to our knowledge by description). If one realizes this, it becomes clear that: (1) Facts *must* be relative to conceptual points of view; and (2) there is *no* foundation of empirical knowledge. Turner (1967), as an arch justificationist in psychology, saw this latter point clearly:

> This is an unfortunate predicament and one that is difficult to avoid. To place raw data in the physical world as independent of any receptor activity is an indefensible metaphysical gambit. Yet to place raw data in the receptor activity is to destroy their neutrality. It would seem that the "counsel of despair" is to regard them as relatively neutral. That is, raw data are coded as sensory input under "optimal" conditions of observation. . . from which we infer that for every punctate input there is a source of physical energy sufficient to elicit firing of the receptor [p. 210].

Hempel originated and still staunchly defends the classic deductive–nomological view of explanation, the "covering law" account. On this account, explanation *is* deduction, and reduction *is* explanation, which is deduction. But this cannot be correct; first, "facts" are not what is deduced in explanation, as Körner argued. Second, the relation is *not* deduction, which would require meaning invariance of the terms (see Chapter 4, this volume).

If it were fully appreciated that factual relativity entailed the denial of meaning invariance, a common factual "basis," the deductive account of explanation, etc., these theorists would likely repudiate justificationism. As it is, their endorsement of factual relativity remains one of the few bright spots in otherwise gloomy positions. And "gloomy" is a very apt word for contemporary logical empiricism. Faced with a forced choice between justificationist rationality and the skeptical justificationist's conclusion that knowledge is not possible (and hence that science is *irrational*), these "sophisticated" empiricists all admit defeat and give in to skepticism. Within the justificationist framework, the skeptic—who holds that no informative knowledge is possible—always triumphs over the "positive" justificationist. The most that positive justificationists can do is delude themselves into thinking that it is a worthwhile task to render the skeptic's acknowledged *victory* as bloodless as possible. Their reasoning is in this vein (Ayer, 1956):

> We should not be bullied by the skeptic into renouncing an expression for which we have a legitimate use. Not that the skeptic's argument is fallacious; as usual his logic is impeccable. But his victory is empty. He robs us of certainty only by so defining it as to make it certain that it cannot be obtained....
>
> This does not means that the use of scientific method is irrational. It could be irrational only if there were a standard of rationality which it failed to meet; whereas in fact it goes to set the standard: arguments are judged to be rational or irrational by reference to it. Neither does it follow that specific theories or hypotheses cannot be justified. ...No proof that we are right can be forthcoming: for at this stage nothing is going to be allowed to count as such a proof. Thus, here again the skeptic makes his point. There is no flaw in his logic: his demand for justification is such that it is necessarily true that it cannot be met. But here again it is a bloodless victory [pp. 68, 75].

No wonder that contemporary empiricists are the best representatives of existentialist despair and dread; by the consistent application of their own criteria of rationality, they have shown that their trust in empiricism was not justified and have retreated to a *faith* in empiricism rather than to a defense of it.

For example, consider Bertrand Russell's (1948) melancholy comment:

> Empiricism as a theory of knowledge has proved inadequate, though less so than any other previous theory of knowledge. Indeed, such inadequacies as we

have seemed to find in empiricism have been discovered by strict adherence to a doctrine by which empiricist philosophy has been inspired: that all human knowledge is uncertain, inexact, and partial. To this doctrine we have not found any limitation whatever [p. 507].

Compare M. B. Turner (1967) in a methodology primer written for psychologists:

It is always a bit ironical when a house which professes to virtue topples under censure by its own precept. . . . Empiricism itself is culpable, yet we have found no reliable substitute for a knowledge supported by the fact of its public communicability. For the empiricist, the alternative to absolute skepticism is the wistful embrace of a principle of convergence [p. 7].

These positions exemplify a *retreat to commitment*; and as Bartley emphasizes, it is no different and no less *irrational* when practiced by the "scientific" empiricist than by the Protestant irrationalist. Whatever rationality there is to science must forever lie *outside* the confines of justificationism.

But now we can understand why the more sophisticated ex-justificationist often becomes a *conventionalist* instead of attempting to buttress one or another inductivist position. The inductivist believes that informative, genuine theoretical knowledge is possible and attempts to show how it can be gleaned from a firm foundation of facts. The conventionalist is far more sophisticated; he or she is aware that informative theoretical knowledge is not possible, given the justificationist conception of knowledge. The dilemma that leads to the assertion that genuine theoretical knowledge is not possible is quite straightfowardly put by Agassi: (1966b):

If we do not go beyond sense experience we have no theoretical knowledge of the world, while if we do go beyond it the margin is not contained in sense experience, and is, thus, a priori.
   This is the logic which led thinkers to abandon empiricism in favour of either apriorism or conventionalism [p. 7].

Sensationalism, the thesis that all our knowledge of the world comes to us through the senses, is incompatible with the view that genuine *theoretical* knowledge exists. But what, then, are our theoretical concepts? Are they mere flights of the imagination? This is indeed the answer provided by conventionalism (Agassi, 1966b):

Conventionalism gives great scope to the imagination, and views both mathematics and theoretical science as admirable structures produced by the imagination. But in admitting that theories go beyond experience conventionalism empties theories of all factual or empirical content. It denies that theories are empirical or factual or informative. It claims that a theory is not informative knowledge but our way of looking at particular facts, our way of classifying particular observed facts. Like mathematics, theoretical science is merely an empty structure to store information in, a way of saying things, a language. Nothing in reality strictly corresponds to abstract or imagined theoretical concepts like 'space curvature' or 'atom'. These words are no more than shorthand symbols with no independent meaning (their meanings are given by implicit definitions), and statements containing them impart no more information than the information procured by sensations alone [pp. 4–5].

Conventionalism can thus become the most sophisticated form of justificationist skepticism. It has traditionally been endorsed by sensationalists as a last-ditch defense of their postion and in practice amounts to a *tu quoque* against criticism. Yet despite their sophistication, conventionalists are still *irrational* justificationists.

But there is another way to conceive of the relation between science and experience. Instead of providing an absolute foundation, experience allows us to construct an "empirical basis." But as Popper (1959) emphasized, this basis is both conjectural and fallible, to say nothing of conventional:

The empirical basis of objective science has thus nothing 'absolute' about it. Science does not rest upon rock-bottom. The bold structure of its theories rises, as it were, above a swamp. It is like a building erected upon piles. The piles are driven down from above into the swamp, but not down to any natural or 'given' base; and when we cease our attempts to drive our piles into a deeper layer, it is not because we have reached firm ground. We simply stop when we are satisfied that they are firm enough to carry the structure, at least for the time being [p.111].

Acknowledging this requires, however, the abandonment of justificationist rationality. As Sellars (1963) noted, "Empirical knowledge, like its sophisticated extension, science, is rational, not because it has a *foundation* but because it is a self-correcting enterprise which can put *any* claim in jeopardy, though not *all* at once [p. 170]." The chapters that follow explore the ramifications of that seemingly obvious statement.

4 Criticisms from Nonjustificational Frameworks

The distinction between (effective) criticisms of justificationism from within and from without is not hard and fast; some could easily be put forth by theorists of either camp. Yet several devastating arguments could hardly have arisen except within a nonjustificational context. In this chapter we examine two major criticisms of justificationism (concerning its quest for instant assessment) that arose from within the framework of Karl Popper's "critical fallibilism," which is historically the first nonjustificational philosophy: Paul Feyerabend's philosophy of proliferation and theoretical pluralism, and Popper's and Lakatos's arguments against any logic of inductive inference in science.

THEORETICAL PLURALISM AND THE ASSESSMENT OF THEORIES

There are two aspects of assessment to be examined: the acceptance of theoretical propositions into the body of science and the elimination or rejection of such propositions. Let us consider the problem of rejection first. The received view, in spite of its occasional acknowledgement of the conceptual nature of facts, portrays science as *literally* proceeding according to *modus tollens* in the rejection of incorrect theories: Given a theory or hypothesis H and a predicted outcome O, if the outcome does not obtain ($\sim O$), then the theory is said to be falsified or refuted according to the logical form *modus tollens*. *Modus ponens* and *modus tollens* are proof procedures —i.e., valid logical inference schemes—from syllogistic logic (see any

$$H \supset O \qquad \text{Hypothesis implies Observation}$$
$$\sim O \qquad \text{Observation does not obtain}$$
$$\therefore \sim H \qquad \text{Therefore reject the Hypothesis}$$

FIG. 4.1. *Modus Tollens* as the "logic" of falsification.

$$(H + A) \supset O \qquad \text{Hypothesis plus auxiliary assumptions implies Observation}$$
$$\sim O \qquad \text{Observation does not obtain}$$
$$\therefore \sim (H + A) \qquad \text{Therefore both the Hypothesis and Assumptions cannot be true at once}$$

FIG. 4.2. Grünbaum's modification of *Modus Tollens*.

competent introductory logic text for their discussion; e.g., Copi, 1954; Rescher, 1964). *Ponens* deals with the confirmation of a proposition that "follows from" another, whereas *tollens* enables one to reject a propostion if its logical consequence does not obtain. Figure 4.1 schematizes the rejection of a theory according to *modus tollens*. Now this picture of rejection is admitted to be a little too simple. In attempting to "correct" the Duhemian thesis that any proposition of science can be held, come what may, Grünbaum (1963) was led to reformulate the test situation as: $(H + A) \supset O$, to take account of "background or auxiliary assumptions" (A) in testing (thus if $\sim O$, it is not yet clear whether it is H or A that is to be rejected) (see Fig. 4.2). But this admission already defeats the justificationist.

For if the conceptual nature of facts is acknowledged, then the hypothesis, the "auxiliary assumptions," and the outcome are *equally* theoretical in nature. *The testing of a theory is a matter of choice between competing theoretical statements*. If there is no "natural" separation of "theoretical" and "observational" levels, then there is no natural separation of theory from background. Thus, one must abandon the conception of testing as a problem of "how to replace a theory that is 'refuted' by the facts" and replace it with the appraisal of "which alternative among many competing theories to accept, when it is known in advance that they are *all* false (because no theory agrees with all its relevant observations)." This is a statement of the switch from a monotheoretical to a pluralistic model of theory assessment. Note that such a switch is *automatically* one from justificationism (with the notion of proof underlying "testing" and "refutation") to one of nonjustificationism (and the problem of acceptance of conjectual assertions that cannot be proven true). According to Lakatos (1968b):

> The problem is then not when we should stick to a '*theory*' in the face of 'known facts' and when the other way round. The problem is *not* what to do when 'theories' clash with 'facts'. Such a 'clash' is only suggested by the

monotheoretical deductive model. Whether a proposition is a '*fact*' or a '*theory*' depends on your methodological decision. 'Empirical basis' is a monotheoretical notion, it is *relative* to some monotheoretical deductive structure. In the pluralistic model the clash is between two high-level theories: an *interpretative theory* to provide the facts and an *explanatory theory* to explain them; and the interpretative theory may be on quite as high a level as the explanatory theory. The problem is not whether a refutation is real or not. The problem is how to repair an inconsistency between the 'explanatory theory' under test and the— explicit or hidden—'interpretative' theories; or, if you wish, *the problem is which theory to consider as the interpretative one which provides the 'hard' facts and which the explanatory one which 'tentatively' explains them.* Thus experiments do not overthrow theories, as Popper₁ has it, but only increase the problem-fever of the body of science. *No theory forbids some state of affairs specifiable in advance; it is not that we propose a theory and Nature may shout NO. Rather, we propose a maze of theories, and Nature may shout INCONSISTENT [pp. 161–162].*

A consequence of the pluralistic model of evaluation is that science *can* progress in the absence of "refutations" altogether. Lakatos (1968b) saw this more clearly than others:

> Let us finally mention that the separation by Popper₂ of the notions of (low-level) 'refutation' and growth, soldered together by Popper₁, is so sharp, that according to Popper₂ science can grow without any 'refutations' leading the way. It is perfectly possible that theories be put forward 'progressively' in such a rapid succession that the refutation of the *n*-th appears only as the corroboration of the *n* + 1-th. According to Popper₁, the growth of science is *linear*, in the sense that theories are followed by eliminating refutations, and these refutations in turn by new theories. According to Popper₂, the growth of science is pluralistic: 'Elimination depends on the condition that sufficiently many and sufficiently different theories are offered'. This pluralistic aspect of Popper₂'s philosophy was elaborated and further developed by Paul Feyerabend [p.166].

(As we detail in the Appendix [Chapter 11], the convenient fictions—Popper₁ and Popper₂—refer to stages in the development of the philosophy of Karl Popper. Popper₁ is a sophisticated justificationist who replaced "confirmation" by "conventional falsification," and Popper₂ is the first real nonjustificationist.)

By now it should be clear that the classic picture of science is crumbling away. First proof and certainty were watered down to "probable truth." But the quest for justification remained. Then the "empirical basis" was seen to be theory contaminated, and factual relativity was admitted. Now it is clear that theories are not evaluated in isolation against neutral facts but rather in a maze of competing alternatives. With this step it must be realized that science can progress in the absence of refutations altogether. This is a giant step away from *any* justificationist picture. The next one can be taken when it is realized that science can progress in the absence of confirmation, also. This we can see in examining the failure of "confirmation theory" or probabilistic inductive logic. But let us conclude this section by noting that all scientific theories are, indeed, *factually false*.

The fact that all theories are or will be falsified can be shown a priori; it is *not* an empirical claim. Bunge (1967, Vol. 1) beautifully summarized why this is so.

> Every scientific theory is built, from the start, as an idealization of real systems or situations. That is, the very building of a scientific theory involves *simplifications* both in the selection of relevant variables and in the hypothesizing of relations (e.g., law statements) among them. Such simplifications are made whether or not we realize that they amount to errors—not mistakes but just discrepancies with actual fact. Moreover, this is not a mere descriptive statement concerning actual habits of theory construction: it is a rule of theory construction that as many simplifications as needed are to be made at the start, relaxing them gradually and only according as they are shown to constitute too brutal amputations. Such simplifications are, of course, deliberate departures from the truth.
>
> The idealizations inherent in the initial assumptions will be propagated to their testable consequences; moreover, auxiliary simplifying assumptions known to be false (e.g., that the earth is flat, or that it is perfectly spherical) must often be added to the axioms proper in order to derive theorems comparable with empirical data. When such theorems are subjected to empirical tests a discrepancy with the outcomes of such tests will sooner or later emerge—the finer the empirical techniques the sooner. And such a discrepancy will force the theoretician to gradually complicate the theoretical picture or even to make an entirely fresh start. But the improved and more complex theory will no less refer immediately to an ideal model than the previous theory. This cannot be helped, because theories are conceptual systems rather than bundles of experiences [p. 388].

THE DEMISE OF INSTANT RATIONALITY

The goal of the theory of instant rational assessment is to provide an algorithm, a mechanical formula, such that *any* proposition may be evaluated on the merits of its evidence. Confirmation theory (a better name than "inductive logic"), even though it may yield "probable" truths, is to be infallible in this methodological sense. That is what is summarized in the formula $P(h,e) = C$: an evaluation procedure that—*although it yields a "probabilified" degree of truth*—is still an *infallible procedure*. Inductive inference, when performed according to the codified rules of confirmation theory, is to guarantee an assessment of the *truth* of a scientific proposition (the probability calculus underlying inductive logic is being taken to assess the *justification* of a proposition = its certainty = it *probability* of being true). Inductive "logic" is to be *the inductive judge*: the judge of the *scientific merit* of a proposition.

If it can be shown that inductive logic or "confirmation theory" *cannot* perform the function of the "inductive judge," then it follows that the quest for a theory of *instant* rational assessment is chimerical. And indeed this is so, as we see in studying the *abdication of the inductive judge*. Once we have seen that there is *no* instant rational assessment possible, then it becomes clear that growth, or scientific progress, is actually the first major topic for a successful metatheory of the scientific endeavor: In nonjustificational metatheories, growth replaces instant assessment as the most crucial concern.

Confirmation theory runs afoul of two major criticisms: First, it presupposes a monotheoretical theory of testing *and* an invariant factual basis (the basis being the evidence for the proposition under assessment). Second, probability, in the form of logical probability or the calculus of probability, *does not apply* to the propositions of science. That is, empirical scientific propositions are equally *improbable* and *unprovable*: That which *is* probable or certain (e.g., tautologies) turns out to be *uninformative* and not empirical. Consider these points in order.

The devastating argument against a theory of rational assessment from the pluralistic nature of the scientific endeavor is simply that the *choice of a language for science implies a conjecture as to what is relevant evidence for what, or what is connected, by natural necessity, to what*. Now, how can the inductive logician choose *the correct language* for science? For instance, Carnap in 1950 thought that "*the* observation language" was the absolute, correct one. When criticized (by, e.g., Putnam and Nagel), he said it was "*the* theoretical language." But it should be clear that there is no *single* theoretical language any more than there is a single observational one. *Confirmation theory can work only if it is possible to exhaustively separate "the" theoretical and observational languages, i.e., in a monotheoretical system with a firm basis*.

But the growth of science, even during normal science puzzle-solving, *changes* its languages and therefore changes the structure of any confirmation theory: The inductive machine, which was to be the infallible algorithm for inference, will require *complete reprogramming* with each language change. But how can the inductive judge tell us which language to choose? Without external, i.e., noninductive, aid, it cannot. Lakatos (1968a) put the dilemma thusly:

> This consideration shows that the essential part of 'language planning' far from being the function of the inductive logician is a mere by-product of scientific theorizing. The inductive logician can, at best, say to the scientist: 'if you choose to accept the language L, then *I* can inform you that, in L, $c(h,e) = q$'. This, of

course, is a complete retreat from the original position in which the inductive judge was to tell the scientist, on the sole basis of h and e, how much h was confirmed on the basis of e: 'All we need for calculating c(h,e) is a logical analysis of the meanings of the two sentences'. But if the inductive judge needs to get from the scientist in addition to h and e also the language of the most advanced, best-corroborated theory, what then does the scientist need the inductive judge for [p. 364]?

Thus, confirmation theory is no less fallible than science itself. Therefore, it is unnecessary as a guide to research practice, and therefore it cannot be a theory of instant rational assessment.

As an aside, note that the fact-correcting and/or refuting nature of science destroys the possibility of an *inductive* logic of scientific *discovery* (growth). We are primarily concerned to refute "confirmation theory as a theory of instant assessment"—our problem (1) in Chapter 1. But it cannot work for problem (2) (growth) either, as Duhem noted at the turn of the century. This is because successor theories often *deny* the facts of their predecessors; is so, they cannot be inductively "founded" upon them. Inductive logicians have failed to notice this—that even if, per impossible, they could provide a theory of instant assessment, it would not automatically solve the problem of growth in science.

Consider now the second objection to confirmation theory. Earlier we noted that it has been unquestioningly assumed that "degree of evidential support" should somehow be equated with probability in the sense of the probability calculus. It was the acceptance of this "identity" that led to the development of a confirmation theory that was to define a countably additive measure function over the entire field of sentences (hypotheses, propositions) of the complete "language" of science. Once such a function is defined, the degree of confirmation of h can be computed by taking $P(h,e) = p(h,e)/p(e)$.

Popper argued—in 1934 one way, in 1954 another (see Popper 1959)—that this implicit equation of degree of evidence and probability is incorrect. Popper's 1934 argument is that the degree of corroboration (*not* confirmation) of a theory is in *inverse ratio* to its logical probability. Scientific hypotheses, if they are good, *informative* ones, are highly novel, bold conjectures that are as logically *improbable* as possible. If you increase the (empirical) content of a theory, its corroborability (possibility of surviving test) increases, but its probability (both prior and posterior) *decreases*. The probability of a tautology is 1 or certainty; it is certain that "white swans are white" is true. But tautologies are uninformative—they tell us nothing new. Scientific factual propositions, however, *are* highly informative; and their "probability" (prior *or* posterior) of being true (*even* if they have survived repeated attempts at disconfirmation) is 0. This is why Popper argues that the aim of science is the construction of bold, highly informative conjectures— that are as improbable as possible. The aim of science is to learn new things—

not to enshrine certainty. The 1954 argument slightly weakened the inverse ratio thesis: It is not always the case that there is a direct ratio between degree of corroboration and content (see Lakatos, 1968a, p. 353ff.). But the point remains: The probability (or provability) of a hypothesis is not equivalent to its (degree of) evidential support, and this is devastating to the entire program of confirmation theory.

It is at this point that confirmation theorists cease talking in terms of the probability of scientific statements and start musing about "degrees of belief" and "rational betting quotients." But regardless of the psychological utility of such strategies, this again signals the end of the program within justification-ism (Lakatos, 1968a):

> It has been a cornerstone of empiricism that the only justification, total or partial, of a hypothesis—and therefore the only rational ground for total or partial belief in it—is its evidential support. And there has also been a longstanding dogma about degrees of belief, namely, that their best touchstone is how much one is willing to bet on them. (Carnap attributed this idea to Ramsey, but Ramsey himself refers to it as an 'old-established' thesis.) But if evidential support was to determine degrees of belief, and degrees of belief were to be measured by betting quotients, then these three concepts natually were merged into one. But now this old-established trinity is split. And this rings the death knell of the *one* concept of 'rational belief', 'credence', 'credibility', etc., in any objective sense of these terms [p. 358].

If the fusion of induction and probability breaks down, the positive program of neojustificationism breaks down, also. If induction cannot assess the merit of a scientific proposition (its validity or truth) in terms of its probability, it cannot assess scientific merit at all. This is because the whole program of neojustificationist philosophy revolves around justifying inductive logic (as a formal codification of all inductive inference) as a means of knowledge acquisition. But with the failure of the justificationist picture of acceptance (inductive inference) and rejection (theory disconfirmation or rejection), nothing is left of this "positive" program. At this point, virtually nothing remains of the received view of the scientific endeavor. Scientific knowledge is neither proven nor probabilified. There is no theory of instant rational assessment, nor could there be one. There are no facts that remain fixed forever; there is no solid "empirical basis" or foundation of knowledge. Science does not test its theories in insolation but rather compares a maze of theoretical formulations and assesses their consistency. Not only does science grow or progress in the absence of confirmation and refutation, but it can progress in the absence of *any* of the justificationist criteria. What remains is to see why this is so.

5 Nonjustificational Conceptions: Knowledge, Rationality, and the Growth of Science

Every thesis consonant with one metatheoretical perspective is simultaneously a criticism of its rivals. Thus this chapter and the next are obviously continuing criticisms of justificational positions. But such criticisms also have a very positve aspect that extends far beyond arguing against the received view: They argue for alternative conceptions that provide solutions to problems that have debilitated justificationism. This chapter begins that positive task by overviewing the nature of human knowledge and rationality and the revolutionary as well as cumulative aspects of scientific growth. It concludes by indicating how the dilemma of ultimate commitment, which eventually stultifies justificationist "ways of life," can be resolved by stepping outside the metatheory to a new conception of rationality and criticism.

THE NATURE OF KNOWLEDGE AND RATIONALITY

Recall that justificationism identifies knowledge equally with proof and authority. It was assumed that *truth* was to be transmitted to the conclusions of scientific explanations via the logical relation of deducibility, also that there are sources of *ultimate authority* for knowledge claims. With the shift to a nonjustificational viewpoint, these assumptions and identifications are rejected. Knowledge becomes a matter of having defensible opinions, or conjectures, that can neither be proven true nor justified by an appeal to *any* ultimate authority.

Knowledge claims, whether scientific or otherwise, are always *fallible*; anything in both common sense and the "body of science" is subject to criticism and consequent revision or rejection, *at all times and for all time*. We may (and often do) reject "well-established" scientific propositions, and we may (and often do) reinstate previously rejected propositions. Thus science is a *comprehensively critical endeavor*; *all* its conjectures, including the most fundamental standards and basic positions, are always and continually open to criticism. Nothing in science is immune to criticism or justified fideistically, by appeal to authority. This leads to a striking change in our conception of the nature and role of criticism (Bartley, 1962):

> The philosophical questions that would have to be asked within such a program would show a striking structural change. The traditional demand for justification—the "How do you know?" question—would not legitimately arise. And if it arose in fact, the philosopher would have to reply: "I *do not know:* I have no guarantees."
>
> If he wanted to be a little more precise, he might elaborate: "Some of the beliefs I hold may in fact be true; but since there are no guarantees or criteria of truth, no ways of definitely deciding, I can never know for sure whether what I believe to be true is in fact so." For such a philosopher, a different question would become important: *How can our intellectual life and institutions be arranged so as to expose our beliefs, conjectures, policies, positions, sources of ideas, traditions, and the like—whether or not they are justifiable—to maximum criticism, in order to counteract and eliminate as much intellectual error as possible*? This concern could hardly clash more sharply with that of the traditional rationalist for whom the main intellectual offense was to hold an unjustifiable belief [pp. 139–140].

The first reasonably consistent nonjustificational philosophy of criticism is due to Karl Popper (see the Appendix, Chapter 11). For Popper, criticism does not rely on the justificational *transmission* of truth to the conclusion but rather on the *retransmission of falsity from the conclusion to the premises*. Scientific propositions remain conjectural through and through, however; even the falsity of a statement does not *establish* or *prove* the refutation of it. "Refutation" is always itself open to criticism. Thus testing can in principle go on forever, and *nothing* is conclusively "established" or "refuted." And this does not lead to an infinite regress—because the *aim* of "justifying" a scientific proposition has been abandoned (Popper, 1963):

> Thus every statement (or 'basic statement') remains essentially conjectural; but it is a conjecture which can be easily tested. These tests, in their turn, involve new conjectural and testable statements, and so on, *ad infinitum*; and should we try to *establish* anything with our tests, we should be involved in an infinite regress. But as I explained in my *Logic of Scientific Discovery* (especially section 29) we do not *establish* anything by this procedure: we do not wish to 'justify' the 'acceptance' of anything, we only test our theories critically, in order to see whether or not we can bring a case against them [p. 388].

Thus the nature of knowledge changes from being proven assertion (or probable assertion) to being *warranted* assertion. Knowledge claims must be defended, to be sure; however the defense of such a claim is not an attempt to *prove* it, but rather the marshaling of "good reasons" in its behalf. And the "good reasons" are never justifications of the claim, only conjectures that are relevant to its assessment. The only way to defend fallible knowledge claims is by marshaling other fallible knowledge claims—such as the best contingent theories that we possess. There are no "ultimate" sources of knowledge or epistemological authorities; everything is equally a potential "source" of knowledge, but none is *the* authoritative one.

The relationship of truth to knowledge in a nonjustificational framework is more complex than their definitional identity within justificationism. Truth is not to be confused with confirmation or the evidence upon which a claim is based; Carnap (1936) showed that clearly in defending the legitimacy of truth as a metalinguistic concept. Truth in science is a regulative ideal; we may aspire to it, but even if we fell upon it, we would be unable to *know it as such*. But if truth is not simply "knowledge," then its exact nature is in doubt; and it requires a *theory of truth* to tell what the nature and role of truth in science actually is. Specification of the nature of truth, and of the approach to truth, poses considerable problems (see Chapter 6, this volume).

If the nature of knowledge changes (from proven to warranted assertion) in the abandonment of justificationism, the nature of rationality does also. For both the justificationist and the nonjustificationist, the rational way is the critical way. To be rational in one's endorsement of a position, one must *criticize* it. But what the justificationist means by being rational, i.e., by being critical, is to be justificational. Criticism within justificationism is fused to proof and to authority in exactly the same manner as knowledge. Methodologically speaking, the heart of justificationism is the fusion of criticism with the ideal of justification (demands for which can be satisfied only by an appeal to the rational authority). A justificationist critically assessing a position attempts to prove it, to establish it—and the rationality of science lies in its justificational nature. (Evading the dilemma that this approach engenders is discussed in the last section of this chapter.)

In contrast to this, the nonjustificational philosophies of criticism locate rationality in criticism rather than in justification. One can be rational without attempting to prove—by criticizing or testing (as severely as necessary)—every position that one entertains. But now it becomes obvious that criticism, far from being an intuitively clear and unproblematic notion, is a matter for intensive study. What constitutes (adequate) criticism may vary from case to case (see Bartley, 1964, p. 22f). Indeed, there are times when being *committed* to a position (even dogmatically) may be an effective means of being critical (see the last section).

THE HISTORIOGRAPHY OF SCIENCE:
THE ROLE OF SCIENTIFIC REVOLUTIONS

For the justificationist, the history of science must be cumulative, continuous, and coherent in the sense that all scientific knowledge in all domains must be compatible. Justificationist historiography thus pictures science as a building-block endeavor that points inexorably toward the present. Writing a history consists mainly of ancestor worship—praising those who led us to the present and condemning those who sidetracked us (see Agassi, 1963). The questions of history are largely those of which ancestors to portray as white knights who amassed truth and which to portray as black knights who led us astray. Such a historian must *ignore* (i.e., write *out* of history) two obvious phenomena: (a) schools and controversies, and (b) the black *and* white nature of even the whitest of white knights. More important, he or she *must* ignore all scientific *revolutions*, for there can be no such thing as fact-*correcting* science that denies the validity of portions of the "eternally certified" edifice of scientific knowledge.

But that is what revolutions are all about; *successor* theories in a domain are *by definition* theories that *deny the validity* of their predecessors (otherwise they would not be successors, but merely refinements). Duhem (1954) appears to have been the first historian to make historiographic mileage of the fact-correcting or refuting nature of science; he used it to argue against the philosophy of inductivism. But Duhem, still a justificationist, gave up the hope of a positive theory of growth and embraced skepticism (actually, the position of conventionalism: the idea that theories are calculation devices, that no *genuine* theoretical knowledge is possible [see Agassi, 1966b]. In contrast, since 1934 Popper used the revolutionary nature of science to argue against both inductivism *and* conventionalism. His thesis, maintained consistently since then, is that no genuine science can resemble the building-block picture sketched by justificationism. Popper's motto for the maximal advancement of science is "revolutions in permanence!" and it is this framework that leads to the pluralistic methodology and the "philosophy of proliferation" defended by Paul Feyerabend (1965a, 1965b).

Thomas Kuhn, in *The structure of scientific revolutions*, wrote an enormously successful historiographic refutation of justificationist history, which literally shocked the scientific and philosophical establishment. For that reason, Popperians were initially in agreement with him and provided an enthusiastic audience. But Kuhn, unlike Popper, emphasizes the indispensability of "normal science" as well as "revolutionary science." Kuhn claims that normal science, as a puzzle-solving tradition that holds "theoretical and philosophical" considerations at arm's length, contains within itself a sufficient mechanism to lead to revolutionary science. This "mechanism" is the perception (and collection) of *anomaly*. Thus, Kuhn claims that in the *mature* sciences, the philosophy of proliferation is *unnecessary* to guarantee progress and can indeed become a drawback. Kuhn (1970b) sees Popper's methodology as relevant to the *immature* or protosciences and the arts but *not* to those sciences where progress is already in evidence:

> My claim has been—it is my single genuine disagreement with Sir Karl about normal science—that with such a theory in hand the time for steady criticism and theory proliferation has passed. Scientists for the first time have an alternative which is not merely aping what has gone before. . . . In the developed sciences, unlike philosophy, it is technical puzzles that provide the usual occasion and often the concrete materials for revolution. This availability together with the information and signals they provide account in large part for the special nature of scientific progress. Because they can ordinarily take current theory for granted, exploiting rather than criticizing it, the practitioners of mature sciences are freed to explore nature to an esoteric depth and detail otherwise unimaginable. Because that exploration will ultimately isolate severe trouble spots, they can be confident that the pursuit of normal science will inform them when they can most usefully become Popperian critics. Even in the developed sciences, there is an essential role for Sir Karl's methodology. It is the strategy appropriate to those occasions when something goes wrong with normal science, when the discipline encounters crisis [pp. 246, 247].

Thus the Kuhn–Popper controversy that permeates recent literature about the methodology of scientific research primarily concerns the necessary and sufficient mechanisms of growth and progress. It is a controversy that abandons our first problem—the quest for instant rationality—for the second—a theory of scientific progress. It is also a clash of *critical* fallibilism and *psychological* fallibilism as instances of nonjustificational philosophies. At the metatheoretical level, the most important question concerns whether the rationality of the scientific endeavor can be reconstructed in solely philosophical terms or whether it will invariably require a socio-psychological reconstruction. Popper attempts a purely philosophical reconstruction; Kuhn opts for an explanation of science-as-an-activity in social–psychological terms. We shall see that the question of the relevance of psychology to epistemology and philosophy of science recurs through all the "current issues" discussions and that it is one of the most important topics in the clash of available nonjustificational approaches to science.

But the historiographic point remains; the justificationist continuity approach, which pictures science as a cumulative record, cannot be correct. The history of science presents a series of revolutionary reconceptualizations of its domain rather than just incremental steps forward.

THE DILEMMAS OF COMMITMENT IN
RATIONALITY AND SCIENCE

Let us now tie together two topics: the dilemma of commitment facing the justificational rationalist and the dilemma of how critical to be in scientific practice. The dilemma of commitment facing conceptions of rationalist identity is that they *oversubscribe* their adherents to an impossible goal and hence force a retreat to commitment *in actual practice*. By proposing an unworkable conception of rationality, one that cannot be lived up to, the justificationist forces himself to embrace rationalism irrationally, as an act of faith. The dilemma of commitment in scientific practice is that rationalist identity demands that the justificational scientist be constantly critical, yet progress seems to occur best when the scientist is firmly committed to a way of seeing reality specified by a normal science research tradition. Being critical in periods of normal science gets in the way of doing good science, and that seems clearly paradoxical.

The dilemma of ultimate commitment concerns the alleged limits of rationality. For the justificationist, rationality requires the justification of not only our knowledge claims but of our ultimate standards of rationality. This poses a problem; there is an infinite regress involved in justifying ultimate standards, for one can always ask "How do you know?" with regard to a putative "ultimate" standard. Thus the dilemma: Either justification comes to an end and we irrationally accept some standard, i.e., retreat to a commitment in rationality; or we are left with skepticism—the view that no knowledge and rationality are possible. We must either succeed in justifying our commitment to rationality, or we shall be forced to conclude that the rational way of life cannot be rationally shown to be superior to its alternatives.

Traditional epistemology has been a succession of proposals of rational authorities that were to be necessary and sufficient for the justification of scientific inference as a rational source of knowledge. In order to avoid skepticism, one or another fideistic commitment to a rational authority was always made. But this, of course, gives comfort to the irrationalists who pin their commitment to faith: Because scientists are also committed to a faith in science, the scientists cannot criticize the irrationalists. The irrationalists have a *tu quoque* reply to criticism, pointing out that their "scientific" critics are equally committed to a point of view that they cannot defend and therefore criticism is useless—all can choose their own commitments and be immune to the criticism of others. Universal conventionalism based upon fideistic commitment has been the result.

Because of its conceptions of rationalist identity, justificationism could not defeat the *tu quoque*. Sophisticated justificationists admitted this and retreated to conventionalism (or its popular variants—instrumentalism or pragmatism) when their position was questioned. When the criticism lessened, they returned from skeptical justificationism to the posture of positive justificationism in one or another form of inductivism [see Agassi, 1966b]. The justificationist conception of criticism is responsible (along with the equation of knowledge with proof) for this predicament. Justificationism fuses criticism to the attempt to justify such that to be critical of a position means to attempt to justify it.

But the consistent justificationist critic is one who *never succeeds* in being critical (because of the power of the *tu quoque*). However, if the key concepts are unfused, the justificationist can be led out of a self-made prison. By abandoning the authoritarian conception of knowledge and the equation of criticism with justification, one can abandon *critical rationalism*—the neojustificationist conception of rationalist identity—for comprehensively critical rationalism and can break the power of the *tu quoque*.

The classic form of rationalist identity is a position that may be called *comprehensive* rationalism. Following Bartley and Popper, it may be characterized by the following requirements:

1. A rationalist accepts any position justifiable by appeal to the criteria or authorities deemed rational;
2. A rationalist accepts *only* positions that can be so justified.

Not suprisingly, such a conception of rationalist identity cannot be attained. As Bartley pointed out, the first principle is itself not capable of rational justification and is thus unjustifiable and irrational. As the second requirement forbids holding unjustifiable beliefs, there now arises an irreconcilable conflict between the two requirements of comprehensive rationalist identity. One of them must go; and the most likely candidate is the second requirement, because it too cannot be justified by appeal to rational criteria or authorities. If true, it must by its own directive lead to its own rejection: It asserts its own untenability. Thus it turns out to be impossible to endorse comprehensive rationalism on purely logical grounds.

At this point, the strategy of minimizing the skeptics' victory arises (Bartley, 1962):

> Although these difficulties have battered rationalists severely, they have driven comparatively few of them into outright irrationalism. Rather, rationalists have sought some way to minimize the importance of their critics' arguments while acknowledging their cogency; to make their critics' *victory* "bloodless" or even "fictitious", as A. J. Ayer puts it. After admitting that their own position contained the germs of irrationalism, they have taken businesslike steps to immunize themselves from further contagion and to prevent the disease from spreading [p. 149].

It is also at this point that the second conception of rationalist identity, *critical rationalism*, appears to water down skepticism. Critical rationalism is endorsed by the sophisticated or neojustificationist as a concession to the untenability of classic justificationism and its conception of comprehensive rationalism. Instead of making the essence of rationality its comprehensiveness, the critical rationalist switches rationality to "the critical approach." By acknowledging the limits of (comprehensive) rationalism, the critical rationalist at least postpones the crisis of integrity. Critical rationalism holds that:

1. Rationality *is* limited, because some things (e.g., standards of rationality) cannot be justified by appeal to rational standards;
2. This concession is claimed to be unimportant, in that the skeptic's victory is somehow "bloodless";
3. The ultimate basis for any position is the *tu quoque*—a retreat to commitment in personal or social standards that are assumed to be beyond challenge.

An excellent example of such a position is Ayer's (1956) attempt to evade the problem of the justification of induction. Ayer grants the failure of comprehensive rationalism to defeat skepticism and takes as his task making the acknowledged victory that the skeptic has won bloodless or fictitious; the honesty of Ayer's approach makes it a *critical* rationalism. But he must show why his approach, *qua* theory of rationality, can allow one to dispense with the justification of ultimate standards. And it is this latter task upon which he fails. Ayer's reason for why standards of rationality require no justification is that such standards *set* the standard and are not to be *judged* by it. Such a standard "could be irrational only if there were a standard of rationality which it failed to meet; whereas in fact it goes to set the standard: arguments are judged to be rational or irrational by reference to it [p. 75]." Later he adds: "When it is understood that there logically could be no court of superior jurisdiction, it hardly seems troubling that inductive reasoning should be left, as it were, to act as judge in its own cause. The skeptic's merit is that he forces us to see that this must be so [p. 75]." Ayer has, very obviously, simply said *tu quoque* to the skeptic; his is a fideistic commitment rather than a reason (a justification). Instead of justification of standards, the philosopher's task is merely to *describe* them. (This is one motivation for the trivialization of philosophy that occurred in British "ordinary language analysis" after World War II.)

The problem with Ayer's defense is that it begs the question at issue (Bartley, 1964):

Ingenious as it might seem, Ayer's argument could not be relevant to the present discussion, let alone valid, *unless* some particular standards and procedures of rationality, such as Ayer's own, which include "scientific induction," are *assumed* to be the correct ones. If some particular standards of rationality *are* the correct ones, then there can exist no other rational standards which are also correct but which can nevertheless invalidate the former as irrational. Yet this "if" marks a very big assumption; for *this is precisely what is at issue in the problem of rationality*. Whether regarded historically or theoretically, the most important criticisms of putative standards of rationality have questioned *whether* they were correct. Alternative conceptions of scientific argument and method, such as Popper's which denies the *existence* of inductive procedure, let alone its rational legitimacy, do claim that there are standards of rationality which positions like Ayer's fail to meet [p. 16].

Because it begs the question at issue and because Ayer's position also *bars criticism in advance* by defining "rationality" such that his standards are automatically rational, it is clearly fideistic in nature; Ayer has retreated to a commitment in "rationality" rather than defeating the force of the skeptic's victory. That is, Ayer has strengthened the skeptic's position by his failure. Critical rationalism, the conception of rationality held by virtually all contemporary philosophers and scientists, "succeeds" only by invoking the power of the *tu quoque*. And to understand that is to understand that it does not succeed at all.

ANSWERING THE TU QUOQUE: COMPREHENSIVELY CRITICAL RATIONALISM

The immense power of the *tu quoque* hinges upon the fusion of concepts to which it refers. Unfuse the key concepts—justification and criticism—and the justificationist prisoners can be led out of their self-made cells. But in leading them out of their dilemma, they will no longer be justificationists.

Such a new, nonjustificational framework permits one to characterize rationalists as those who hold *all* their beliefs open to criticism *all* of the time. Comprehensively critical rationalists will never hold a belief or fundamental standard immune to criticism; they will never resort to faith or irrational commitment to justify acceptance of any belief. Most especially, they will never cut off criticism of their conception of rationality; comprehensively critical rationalism is itself an approach that is open to criticism. That is, this conception of rationalist identity does not lead to a crisis of integrity; it is, according to its own formulation, rational. According to Bartley (1962):

Surprising as it might seem, the practice of critical argument can be criticized without paradox, contradiction, or any other logical difficulty. Just as it is possible for a democracy, through democratic processes, to commit suicide (e.g., through a majority vote to abolish democracy in favor of totalitarianism), so a comprehensively critical rationalist who was *not committed* to the belief that his position was the correct one could be argued, or argue himself, out of his rationalism.

For example, someone could devastatingly refute thing kind of rationalism if he were to produce an argument showing that at least some of the unjustified and unjustifiable critical standards necessarily used by a comprehensively critical rationalist were uncriticizable to boot, that here too *something* had to be accepted as uncriticizable in order to avoid circular argument and infinite regress [p. 149].

This conception of rationalist identity, which *locates rationality in criticism rather than justification*, is sufficient to break the power of the *tu quoque*. The power of the *tu quoque* is broken when the structure of the infinite regress is dissolved by identifying the essence of rationality with criticism rather than justification. One can be critical *forever*, never shutting off debate, without ever justifying or failing to justify a position or belief. If criticism is the essence of rationality, it is rational to hold an unjustified belief and *even an unjustifiable* one (so long as criticism is never cut short)! Indeed, justification is not *always* desirable (or undesirable) for the comprehensively critical rationalist; its merit in any given case is always "open to criticism."

But is Bartley's conception of rationality "nothing but" the idea of being constantly critical? The answer is emphatically "no." For on this account, criticism of commitment no longer boomerangs into a *tu quoque* to end criticism with fideism. Bartley's conception rules out *fideistic* commitment, to be sure, but it does not rule out commitment *simpliciter* (1962):

First, the claim that a rationalist need not commit himself even to argument is no claim that he will not or should not have strong convictions on which he is prepared to act. We can assume or be *convinced* of the truth of something without being *committed* to its truth. As conceived here, a rationalist can, while eschewing intellectual commitments, retain both the courage of his convictions and the courage to go on attacking his convictions—the courage to think and to go on thinking. . .

Second, a comprehensively critical rationalist, like other men, holds countless unexamined presuppositions and assumptions, many of which may be false. His rationality consists in his willingness to submit these to critical consideration when he discovers them or when they are pointed out to him. When one belief is subjected to criticism, many others have to be taken for granted—including those with which the criticism is being carried out. The latter are used as the basis of criticism not because they are themselves justified or beyond criticism, but because they are unproblematical at present: we possess no criticisms of them. For the time being these are, in that sense alone, beyond criticism. And one belief that is nearly always taken for granted when one or another belief is being criticized is the belief in criticism itself. But the fact that most of a man's beliefs are beyond criticism at any one time does not mean that any of them has to be beyond criticism all the time: this is not so logically, and probably not even practically. Nor does it mean that the belief in criticism itself may not come up for critical review from time to time [pp. 151–152].

Indeed, one thing that is most illuminating in Bartley's formulation is his insistence that *what counts as criticism*, in a nonjustificational point of view, *is far from obvious*. For example, abandoning the idea that criticism equals justification or proof entails abandoning the attempt to prove or disprove conclusively. Thus there is no instant rationality (or instant objectivity, as writers such as Trigg, 1973, have sought), as the inductive logician and the justificational falsificationist had hoped; to criticize a position is neither to prove nor to refute it. In a broad and vague sense, to criticize a position or theory (scientific or otherwise) is to work within it, to explore and articulate it and examine its consequences. For Bartley and other nonjustificational falsificationists, the detection and elimination of error is of prime importance; one articulates and examines a position to weed out error or at least to hold error in check as much as is possible.

But it does not follow that even the goal of eliminating error is best served (or even served *at all*) by being instantly or constantly critical. The shift to a nonjustificational approach abandons theories of instant rational assessment for once and for all. It is no longer *rational* to reject a view as erroneous and to eliminate it, *simply because it is falsified*. As we noted in Chapter 4, all theories *are* erroneous—i.e., falsified—all of the time. As Lakatos (1970) emphasized, one must treat budding research programs that go against established traditions leniently, for they may tell us much of importance despite the fact that they clash with currently held beliefs as to what is "rational." Indeed, if we were always constantly critical, there could be no revolutionary reconceptualizations in science, for we would—according to presently held canons of what is rational and what is critical—reject any position that clashed demonstrably with an accepted body of scientific theory and fact.

This reasoning, when applied to assessing the rationality of the scientific endeavor, leads to what appears to be a highly paradoxical result: In most cases in actual scientific practice, the most effective means of criticism available to a researcher is to remain committed to a position in order to fully articulate it and explore its consequences. The common conception of science as a constantly and instantly critical endeavor is an instance of residual justificationism, a hangover from the theory of instant rational assessment. In emphasizing the tenacity of normal science puzzle solving, both Thomas Kuhn and F. A. Hayek (especially 1948) have a conception of scientific rationality far more in keeping with the essential features of nonjustificational philosophies of criticism than does Karl Popper (see Chapter 8, this volume). One can be committed to conceiving the world in terms of a given normal science research tradition and still be rational; comprehensively critical rationalism is sufficiently flexible to allow for commitment. But to be rational, the sort of commitment that occurs in science must *not* be an irrational retreat ot commitment as in the *tu quoque*. By adopting a nonjustificational framework, the comprehensively critical rationalist can have a conception of rational identity that is not threatened by a crisis of integrity *and* also can admit the rationality of certain forms of commitment.

6 Nonjustificational Conceptions: Evidence and Support, Demarcation, and Truth in Conjectural Knowledge

Nonjustificational approaches to traditional problems rarely result in answers that are satisfactory to traditional thinkers; both the character of the problems and the possibilities of resolution are often different. A most characteristic result is the relocation of problems in different areas from which they originated. Then an old problem may be transformed into one or more new ones or indeed disappear as no longer a problem. This chapter traces transformations in the problems of assessment, demarcation, and truth. What we shall see is that the problem of support both disappears from philosophy and reappears transformed in psychology; demarcation turns out not to be a problem in the usual sense; and verisimilitude, as an approach to truth, is actually a matter of corroboration.

THE PROBLEM OF SUPPORT IN SCIENCE: EMPIRICAL CONTENT AND CORROBORATION

If scientific propositions can be neither verified nor falsified conclusively, and if science can progress in the absence of even conventionalized refutations, what then is their "positive" support? Popper's answer has been his theory of corroboration, which is an analytic appraisal of the status of a theory. Let us "assess" the merit of this theory.

Corroboration has to do with the "empirical content" and "excess empirical content" of a theory, and its focus is upon *growth*, not *confirmation*. It is neither another form of inductive inference nor—as confirmation theory was supposed to be—a "guide to scientific life" or an "inductive judge."

The *empirical content* of a theory consists of the class of its potential falsifiers. A theory is the more empirical for Popper, the more observations it *forbids*. If a theory has empirical content, it is *refutable*. *Excess* empirical content has to do with a theory's *boldness* and its ability to survive *severely* critical testing. But excess relative to what?—to the combination of rival theories that constitute the "background" of the testing (evaluating) situation. To corroborate a theory, one must test it and accept it by failing to reject it. A theory is corroborated if it has defeated some (potentially) falsifying hypothesis when subject to "testing." *Excess corroboration* occurs when it has excess empirical content (that is tested successfully) over its background theory (theories). That is, a theory has excess corroboration when it is shown to entail *novel* outcomes.

Corresponding to these two notions of corroboration are two of (tentative) acceptance for theories. Corresponding to corroboration is what Lakatos (1968a) called acceptance$_1$. A theory is judged acceptable$_1$ (prior to testing) if it *has* empirical content in excess of its background theory—i.e., if it is *not* ad hoc but genuinely "empirical." A theory is acceptable$_2$ if it predicts novel "facts" (relative to the background theories) that are corroborated in testing (this corresponds to excess corroboration).

It is clear that Popper's emphasis is on the growth of conjectural knowledge rather than refutation. The crucial characteristics of growth are excess content rather than content and excess corroboration rather than corroboration. This becomes clear when one asks when a theory is to be *eliminated* from the body of science. Refutation *alone* is definitely not sufficient, because *all* theories are born refuted. Rather, one eliminates (tentatively, subject to critical reassessment) a theory *only* when there exists an alternative theory that achieves *excess* corroboration (relative to the eliminated theory).

Consider how different this is from the justificationist outlook. The Popperian may accept$_1$ and accept$_2$ some theories *even when known to be false* but likewise reject some theories even if there is no evidence against them (if they have no excess content relative to their alternatives). The Popperian may accept them if they indicate *growth*, reject them if they do not.

The justificationist had only one notion of acceptability for scientific theories, and it is *neither* of the above. The necessary and sufficient notion of acceptance for the justificationist is that of *trustworthiness*—defined as *the degree to which it has been proved.* The nonjustificationist rejects this "monolithic" notion in toto but does have a third sense of acceptability that reinterprets trustworthiness. Acceptability$_3$ has to do with trustworthiness defined as *instrumental utility.* Acceptability$_3$ is required for an appraisal of the *future performance* of a theory. A theory is accepted$_3$ if it yields *reliable* predictions.

Something like acceptability$_3$ is at the heart of the justificationist's monolithic notion of acceptance. The theory of instant rational assessment was thus the means of achieving "acceptability." It is in this manner that *instrumentalism* becomes so dominant a picture of science in the received view. But Popper's methodology *requires* neither "inductive" assessment *nor* acceptability$_3$ (see Lakatos, 1968a, p. 392); he can evaluate theories on "nothing but" their acceptability$_1$ and acceptability$_2$.

Yet as Lakatos proposed, Popper can easily talk of acceptability$_3$ in terms of "total corroboration" or verisimilitude. Versimilitude is the difference between the truth content and the falsity content of a theory. Popper's reasoning would be (according to Lakatos) that a theory would be more acceptable$_3$, the nearer it comes to the "truth." This allows the body of "actual theoretical" science to be *inconsistent* (it will contain acceptable$_1$ and acceptable$_2$ theories, which may conflict) while retaining a consistent body of "instrumentally proven" acceptable$_3$ theories. Newton's mechanics "builds better bridges" than Einstein's (is more practically useful or acceptable$_3$), even though it is less acceptable$_2$.

But any "criterion" of acceptability$_3$ has serious shortcomings, as Lakatos (1968a) indicated:

> But whichever criterion of acceptability$_3$ we choose, it will have *two very serious shortcomings*. The first is that *it gives us very limited guidance*. While it offers us a body of 'most reliable' theories we cannot compare with its help the reliability of any two theories among these 'most reliable' ones. One cannot compare Popper's (total) 'degree of corroboration' for two unrefuted theories which have stood up to severe tests. All that we can know is that the theories in our latest body of accepted$_3$ theories have higher degrees of corroboration than their 'predecessors' in any past, discarded body of accepted$_3$ theories. A theory T_2 that supersedes T_1, inherits from T_1, the set of theories which T_1 had defeated: the corroboration of T_2 will clearly be higher than the corroboration of T_1. But the corroborations of two theories T_1 and T_2 can only be compared when the set of defeated theories in T_1's past is a subset of the set of defeated theories in T_2's past: that is, when T_1 and T_2 represent different stages of the same research programme. This circumstance reduces drastically the practical, technological use of corroboration as an estimate of reliability for competing technological designs. For each such design may be based on some theory which, in its own field, is the most advanced; therefore, each such theory belongs, in its own right, to the 'body of technologically recommendable theories', of theories accepted$_3$; and therefore, their degrees of corroboration will not be comparable. There is not, and cannot be, any *metric* of 'degree of corroboration'—indeed the expression 'degree of corroboration', in so far as it suggests the existence of such a metric, is misleading [pp. 395–396].

The Popperian conception of "reliability," in keeping with the nonjustificational approach, is *not certain*—i.e., is *not itself* perfectly reliable. Popper's theory of corroboration (which is all he stresses), maintains a stony silence about the future prospects of a theory. Future success is a practical matter of no concern to the acceptability$_2$ of a theory. The questions concerning the guidance of scientific life remain open; pragmatic action is the most pressing issue on the current scene (see Chapter 7).

THE PROBLEM OF SUPPORT IN SCIENCE:
THE NATURE AND ROLE OF POSITIVE EVIDENCE

The philosophical approach to corroboration just outlined is based upon the Popperian conception of trial and-error learning and is tailor-made to reflect Popper's slogan, "We learn from our mistakes." One can grant that science does indeed learn in the process of rejecting one theory in favor of another; but what is the point of positive evidence, i.e., data that agree with a particular position?

The justificationist thought that positive evidence could prove a theory to be true or prove it to be probable. The critical fallibilist rejects this interpretation and leaves positive evidence in limbo as far as science is concerned: Accumulating positive evidence merely indicates that one has not yet refuted a position. Some Popperians (Agassi, 1966a; and Settle, 1969, 1974) have argued, without great conviction, that positive evidence is relevant only in *technology*—which may indeed be "inductive" in character,—in contrast to science (which is noninductive and has no use for such support). Thus positive support would be limited to the realm of acceptability$_3$. But is there any other way to regard evidence that is consonant with a position?

One can shed some light on this problem by looking at the psychological role of evidence in scientific concept formation. Historically, it is obvious that supporting evidence, whether construed as proof or not, is far more appreciated and sought after by scientific research communities than refuting evidence. Kuhn portrayed this admirably in characterizing normal science research as puzzle-solving activity that holds theory (and thus the problems of assessment) at arm's length. This conception also removes evidence (at least in nomal science) from the methodological realm; but unlike the Popperians, Kuhn does not relegate it to technology. Instead, Kuhn moves the role of evidence from assessment to scientific concept formation, from methodology to scientific education or tuition and communication. What the scientist learns in working with exemplars is how to see disparate phenomena as manifestations of common underlying principles. The role of positive evidence is in the unpacking of generative conceptual schemata and their subsequent communication within the research community. What evidence does, how it functions, is to provide the scientist with surface structure manifestations of abstract, underlying rules of determination for the formation and extension of concepts. Data in this sense is the instantiation of theory and the means by which it is extended to new domains; it is how we "see" theoretical principles and subsequently see that their range of application can be extended.

Note that this points away from philosophy and toward psychology in the understanding of scientific practice. Two points are at issue. First, all extant nonjustificational theorists agree that evidence plays no logical or methodological role in growth and at best a minor role in assessment. Popper developed the concept of corroboration into a post hoc appraisal that says nothing about the future and that "assesses" theories only after they have been developed and used (by other means). Kuhn sees no assessment at all in normal research periods and thus reinforces the Popperian position on this point. Second, the psychology and sociology of scientific concept formation becomes of crucial importance to the growth of knowledge for at least two areas: the critical genesis of ideas (Popper's guesses or bold conjectures) and the tuition of ideas within the research community. Evidence in support of a theory is psychologically indispensable to the extension and communication of a theory, but it is methodologically irrelevant. Researchers are never persuaded to or converted from a position solely on the basis of "evidential support." Only justificationists accord an indispensable methodological role to data, since they cannot understand how science can either be "scientific" or grow except in terms of evidential support.

THE FUTILITY OF DEMARCATION DISPUTES

If science is not "based" upon evidence and there is no unique (or infallible) method that it employs, then how can it be distinguished from other endeavors? We must pause to note that the history of attempts to demarcate science from its rivals is as long and honorable as the failures of all such attempts have been obvious to anyone who looks at their basic structure. There are only two kinds of such attempts in the literature: (a) monolithic criterion proposals, which claim that *one* criterion is sufficient to demarcate science from nonscience; and (b) shotgun criteria proposals, claiming that a total configuration or a plurality of indices is the only demarcation available.

The logical positivists' verifiability theory of cognitive meaning is the most famous example of class (a). This was an attempt (1) to: equate the science versus nonscience problem with that of meaningful versus meaningless; and (2) to solve the latter by *defining* the meaningful as the verifiable. Neither half of this program will work. As Popper and his associates never tire of demonstrating, science cannot survive without "meaningless" metaphysics as an integral component of the scientific endeavor. Criteria of meaning are invariably too wide and too narrow; more than science is meaningful, and/or not all of science is. The problem that drove Hume to skepticism invariably recurs in such attempts: Throw metaphysics into the fires of empiricism and science is burned also; rescue it from the flames and metaphysics always creeps back (see Hempel, 1959).

Popper's classic, *The logic of scientific discovery*, proposed another monolithic criterion, specifically aimed at demarcating science from its rivals and pseudoscience. His criterion was *testability*; his claim was that only science attempts to falsify its predictions (and that it learns from its mistakes). But Kuhn (1970a) has argued convincingly that testing does not separate "science" from, e.g., Popper's paradigm pseudoscience of astrology. Astrologers habitually tested their predictions *and acknowledged their failures*. Popper$_1$'s monolithic criterion is as futile as all the other justificationist criteria; Kuhn wrote (1970a):

> The occurrence of failures could be explained, but particular failures did not give rise to research puzzles, for no man, however skilled, could make use of them in a constructive attempt to revise the astrological tradition. There were too many possible sources of difficulty, most of them beyond the astrologer's knowledge, control, or responsibility. Individual failures were correspondingly uninformative, and they did not reflect on the competence of the prognosticator in the eyes of his professional compeers. Though astronomy and astrology were regularly practiced by the same people, including Ptolemy, Kepler, and Tycho Brahe, there was never an astrological equivalent of the puzzle-solving astronomical tradition. And without puzzles, able first to challenge and then to attest the ingenuity of the individual practitioner, astrology could not have become a science even if the stars had, in fact, controlled human destiny.
>
> In short, though astrologers made testable predictions and recognized that these predictions sometimes failed, they did not and could not engage in the sorts of activities that normally characterize all recognized science. Sir Karl is right to exclude astrology from the sciences, but his over-concentration on science's occasional revolutions prevents his seeing the surest reason for doing so [pp. 9–10].

Kuhn proposed the first qualified, *cluster* proposal and only for one kind of scientific practice rather than for all of scientific practice. Kuhn acknowledges the futility of monolithic criteria and proposes that perhaps the *most important* (but not necessarily the *only*) criterion of demarcation, for *normal science only*, is puzzle solving. (He sees no clear-cut criteria at all for revolutionary science.) Kuhn sees normal science as inherently a puzzle-solving endeavor and argues that, for example, although astrologers had tests to make and failures to acknowledge, they had no puzzles to solve as "normal sciences" do.

With the shift to Kuhn's position, we have one nonjustificationist's approach to the problem. The Popper who is the author of *Conjectures and refutations* (1963) is also a nonjustificationist, and his approach is slightly different. This theorist, called Popper$_2$ by Lakatos, demarcates *series of theories* (in a pluralistic methodology) that are *progressive* (i.e., that grow) from those series that are not. Lakatos (1968b) formulated this position clearly. But with this move, the empirical character of a theory—its testability—is seen to be insufficient. And Popper has yet to precisely specify any new, "cluster" criteria.

Nor did Lakatos specify any such criteria, even though he took a significant step beyond Popper$_2$; for Lakatos (1970) demarcated scientific *research programs* from nonscientific research programs.

> Let us take a series of theories, T_1, T_2, T_3,... where each subsequent theory results from adding auxiliary clauses to (or from semantical reinterpretations of) the previous theory in order to accommodate some anomaly, each theory having at least as much content as the unrefuted content of its predecessor. Let us say that such a series of theories is *theoretically progressive* (or *'constitutes an empirically progressive problemshift'*) if some of this excess empirical content is also corroborated, that is, if each new theory leads us to the actual discovery of some *new fact*. Finally, let us call a problemshift *progressive* if it is both theoretically and empirically progressive, and *degenerating* if it is not. We *'accept'* problemshifts as 'scientific' only if they are at least theoretically progressive; if they are not, we *'reject'* them as 'pseudoscientific'. Progress is measured by the degree to which a problemshift is progressive, by the degree to which the series of theories leads us to the discovery of novel facts. We regard a theory in the series 'falsified' when it is superseded by a theory with higher corroborated content.
>
> This demarcation between progressive and degenerating problemshifts sheds new light on the appraisal of *scientific—or, rather, progressive—explanations*. If we put forward a theory to resolve a contradiction between a previous theory and a counterexample in such a way that the new theory, instead of offering a content-increasing (scientific) *explanation*, only offers a content-decreasing (linguistic) *reinterpretation*, the contradiction is resolved in a merely semantical, unscientific way. *A given fact is explained scientifically only if a new fact is also explained with it.*
>
> *Sophisticated falsificationism thus shifts the problem of how to appraise theories to the problem of how to appraise series of theories.* Not an isolated *theory*, but only a series of theories can be said to be scientific or unscientific; to apply the term 'scientific' to one *single* theory is a category mistake [pp. 118–119].

Be this as it may, we are drifting further and further from the original concern of demarcation. But this is only to be expected. Bartley made a strong case for the demarcation *problem* being considerably less significant than the philosophers (including Popper) who concentrate upon it would have us believe (1968):

> An important evaluatory problem is not to demarcate scientific from nonscientific theories but to demarcate critical from uncritical theories or from theories that are protected from criticism—particularly pseudo-critical theories One might, if useful, call a pseudo-critical theory which purported to be scientific a pseudo-scientific theory. But in this broader context the demarcation of science and nonscience is, *per se* unimportant [p.49].

Consider the need for separation of scientific from nonscientific theories (Bartley, 1968):

> The question whether a theory is irrefutable or nonscientific in Popper's first sense does not materially contribute, and may often be irrelevant, to the question of its desirability, acceptability, rationality, legitimacy, seriousness, interest (to all of which problems Popper's theory of demarcation was directed).... What now become needed are more general criteria, applicable to the whole range of logically interrelated claims—metaphysical, scientific, theological, ethical—which help sift theories of dubious interest from those which deserve further discussion [pp. 53–54].

The moral is fairly clear: Demarcation of science from nonscience will result only as a by-product of a completed theory of the rationality of the scientific endeavor. As such, Kuhn and Bartley have the more reasonable positions. But the point remains: Attempts aimed specifically at demarcation are misguided; an adequate characterization of the scientific endeavor is much more important.

TRUTH AND THE QUEST FOR TRUTH IN CONJECTURAL KNOWLEDGE

For Popper$_2$, the critical fallibilist, the *aim* of science is the *search for truth*. His most eloquent statement of philosophical realism that is guided by truth as a regulative ideal of inquiry is in "The aim of science" (Popper, 1972, Chapter 5). But can science ever *attain* the truth? Indeed, what is the nature of truth in conjectural knowledge? Popper defines knowledge as a matter of having defensible conjectures *that are true*. But as long as contingent knowledge remains conjectural, *we can never know*; *we can only guess*. Still, Popper thinks science can make demonstrable progress in its search for truth—that we can know science to be advancing toward it. He developed the concept of *verisimilitude* to indicate how scientific advances approach the truth *by degrees*. Popper (1963) defined the verisimilitude of a theory as its truth-content minus its falsity-content: $Vs = Ct_T - Ct_F$. (Both Ct_T and Ct_F are defined from empirical content.)

> If we now work with the (perhaps fictitious) assumption that the content and truth-content of a theory a are in principle *measureable*, then we can go slightly beyond this definition and can define Vs(a), that is to say, a measure of the *verisimilitude* or *truthlikeness* of a. The simplest definition will be Vs(a) = $Ct_T(a)$ - $Ct_F(a)$ where $Ct_T(a)$ is a measure of the truth content of a and $Ct_F(a)$ is a measure of the falsity-content of a [pp. 233–234].

Popper wishes to compare theories with respect to their verisimilitude; the use of the concept is in the assessment of theories that are already at hand, as a post hoc appraisal to give substance to the notion of corroboration.

Ever since Tarski's (1944) monumental paper on the semantic conception of truth, Popper assumed that the correspondence theory of the nature of truth has been sufficiently rehabilitated to vindicate both his notion of verisimilitude and the idea that the aim of science is the quest for truth. But this is not quite so. Tarski's conception of truth is a diacritical definition of the notion in terms of "correspondence," but it is *not* a theory of what correspondence is. That is, Tarski's approach renders the correspondence approach to truth a tenable one, but it does not provide a correspondence *theory*—i.e., an explication of what truth-as-correspondence is. Although we may accept truth as the aim of science on the basis of Tarski's (and Carnap's) work, the situation is different with regard to verisimilitude. This becomes clear when we explore the correspondence theory of truth in detail.

Wilfred Sellars (especially 1968, Chapters 3 through 5) has the best conception of truth-as-correspondence that I have found. He regards generic truth as a matter of *semantic assertibility* within a conceptual (language) system. For a proposition to be true, it must be *correctly* assertible; truth statements are *authorized performances* in a language "game." Truth is a matter of license and performance. Factual truth, as a species of truth-as-semantic-assertibility, is a matter of warranted assertibility. As such, a factual truth is a matter of linguistic formulations correctly picturing (or, less iconographically, representing) non-linguistic "objects" (states of affairs, etc.).

Neglecting many puzzles and problems for the moment, and without defending this conception of factual truth at all, notice that it has a devastating effect upon the Popperian definition of knowledge. Knowledge now becomes a matter of having warranted assertions that are warranted assertions; adding "that are true" to "knowledge is a matter of warranted assertions" adds nothing but redundancy. If Sellars's conception of factual truth is tenable, then contingent knowledge is "nothing but" warranted assertion. The bond between knowledge and truth now reappears, but in nonjustificational form. Whereas the justificationist equated both knowledge and truth with proof, Sellars's conception of the nature of truth allows both knowledge and truth to be identified with warranted assertions within a conceptual framework.

But what of verisimilitude if factual truth is warranted assertibility? Truth as semantic assertibility admits no degrees: Truth is always absolute truth (and the switch to warranted assertibilty does not change this). (Absolute) factual truth would result when the model of reality that constitutes the scientist's theory isomorphically matched the reality that it models. There may be degrees of adequacy of representation (or modeling), but truth itself remains an all–or–none concept. Even if we had the true representation of reality, we could not know it *as such*, for we could never know that our model was true; we could only appraise it relatively, against its competitors.

This puts Popperian verisimilitude in a new light. Instead of appraising *truth*, it actually appraises *corroboration*—and specifically corroboration relative to background and rival theories. But there cannot be any *metric* of corroboration—or "degrees" of corroboration. Lakatos (1968a) put one reason why clearly:

> One can easily conceive of conditions which would make the estimate of verisimilitude by corroboration false. The successive scientific theories may be such that each increase of truth-content could be coupled with an even larger increase in hidden falsity-content, so that the growth of science would be characterized by increasing corroboration and decreasing verisimilitude. Let us imagine that we hit on a true theory T_1 (or on one with very high verisimilitude); in spite of this we manage to 'refute' it with the help of a corroborated falsifying hypothesis f_1, replace it by a bold new theory T_2 which again gets corroborated, etc., etc. Here we would be following, unknowingly, the twists and turns of a disastrous problem-shift, moving even further from the truth—while assuming that we are soaring victoriously towards it. Each theory in such a chain has higher corroboration and lower verisimilitude than its successor: such is the result of having 'killed' a true theory [p. 307].

As long as Popperian verisimilitude is aimed at corroboration rather than at degrees of adequacy of representation, it is strictly a practical rather than a logical notion. Such "verisimilitude" has nothing to do with truth at all, but only with the analytic, *post hoc* appraisal of a theory. Verisimilitude is only a weak, and indeed a *fallible*, measure of acceptability—specifically, instrumental acceptability. Popper has confused truth with confirmation (or corroboration) exactly as Carnap (1936) warned us not to do.

Because verisimilitude is a fallible indicator of corroboration rather than truth, one form of scientific realism—which holds that science aims at truth *and* can *know* that it is approaching truth—must be abandoned. This form of realism might be called an ontological realism; it claims that the existents that contemporary science discloses are "closer to the truth" than earlier formulations—i.e., that current theory reflects "what is real" more truly. Kuhn (1970c) put the reason for discounting such an ontological realism clearly:

> One often hears that successive theories grow ever closer to, or approximate more and more closely to, the truth. Apparently generalizations like that refer not to the puzzle-solutions and the concrete predictions derived from a theory but rather to its ontology, to the match, that is, between the entities with which the theory populates nature and what is "really there".
>
> Perhaps there is some other way of salvaging the notion of 'truth' for application to whole theories, but this one will not do. There is, I think, no

theory-independent way to reconstruct phrases like 'really there'; the notion of a match between the ontology of a theory and its "real" counterpart in nature now seems to me illusive in principle. Besides, as a historian, I am impressed with the implausibility of the view. I do not doubt, for example, that Newton's mechanics improves on Aristotle's and that Einstein's improves on Newton's as instruments for puzzle-solving. But I can see in their succession no coherent direction of ontological development. On the contrary, in some important respects, though by no means in all, Einstein's general theory of relativity is closer to Aristotle's than either of them is to Newton's [pp. 206–207].

Instead of an ontological realism, one must endorse an epistemic realism: We may retain the search for truth as a regulative ideal of scientific inquiry, but we must abandon the idea that we can know scientific change as progress toward the truth. The faint hope of "ultimate convergence" in a "concilience of inductions" that guides reductionists such as Turner (1971) remains chimerical. The degree of adequacy of representation of our theoretical models is an enormous problem, which is roughly the problem of assessment in science; and we must tackle it without supposing that the assessment of merit of scientific propositions is an assessment of truth. For this reason, the development of a contingent theory of what constitutes support (or confirmation) is of prime importance for the methodology of scientific research (see Maxwell, 1975). But such a contingent theory of what constitutes confirmation will be a far cry from the present neojustificationist "confirmation theory"; specifically, it will not even attempt to justify inference; and truth, proof, and probability of being true will not figure in its formulation. Ultimately, the problems of the growth of our knowledge, because they are pragmatic and epistemic problems, will lead us into the psychology of knowledge and its acquisition (see Chapter 7).

To conclude this section, we must note that the untenability of Popper's conception of versimilitude is no more devastating to a non-justificational metatheoretical approach than is the inadequacy of his attempts at demarcation. One cannot argue from the incorrectness of a given aspect of a philosopher's system to the inadequacy of the system itself unless it can be contended that the aspect is *indispensable* to the system. Despite Popper's emphasis on the concept of verisimilitude, little is lost by abandoning it (as did Lakatos). And one need not suppose (as does Grünbaum, 1976) that the untenability of verisimilitude and the (obvious) inability of a nonjustificational approach to *justify* that "conjectures and refutations" is the method of science constitute an admission that "it may be unavoidable to resort to inductivistic devices (Grünbaum, 1976, p. 106). The distinction that must be kept in mind is between inductive methodologies of science on the one hand and (psychological, sociological) explanations of inference in science on the other. What is required is an explanation of inference in science that does not resort to inductivist methodologies.

7

The Reemergence of the
Problem of Pragmatic Action

For the justificationist, in possession of "*the* true method" of assessment, pragmatic action is no problem at all. But life is not so simple for a nonjustificationist; if there is no *a priori* "guide to scientific life," if corroboration says *nothing* of future success, then the problem of pragmatic action simultaneously becomes extremely crucial and is removed from the philosophical scene to the socio-psychological one. Popperians have failed to emphasize either point, although Lakatos (1971, 1974) admitted he had nothing but "authority" to guide choice in questions of pragmatic action. Kuhn (1963, 1970a, 1974) has seen the necessity for (empirical *and* conceptual) study of science by sociology and psychology as clearly as anyone. Predicting the future success of either a theory or a Lakatosian "research program" cannot be done in a nonjustificational approach (nonjustificationists admit this freely; justificationists thought that confirmation theory *could* predict).

LEVELS OF ANALYSIS AND
THE UNDERSTANDING OF SCIENCE

The problem of pragmatic action can be brought forcefully to the fore by examining the quest for an adequate level and unit of analysis for the understanding of the scientific endeavor. Let us trace this quest from its simplistic formulation in justificationism through to the multi-dimensional analysis that is at present recognized to be necessary (but still *not* sufficient).

For justificationism, there is only one *level* of analysis for science—that within a single theory—and one *unit* of analysis—the particular hypothesis or

NATURE OF SCIENCE

All science is *normal* science

LEVEL OF ANALYSIS

Within theory

> Testing of single predicted outcomes against a firm foundation of (authoritative) facts.

FIG. 7.1.   The justificationist conception of rational scientific activity.

prediction under test. Testing, of course, is *proof* via *deduction* from the appropriate *authority*; and all science is Kuhnian normal science. Schematically, this (oversimplified) picture emerges (what goes on in science is characterized inside the box) in Fig. 7.1.

For Popper, all "interesting" science, all genuine science worthy of the name, is revolutionary science. Normal science is "hackwork" (Watkins, 1970, p. 27). But the Popperian critical fallibilist acknowledges theoretical pluralism and the existence of research programs. The basis of science is still problems, and testing is still of predicted outcomes; but factual relativity is explicitly acknowledged (see Fig. 7.2). Thus for the Popperian, two levels of analysis are needed for the understanding of the scientific endeavor rather than just one; and what goes on during the practice of science is different at each level. Thus when a Popperian critical fallibilist and a neojustificationist fight about science, the conflict may concern either the appropriate level of analysis, or the nature of science, or both.

Lakatos, in attempting to answer criticisms of Popper's views and to incorporate aspects of Kuhn's conception of science, switched from a critical to a conventional fallibilism. Though agreeing with Popper that science should be critical rather than justificational, Lakatos acknowledged that

NATURE OF SCIENCE

All science is *revolutionary* science

LEVEL OF ANALYSIS

Within theory

> Testing of outcomes against a conventionally accepted unproblematic background; if a 'refutation' occurs, the background is also scrutinized.

Between theories

(in a research program)

> *Evaluation* (not testing) of competing theories that are equally problematic; goal is to pick the least "black" lie.

FIG. 7.2.   The Popperian conception of rational scientific activity.

researchers are committed to aspects of their practice (in opposition to Popper, for whom commitment is always unscientific) and that what Kuhn has called "normal science" does indeed occur. He attempted to account for the tenacity of normal science commitment and "come what may" devotion to a position during revolutionary upheaval by emphasizing the conventional nature of falsification while abandoning Popper's dictum that a theory must be abandoned when it is falsified. Thus Lakatos emphasized that one cannot assess the rationality of a theory in isolation and that it is perfectly rational to remain committed to a position when it has been refuted. In doing so, he used Popper's conception of a research program—defined as an interrelated series of theories within a domain—as a focal concept to explain both normal scientific practice and scientific revolutions. Lakatos held that the "committal" aspects of normal science practice are rational (and hence critical) if they result in the successive modification of a research program in terms of a "progressive problem-shift" (a content-increasing, even if ad hoc, evolution in the research program). However, due to the conventional nature of falsification, Lakatos was forced to argue that it is also rational to stick to a research program in a degenerating (content-decreasing) problem-shift. Thus on Lakatos's conventional fallibilist account, the rationality of science is to be reconstructed as in Fig. 7.3. Having sketched this framework for understanding science, Lakatos went on to propose criteria of evaluation for not only "problem-shifts" and research programs but also for methodologies of science. But in order to assess his proposals, let us first look at the levels of analysis required for reconstructing the rationality of science if Kuhn's ideas are combined with those of Popper and Lakatos.

(Watkins [1975] has begun to sketch an alternative to Lakatos's methodology of research programs that emphasizes the scientific status of metaphysical ideas. His chief aim appears to be to emphasize that there need not be a ban on theory appraisal even if one admits research programs and

NATURE OF SCIENCE

LEVEL OF ANALYSIS	Normal science	Revolutionary science
Within theory	Testing hypotheses against the conventionally determined background of a research program.	Collection of 'refuting' instances for public display.
Between theories	Evaluation of competing theories within a developing research program.	Conflicts of rival research programs.

FIG. 7.3.   Lakatos's conventional modification of Popperian critical fallibilism.

NATURE OF SCIENCE

LEVEL OF ANALYSIS	Normal science	Revolutionary science
Within theory	Testing of consequences of particular theories within a research program.	Anomaly collection.
Between theories	Evaluation of particular theories that constitute a research program.	Systematic rejection of all available research programs.
Beyond (or behind) theories	Presupposed background— never articulated or consciously acknowledged.	Paradigm clashes— of incommensurable points of view.

FIG. 7.4.   A more psychologically adequate conception of scientific activity.

theoretical pluralism. Watkins also has a peculiar idea that *rational* assessment should range over "small" units of analysis: "I take it that we want our units of appraisal to be as small as possible, so that the process of amendment and revision in science may be as rational as possible" [Watkins, 1975, p. 108]. As no argument supports this claim and as Watkins appears to accept much of Lakatos's account, I shall ignore his views in favor of the better known, more fully fleshed out view of Lakatos.)

Somewhat more inclusive is the picture that emerges in Fig. 7.4, when one admits, as Kuhn does, that both normal and revolutionary science occur *and* that "paradigm clashes" are often present. The problem of pragmatic action reemerges with the admission of significant paradigm clashes (or at a lower level, with Lakatos's clashes of research programs), for it turns out that *all extant traditional criteria of scientific methodology and growth are incapable of arbitrating in paradigm clashes.* It is at this point that other domains become indispensable to scientific growth or, put another way, that the purely philosophical rationality of science disappears.

Let us examine criteria of assessment for a moment. One might assume that because the assessment of theories is without doubt one of the central tasks of methodology, there would be considerable literature devoted to the topic. Examination of the traditional literature, however, discloses that such discussion is all but nonexistent; for instance, Nagel (1961), Turner (1967) and Wartofsky (1968) mention assessment problems only in passing, as do most contributors in Suppe (1974). Why should this be the case? Several factors are relevant. First, the "weight of evidence" is assumed to be the central criterion, and the assessment of evidence hinges upon the development of confirmation theory. Hence justificationists have never gotten around to discussing assessment criteria independently of inductive logic. But it is clear that all theories have evidence in their favor, and we often reject a theory with much positive evidence (Newton) in favor of another (Einstein) on the basis of *nonempirical* factors. Testability, no matter how formulated, is not an adequate criterion of scientific merit.

Numerous nonempirical criteria have been touted as essential additions to testability: simplicity, comprehensiveness, consistency, reducibility, etc. All such criteria have been employed to rescue a rational conception of theory choice when empirical criteria have failed to account for the allegiances of scientific researchers. Utilization of such criteria (of ex post facto rationalization, rather then "assessment") is often linked to desirable characteristics of confirmation theory; Nagel and Turner, for example, defend reductionism as a criterion of theory *evaluation* (rather than something else—e.g., merely a strategy), because it reinforces the "faint hope" of convergence in a unified, building-block picture of science.

A second factor in the paucity of discussion of criteria of assessment in traditional philosophy of science is that the only criteria that the justificationist could acknowledge had to be concerned with, *at most*, the box in the upper left corner of Fig. 7.4. Received view theorists could not acknowledge criteria of assessment for the other levels of scientific activity on pain of giving up the within-theory conception of scientific rationality. Thus it should not be surprising that in-depth discussion of the uses and limitations of criteria of assessment should come from nonjustificational philosophers who acknowledge other levels of analysis and types of scientific activity (Bunge, 1967, Vol. II, provides one of the best discussions of assessment proposals I have encountered).

To relate criteria of assessment to the problem of pragmatic action in actual research, one need only observe that all the extant philosophical criteria pertain to no more than the first two levels of analysis portrayed in Fig. 7.4, even those discussed by the nonjustificational philosophers. The philosophical conception of the rationality of science does not yet extend beyond the between-theories level of analysis. Seeing that Popper's methodology implied this level of analysis, Lakatos (1968b, 1970) elaborated his methodology of research programs as a simultaneous thrust against both residual justificationist accounts and Kuhn's conception, which Lakatos assumed to be "merely psychological." Lakatos attempted to encompass all the rationality of science at these two levels and to deny as irrational any factors that transcended the level of clashes of research programs. Let us assess this methodology for a moment.

Consider what Kuhn called in 1962 a paradigm clash, which is literally a conflict of preferred ways of "seeing" a domain. What criteria could arbitrate in a paradigm clash? *Testing* cannot separate two paradigms—both will be supported in places, refuted in others; empirically they will both be lies, but of indeterminate degrees of blackness. Simplicity and reducibility cannot be defined except within a given paradigm. Even the authority of the practitioners (the criterion emphasized by Polanyi, 1958) cannot mediate the dispute. For example, in the recent clash in psychology and linguistics, Chomsky is as authoritative in his "paradigm" as Skinner is in his. Both paradigms have successful research programs, which are sometimes in conflict, often simply orthogonal. To which should a researcher pledge allegiance? Lakatos had no answer, and Feyerabend (1970a, 1070b, 1970c) argues persuasively that no philosophical reconstruction can provide an answer. At present there is no criterion to be found in the philosophical domain that will do the job; nor will any cluster of criteria, no matter what combination is tried. From the philosophical point of view, competing paradigms cannot be evaluated; they are equally black, but quite orthogonal, lies.

It is not by accident that Kuhn, Feyerabend, and Hanson (especially, 1958, 1970) often resort to the metaphor of perceptually ambiguous figures when discussing the "incommensurability" of conflicting "paradigms." An appropriate model for 'incommensurability' is the phenomenon of deep-structural ambiguity in language and perception (Weimer, 1974b). Incommensurable scientific paradigms (or research programs stemming from them) are analogous to the two interpretations of the Necker cube or the two readings of a deep structurally ambiguous sentence. Consider Fig. 7.5: In such instances, what is involved are two alternative and incommensurable ways of seeing (or conceiving) *the same domain* (whether perceptual or conceptual). Everything is different in the alternative perceptions, and yet nothing is changed. And there are no philosophical criteria that enable one to choose to "see" one or the other interpretation. At this point the Popperian philosophers despair for rationality: Popper, Lakatos, and Watkins argue that paradigm choice is irrational because it resembles the Necker cube and propose to exclude this aspect of science from methodological reconstruction; Feyerabend, agreeing that paradigm allegiance is psychological but seeing that it is an indispensable part of science, now sings praises to the irrationality of science.

But what "criteria" could differentiate between paradigms in clashes? Surely there are none that can uniformly command assent to one paradigm. For if there were such an entity, it would be a prescriptive rule telling one *how to see*, for paradigm clashes are just that: clashes in ways of seeing *the same* domain (or world). Thus the "criteria" that will aid in our *understanding* of paradigm clashes are not properly traditional criteria *of choice* at all, for they

The police were ordered to
stop drinking after midnight.

Flying planes can be dangerous.

FIG. 7.5. Perceptual and linguistic examples of deep structural ambiguity.

will not enable one to "accept" or "reject" a particular paradigm or research program. Nor can they even tell one whether or not a particular research program is worth pursuing, in the light of the relevant background information (which consists of the entire body of science, but especially the history of the domain in question).

The "criteria" that render paradigm clashes explainable (intelligible) will be disclosed in the formulation of an adequate socio-psychological account of knowledge acquisition. Ultimately, the growth of scientific knowledge becomes nothing more, nothing less, than the socio-psychological problem of knowledge acquisition. One who understands the nature of our knowledge and the processes involved in its acquisition will understand paradigm clashes—and will be a (Utopian) *psychologist* (Weimer, 1975). But regardless, the problem of pragmatic action remains the focal point of the clash between the nonjustificational metatheories. Psychological fallibilism (as I have tentatively reformulated Kuhn's position) merely has the advantage of locating the problem. Critical and conventional fallibilism try to ignore it; in falling back upon authority to mediate paradigm disputes, Lakatos (1971) admitted that he had no *theory* of pragmatic action at all. Indeed, nobody has such a theory; all we have are tentative maxims derived from the case history study of the revolutionary thinkers of the past. This is the single most important area for future research directed at understanding the scientific enterprise. Intellectual honesty demands that we give it the attention it deserves.

If there is a moral in this story, it is that the psychological sciences (and rhetoric: see Chapter 8) are indispensable for epistemology. This is because there is no difference in kind between scientific knowledge and our "garden variety" knowledge. (This is not, of course, an endorsement of common sense-based theories of knowledge; they are just plain wrong, for reasons that Sellars (1963) admirably portrays. It is rather the claim that a correct characterization of the nature of scientific knowledge is also a correct characterization of knowledge, *simpliciter*.)

METHODOLOGY AND THE PROBLEM OF THE GUIDANCE OF SCIENTIFIC LIFE

Another way to emphasize the centrality of the problem of pragmatic action is by looking at the practical methodological problem of the guidance of future research in scientific inquiry. For the justificationist, confirmation theory was to assess the scientific merit of propositions and also to provide guidance to future research. The second function of the inductive judge was to guide scientific life; if inductive inference could be justified, then one could, by examining the accepted body of scientific knowledge, infer where future research ought to go. The logic of induction was to provide not only a theory of instant rational assessment but also one of instant guidance. But without a justified logic of inductive inference, there can be no guidance; the justificationist theory of guidance collapses with the rest of the metatheory.

If we abandon the justificationist's quest for a theory of instant rationality, in favor of the nonjustificational problem of the growth of conjectural knowledge, what approaches to guidance are there? The critical fallibilist has nothing to say about guidance; as Lakatos pointed out, the concept of corroboration, as an analytic appraisal, has nothing to do with guidance. For Popper, the logic of scientific discovery consists in the critical function of refutation directed at already extant conjectures; How one gets a conjecture in the first place is beyond the pale of Popperian methodology.

The methodology of scientific research programs that Lakatos advocated as an improvement of Popper fares no better with respect to the problems of guidance. The only explicit mechanism Lakatos proposed is the authority of the research director; "guidance" becomes the direction of the program's research. The creativity of the director of research remains unexplained. His last paper on induction (Lakatos, 1974) urged Popper to accept "a whiff of inductivism" and to connect the game of science (in its methodogy) to the concept of verisimilitude by some quasi-inductive postulate. The intent of such a hookup is to legitimate (i.e., to justify) science as a rational source of knowledge in opposition to other potential sources of knowledge such as voodoo, religion, etc.

There are two reasons why defenses of the scientific "game" cannot connect methodology, even synthetically via a contingent theory, with epistemology. The first of these concerns concepts such as verisimilitude, which are ultimately defined in terms of the empirical content of a theory. The problem here is that one cannot bridge the gap between *empirical* content and *truth* content. There is no way to *know* that one can arrive at truth content from empirical consequences; the appraisal of a theory and its truth are not related in any straightforward manner. Pace Carnap (1936), truth cannot be equated with confirmation. The second problem with inductive justifications of scientific "inference" as a source of knowledge is that the methods and patterns of inference are common to human beings *qua* sentient organisms and are not possessed by scientists alone. What guides scientific life (its inferences) is the way scientists form concepts—not any set of philosophical rules of the scientific game.

Rational philosophical *re*construction of scientific methodology must give way to the psychology of inference and expectation when the problem to be addressed is that of the scientific *construction* of reality (Weimer, 1975). Once we step beyond justificationism, the guidance of scientific life is not a problem for philosophical method; it remains for the psychologist and sociologist to explicate how scientific concept formation occurs and how the knowledge we possess constrains the inferences we will make. Put another way, the problems of "induction" are *what* and *how* we learn from gathering scientific data, and both of these problems require psychology (and then sociology) for their solution. (There are enough legitimate problems for philosophy that we should not burden it with others it has no hope of resolving.) Both the nature of our knowledge and the means of its acquisition are ultimately problems for the psychological sciences. If we can understand how human beings generate their concepts, we will understand the method of inference employed by both scientific and common sense reasoning; put another way, the *nature* of knowledge acquisition does not change with the change from common sense to science; it is only the end products that change.

Scientific concept formation is an exhibition of what Polanyi (1958, 1966) aptly called *tacit knowledge*; it is a graphic illustration of the fact that we can know and do more than we can tell. Consider our ability to recognize human faces *as* faces: We can recognize an indefinitely extended domain of particulars as instances of faces, despite the fact that we have never experienced them before. And no one is aware of or can tell how he or she can do this (see Turvey, 1974). Concept formation operates according to psychological principles of determination, but we do not presently know what these principles are. However, the striking point to emphasize is that even if we knew the completed psychology of inference and expectation, the knowledge of the principles of determination according to which concept formation occurs could not enable a methodologist to teach student scientists how to be good methodologists. Human skills learning can be demonstrated, but it cannot be taught explicitly; the student either will learn from examples of good scientific practice "how it is done" or will not; and if the latter, no amount of further training in method will make that student more proficient at doing science.

There need be nothing mystical or obscurantist in the thesis of tacit knowledge. It is no more obscurantist than the fact that scientists can recognize scientific problems as such in just the way one can recognize faces as such. What is required is a theoretical explanation of how either can be done; and it is the burden of psychology, rather than philosophy, to provide this theory. The charge of "obscurantism" and "irrationality" *really* arises when the second half of the tacit knowledge claim, that no amount of explicit training will improve performance appreciably, is advanced. Yet this should not be terribly surprising, for there are many "skills" that we possess that can be learned only by doing and that certain people can learn to do better than others. Talking to athletic coaches provides an instance. They will tell you that ballplayers learn by playing ball and that coaching cannot "teach" anything other than (a) basic fundamentals and (b) relatively tangential things like good "health" and "moral character." Doing science is analogous to playing skilled games in this sense: One can be shown *by example* how to do it; and *if* one has the innate ability and is perceptive enough to learn by doing, one will succeed. Otherwise one will fail, no matter how explicit the memorization of the "rules of practice." This phenomenon of learning by doing instead of by rules of practice has an analogy in such things as a mother's giving birth to a child. All the "book learning" in the world cannot substitute for the experience of having a baby. By the same token, nothing can substitute for the experience of doing science, and the only way to "learn" how it is done is by doing it.

This leads directly to the nature of scientific knowledge acquisition and transmission as instances of generative concept formation. Here the only "philosophical" theory that can even address the problems of the acquisition of knowledge is Kuhn's (1974) thesis of learning from exemplars, which we must now discuss.

8 Beyond Philosophical Reconstruction

Philosophy at one time or another has been the mother of virtually all intellectual disciplines, including the physical sciences and the nascent psychological sciences. In most cases, the birth pangs have been traumatic, with the mother jealously trying to retain sovereignty in the new domain and the offspring childishly distantiating itself from its intellectual heritage. Again and again, it is necessary for both sides to learn that philosophical analysis does not diminish because a new science is in practice and that science can never eschew philosophy. Science enriches philosophy, and vice versa; their relationship, although often painful, is symbiotic rather than antagonistic or parasitical. Thus scientific accounts should supplement, rather than replace, philosophical analysis of a domain. This is so even when the domain of inquiry is the understanding of science itself. This chapter addresses topics that show limits in current philosophical analysis and point to other domains for tentative solutions. First we consider the nature and role of theories, tuition in science, and then the rhetorical and sociological side of science. Next we comment on a clash between historians and philosophers concerning "internal" and "external" reconstructions of science as an illustration of one controversy that need not have arisen if philosophers had not attempted to protect their vested interests. We conclude by reconsidering the nature of rationality.

THE ROLE OF THEORIES IN SCIENTIFIC PRACTICE

To what extent is the philosophical account of the structure of scientific theories a good one, and what is the role of "theory" in actual scientific practice? The received view thought that inductive logic was a "guide to scientific life," in the sense that it both guided research and provided a basis for "true" knowledge claims. We have argued, following Popper, that confirmation theory or "inductive logic" is unattainable and that consequently its alleged role as a guide to scientific life must be seen as incorrect. We have also indicated that the problem of guidance is one for (primarily) psychologists to explain, when they are able to explicate the nature of concept formation and tacit knowledge. Now, what about the role of theories in actual practice? Could it be the case that—as both the received view theorists *and* Popper claim—the nature of our scientific knowledge is *determined* and *transmitted* by our theories? To test this claim, the following reasoning suggests itself: "*If* the notion of 'theory' is correctly supposed to account for what it is that scientists possess that enables (and guides, etc.) them in ascertaining the nature of reality, *then* the concept of theory ought to be mirrored in actual scientific practice." One can then ask, as a historian or socio-psychologist, "Does the notion of theory play the role in actual scientific practice that philosophers attribute to it?" The answer, not suprisingly, is "No."

Michael Polanyi and Thomas Kuhn are two of the very few theorists who have asked this question concerning the role of "theory" in scientific practice. Consider this comment of Kuhn (1970c):

> Philosophers of science have not ordinarily discussed the problems encountered by a student in laboratories or in science texts, for these are thought to supply only practice in the application of what the student already knows. He cannot, it is said, solve problems at all unless he has first learned the theory and some rules for applying it. Scientific knowledge is embedded in theory and rules; problems are supplied to gain facility in their application. I have tried to argue, however, that this localization of the cognitive content of science is wrong. After the student has done many problems, he may gain only added facility by solving more. But at the start and for some time after, doing problems is learning consequential things about nature. In the absence of such exemplars the laws and theories he has previously learned would have little empirical content [pp. 187–188].

And in another location (1970b) he adds:

> Ordinarily problem-solutions of this sort are viewed as mere applications of theory that has already been learned. The student does them for practice, to gain facility in the use of what he already knows. Undoubtedly that description is correct after enough problems have been done, but never, I think, at the start. Rather, doing problems is learning the language of a theory and acquiring the knowledge of nature embedded in that language [p. 272].

Kuhn's point is obvious: The actual practice of science is *not* guided or directed by explicitly (or even implicitly!) formulated *theories*; rather it is much more like coming to learn a second (conceptual) language, and language learning is done by speaking—not by inculcating *any* "theory." *Tacit knowledge is the basis of normal scientific practice*, and it is manifested primarily in learning from exemplary puzzles and their solutions (Kuhn, 1974).

The theme of "tacit knowledge" immediately leads to the work of Michael Polanyi. Consider the similar conclusion that Polanyi (1966) reaches from a slightly different perspective than Kuhn's:

> To rely on a theory for understanding nature is to interiorize it. For we are attending from the theory to things seen in its light, and are aware of the theory, while thus using it, in terms of the spectacle that it serves to explain. This is why mathematical theory can be learned only by practicing its application: its true knowledge lies in our ability to use it. ... A mathematical theory can be constructed only by relying on *prior* tacit knowing and can function as theory only within an act of tacit knowing, which consists in our attending *from* it to the previously established experience on which it bears. Thus the ideal of a comprehensive mathematical theory of experience which would eliminate all tacit knowing is proved to be self-contradictory and logically unsound [pp. 17, 21].

Theoretical physicist David Bohm (1965, 1974) has reached conclusions consonant with those of Kuhn and Polanyi. He argues (1974) that:

> Science is *primarily* an activity of extending perception into new contexts and into new forms, and only secondarily a means of obtaining what may be called reliable knowledge [as codified in theory]. ... The very act of perception is shaped and formed by the intention to communicate. ... It is generally only in communication that we deeply understand, that is, perceive the whole meaning of what has been observed. So there is no point to considering any kind of separation of perception and communication [p. 374].

Bohm regards science as perception-communication, in which information is assimilated into the entire tacit knowledge system of the scientist (1974):

> Theories are changing all the time; ... each new step may introduce something novel and "incommensurable" with what came before. Indeed, even to read an article and to understand it is, in general, to change it significantly. For understanding something is assimilation, that is, making it a whole with oneself. ... So the basic action of science is seen to involve *perception of what is new and different* from moment to moment. In this regard, it is similar to the relevant activity in everyday life, which is also such a kind of perception [p. 388].

Bohm has come to regard the difference between conceptual points of view in science as so pervasive that to speak of the "incommensurability" of theories is misleading, because it implies that other "theories" can be said to be commensurable (Bohm, 1974):

> Each theory is itself a whole, in which analysis into disjoint components or elements is not relevant (just as in the case of perception-communication). This is because all the terms in such a theory can have their meanings and their criteria of factuality and truth only in the total context given by *that* theory. There is, therefore, actually no way to "measure" or "evaluate" the basic concepts and notions of any one theory in terms that are common to those of another theory, so that one could meaningfully compare the theories and thus establish whether they are commensurable or incommensurable [pp. 375–376].

So long as one remains at the within-theory level of analysis, Bohm's point is well taken: The only way in which aspects of science at one level of analysis can be compared is by moving to a higher, more inclusive level. Analysis of a theory requires thorough understanding of the relevant research program(s); analysis of research programs requires understanding of the paradigm, etc. Thus, understanding in science is in a very important sense the comprehension of a structured whole; unless we know all of it, we actually know none of it (as well as is necessary). This makes the task of the methodologist as difficult as any ever faced in human intellectual endeavor.

There is a moral to be drawn here. He who understands Kuhn's, Polanyi's, and Bohm's claims understands that *science, rather than philosophy*, is the domain that will ultimately be most relevant to the understanding of the scientific endeavor. Indeed, if we are ever to understand *normal science* practice, we must have a psycho-sociological account of "learning from exemplars" or generative concept formation; that is Kuhn's claim. I claim if we are ever to have an adequate understanding of *revolutionary science*, we shall require a psychological theory of concept formation adequate to understand "points of view" and their generation by the human concept former. Bohm's contention that science is perception-communication requires an understanding of rhetoric and the manner in which science is a rhetorical transaction. In addition, the understanding of both normal and revolutionary science will require an adequate sociology in order to understand the workings of congeries of specialist groups and of individuals within those groups (e.g., Hagstrom, 1965; Mitroff, 1974; Mulkay, 1972; Ravetz, 1971). At this point the study of the scientist as subject becomes, as Mahoney (1976) noted, a psychological imperative.

Parenthetically, we must note that some theorists have proposed that interpreting theories in terms of Tarski's (1956) conception of semantic analysis will provide illumination that is unavailable in either the classic logical empiricist account or in the accounts examined in this section. Suppe (1974) had made extravagant claims for such *model theoretic* interpretations, arguing from the point that traditional analysis "reveals nothing about what is characteristic of theories except that their formulations have certain characteristics; a direct examination of theories themselves is likely to result in a more detailed and more accurate analysis [pp. 221–222]." A theory *itself* turns out to be a model theoretic interpretation: "Scientific theories have as their subject matter a class of phenomena known as the intended *scope* of the theory. The task of a theory is to present a generalized description of the phenomena within that intended scope which will enable one to answer a variety of questions about the phenomena and their underlying mechanisms [p. 223]." Thus theories ultimately become structures in a phase space rather than linguistic formulae or traditionally axiomatized systems. This conception of theory may be more informative than traditional ones, but it says nothing when faced with the criticisms in this section: Regardless of how they are reconstructed in after-the-fact analysis, theories in practice are tacit knowledge structures within the scientist. Because what philosophers have assumed theories to be does not guide scientific practice, it is presently far more important to look to epistemology, as one of the psychological sciences, to find out what does.

INJUNCTION AND THE COMMUNICATION
OF ARGUMENTATIVE DISCOURSE

Traditional accounts portray the language of science as purely descriptive. Taking their departure from the truism that theories describe the nature of reality, such accounts ignore the argumentative nature of explanatory discourse and assume that representation, the essential characteristic of science, is just description. But not only is such an account deficient with regard to the argumentative force of theoretical explanation; it also cannot account for communication in science, either among established practitioners or between apprentice and master.

At the observational level, pure description fails to provide a sufficient specification of factual data. One cannot see a fact in any descriptive sense; to see facts *as such* requires an interpretative framework—that is the essence of factual relativity. But how is such information as is required to see facts communicated? To be sure, facts can be described within a conceptual framework, but how does one learn and then communicate the conceptual framework?

Kuhn's account of learning, in terms of generative concept formation resulting from practice with exemplary puzzles and their solutions that the metaphysical–sociological paradigm sanctions, is the best account of this tacit knowledge acquisition that we presently possess. If we grant that science is largely tacit in this regard, there is still the problem of explicating how science tells its practitioners what to do in order that the world will be seen in the terms prescribed by the metaphysical "paradigm." The paradigm, as a conceptual point of view, cannot merely describe reality to the individual scientist any more than the skilled researcher can merely describe research practice to the novice; in both cases the language of science is intrinsically *argumentative*. What is being conveyed is that reality *must* be seen in a certain way.

In both communication between initiates within the scientific community and in the instruction of apprentice researchers, *the argumentative mode of discourse requires injunction rather than description*. Communication in science is primarily a matter of *commands*: The correct description will not be attained unless an injunction is obeyed. Both scientific articles and research training instruction given to novices *enjoin* their audience to behave in a certain way. In this regard science very literally is a "cookbook" endeavor; it is a matter of recipes for conceiving, perceiving, and doing, and the recipes are given as injunctions. In terms of the contrast between knowledge by description and acquaintance, scientific communication becomes a set of commands, given in terms of description, that will enable the researcher to have the appropriate experience or acquaintance: "Do this, and you will experience the world correctly!" The descriptive commentary of the scientific report only becomes a description within this injunctive framework. G. Spencer Brown (1972) conveys this with admirable clarity:

> Natural science appears to be more dependent upon injunction than we are prepared to admit. The professional initiation of the man of science consists not so much in reading the proper textbooks, as in obeying injunctions such as 'look down that microscope.' But it is not out of order for men of science, having looked down the microscope, now to describe to each other, and to discuss amongst themselves, what they have seen, and to write papers and textbooks describing it. Similarly, it is not out of order for mathematicians, each having obeyed a given set of injunctions, to describe to each other, and to discuss amongst themselves, what they have seen, and to write papers and textbooks describing it. But in each case, the description is dependent upon, and secondary to, the set of injunctions having been obeyed first [p. 78].

Understanding in science, on this account, is a matter of illustrating to ourselves the commands of the paradigm (in both Kuhn's exemplary and metaphysical senses). The scientific report is a recipe for the creation of meanings in our acquaintance (Spencer Brown, 1972):

> When we attempt to realize a piece of music composed by another person, we do so by *illustrating*, to ourselves, with a musical instrument of some kind, the composer's commands. Similarly, if we are to realize a piece of mathematics, we must find a way of illustrating to ourselves, the commands of the mathematician. ... In this respect it is comparable with practical art forms like

cookery, in which the taste of a cake, although literally indescribable, can be conveyed to a reader in the form of a set of injunctions called a recipe [pp. 77–78].

SCIENCE AS A RHETORICAL TRANSACTION

Classic thinkers distinguished between patterns of reasoning that were self-evident and necessary on one hand and those in which deliberation and argumentation were involved on the other. It was assumed that self-evidence characterized the domain of logic and that argumentation and persuasion characterized an inferior art form called rhetoric. Until very recently, the essential aspects of scientific thought were presumed by all to be modeled by logic; indeed, the classic justificationist quest is to exhibit the "logic" of scientific inference. Rhetoric was assumed to be concerned with persuasion and flattery, with the attempt to win adherence when logic and self-evidence did not apply. But with the abandonment of justificationism, it becomes "self-evident" that the logic of science is actually rhetoric. We are thus ready to propose a new role for rhetorical theory (or rhetorical criticism): In order to understand the rationality of science as communication, we must have a theory of the rhetoric of argumentative discourse and injunctive tuition. When we understand the rhetorical nature of the various uses of the argumentative mode of discourse (which is literally the essence of science), we will understand the growth of scientific knowledge. Rhetoric will be a key to understanding science, simply because its domain is all of pragmatics and the argumentative use of behavior (including language).

This conception of the domain and scope of rhetoric reintegrates science with other forms of human activity that have heretofore been (on justificationist accounts) purposely distantiated from it. But insofar as they instantiate rhetorical activity within the argumentative function of discourse and action, science, art, education, philosophy, even rational theology are all on a par. Although principled distinctions between such domains can easily be effected, they can no longer be distinguished because some are "merely" rhetorical and suasory rather than logical (or dialectical). But perhaps most important, this conception of rhetoric emphasizes the intrinsic valuational or ethical dimension inherent in all scientific activity. Knowing and valuing are inseparable; according to Lewis (1946):

The primary and pervasive significance of knowledge lies in its guidance of action: knowing is for the sake of doing. And action, obviously, is rooted in evaluation. For a being which did not assign comparative values, deliberate action would be pointless; and for one which did not know, it would be impossible [p. 1].

In the past, both scientists and rhetoricians have accepted, seemingly as revealed truth, the idea that science and logic are value free, in contrast to properly rhetorical concerns (where values were grudgingly admitted). But knowing, doing, and valuing can and must be reunited. Insofar as all involve the argumentative function, rhetoric is the domain in which that unification must occur (note that from the rhetorical perspective, much of the overlap between sociological, philosophical, and psychological analyses of science concerns the use of the argumentative mode of behavior).

The object of communication in science is always to educate the members of the research communities involved. Science instructs us in how to conceive the universe in which we find ourselves, and it does so rhetorically because the claims of scientific theory can only be given support by argument. The *modal* reasoning in which the scientist engages is inextricably linked to injunction in tuition addressed to other scientists (and students). Scientific description can only be descriptive in virtue of being embedded in an explanatory framework; explanations can only be explanatory in virtue of being argumentative; and arguments can only be learned by injunction. Hence, to state a fact is to argue for the warrant of the theory that necessitates it, and to teach others that it is a fact is to enjoin them to see reality as that theory commands one to see it. Whenever scientists communicate, even the most mundane and seemingly innocuous descriptions, they are persuading their audience, literally commanding them, to adopt their point of view.

The rhetorical nature of theory choice and revolutionary reconceptualization is easy to see (and is noted later); but what must be emphasized is that there is absolutely no difference between revolutionary and normal science in this regard; tuition and communication are injunctive in both. Indeed, Spencer Brown's remarks refer specifically to normal science tuition; and Kuhn, Polanyi, and others have discussed this aspect of scientific communication at length. Perhaps it suffices to point out that this aspect of scientific tuition has been known since the time of Plato, as a look at the interchange between Socrates and Meno's slave in the *Meno* makes clear.

In order to press the claim that science is a rhetorical transaction, one must be clear on the nature of rhetoric. Historically, rhetoric has not been given much in the way of a domain; justificationist thought has accorded considerably more prominence to logic and dialectic. Let us sketch the historical background enough to make clear the sense in which a nonjustificational conception of rhetoric aids our understanding of science.

Aristotle is generally regarded as the father of rhetoric, and after him attention usually focuses upon the Romans Cicero and Quintilian. But even though Aristotle is the classic father of rhetoric, the distinction between rhetoric and dialectic was already sharp by the time of his mentor Plato; and it is the divergence between rhetoric and dialectic in Plato's thought, shaped by the justificationist metatheory, that we must examine. Since the quest of science is for true knowledge, we must see how rhetoric and dialectic were assumed to function in the acquisition of knowledge.

As a classic justificationist, Plato held that genuine knowledge was proven truth and consisted in the intuition of essences or Forms by the immortal soul. There is no learning as opposed to recollecting or remembering; Plato's theory of knowledge acquisition is the doctrine of *Anamnesis*, which holds that under the correct conditions, man's immortal soul can recollect the truth with which it is already acquainted. Tuition in such a framework is quite different from our current notion of learning: Learning, as exemplified in Socratic maiutic, becomes a matter of aiding the soul's recollection. Thus we must ask about the relative roles of rhetoric and dialectic in achieving the soul's recollection of essences.

In the *Gorgias* (503), Plato acknowledged two forms of rhetoric: the art of persuasion and flattery and an ennobling art of tuition.

> If this matter is really two-fold, part of it will doubless be a form of flattery and a shameless method of addressing the public; the other may well be beautiful, a genuine attempt to make the souls of one's fellows as excellent as may be. . . . But a rhetoric such as this you have never encountered [Helmbold, 1952, p. 77].

Unfortunately, this second form of rhetoric is never discussed, and in the *Phaedrus* rhetoric reverts to "an artless routine" of persuasion and flattery that is never a means to genuine knowledge (proven truth). Here the true art of speech is seen to be dialectic. Dialectic, as the *Meno* and subsequent dialogues disclose, is the discovery of knowledge through the discussion of two or more viewpoints, a moving from the known (premises) toward the unknown (conclusion), or not yet recollected. Whereas rhetoric can at best provide only true opinion, genuine knowledge—which is certain truth unshakable by persuasion—can be achieved only by dialectic. The *Republic* (533–535) makes this clear:

> Dialectic, and dialectic alone, goes directly to the first principle and is the only science which does away with hypotheses in order to make her ground secure; the eye of the soul. . . is by her gentle aid lifted upwards. . . Dialectic. . . is the coping-stone of the sciences, and is set over them; no other science can be placed higher. . . [pp. 361–62].

Thus rhetoric produces only *belief* by argument and persuasion, and belief can at best be true opinion. But genuine knowledge is produced only by dialectic. Thus Socrates is a master dialectician in the maiutic technique, and Plato's dialogues are cast such that they reflect dialectic rather than rhetoric. It is from this framework that Aristotle fathered rhetoric, giving it the classic definition of a methodological technique of persuasion independent of any substantive content area.

This conception of dialectic and rhetoric has had over twenty centuries worth of pernicious consequences. By establishing an ideal of reasoning that cannot conceivably be attained, it forced theorists who recognized the futility of "dialectic" or "scientific method" to attain centainty and proof to abandon a rational conception of contingent disciplines. It has thus fostered the idea that rhetoric represents a retreat from ideal, but unfortunately unattainable, critical standards. Rhetoricians accepted the second-rate status of their discipline in comparison to both logic and dialectic and either concluded that rhetorical argument is not rational or that rhetoric is not as rational as the "sciences," which employ logic and dialectic (which are assumed to be different from rhetoric).

Neither conclusion is warranted, however, for both rest upon an untenable conception of rationality and an unwarranted separation of dialectic and rhetoric. Consider first the rationality of rhetorical argument and the nature of criticism. Here the accepted premise is that if one cannot be critical, then argument is not rational. But what constitutes criticism? According to the most prevalent view, criticism consists in the search for contradictions and then attempt to eliminate them. The rationality of science is thus criticism, which is the motive force of theory change (Popper, 1963):

> Criticism invariably consists in pointing out some contradiction; either a contradiction within the theory criticized, or a contradiction between the theory and another theory which we have some reason to accept, or a contradiction between the theory and certain facts. . . . Criticism is, in a very important sense, the main motive force of any intellectual development. Without contradictions, without criticism, there would be no rational motive for changing our theories: there would be no intellectual progress [p. 316].

Popper's reason for endorsing this strong stand on the nature of criticism and its centrality to rationality is that (1963) "if we were to accept contradictions then one would have to give up any kind of scientific activity. . . . This can be shown by proving that *if two contraditory statements are admitted, any statement whatever must be admitted*; for from a couple of contradictory statements any statement whatever can be validly inferred [p. 317].

But despite the validity of the proof that Popper then outlined, this identification of criticism with the search for contradictions (and of both with scientific rationality) is incapable of accounting for the growth of science. No one has delighted in detailing the growth of science on *inconsistent* "foundations" or theories as much as Paul Feyerabend (1970a, 1970b, 1970c), but Kuhn and Lakatos have also convincingly documented this charge. Paradigm exemplars of rational scientific progress discussed by virtually every historian have utilized inconsistent premises and thus *could have* "logically deduced" any conclusion whatsoever.

Rhetoricians have reached a similar conclusion about the role of criticism (defined according to Popper) in argument. Consider Johnstone (1971):

> I used to think of philosophical criticism primarily as the attempt to expose an internal inconsistency in the position criticized, forcing the holder of the position to revise or abandon it. ... This interpretation assumes that consistency is the highest aim of anyone taking a philosophical position... [pp. 87–88].

But now the question arises: Having seen the inadequacy of identifying rationality with criticism and criticism with consistency, what is to be done? Johnstone provides one answer—the abandonment of rationalism (1971):

> My rationalism... is now a thing of the past. I no longer see philosophical argumentation as an attempt to appeal to a standard of consistency in order to get an interlocutor to revise or abandon his position.... It is an attempt to evoke on his part a fuller consciousness of presuppositions that may have been merely implicit in his philosophical position.... Thus the abandonment of rationalism has made it possible for me to adopt a view of philosophical argumentation according to which rhetoric has a natural and proper place in the discussions and debates of philosophers [p. 88].

Johnstone, like the majority of contemporary rhetoricians and philosophers, takes *critical rationalism* to be the only conception of rationalist identity. Like other neojustificationists, he assumes a forced choice between two exhaustive alternatives: critical rationalism or irrationality. Faced with this choice, he abandons rationalism in favor of an existential–phenomenological irrationalism, in a *retreat to commitment.*

But comprehensively critical rationalism allows philosophical argument (and rhetoric) a place *within rationalism.* Within comprehensively critical rationalism, the concept of criticism has no fixed, a priori definition; what constitutes criticism, or better—*appropriate* criticism—can only be determined in the given case. There is no statute law of criticism, only case law. Further, even in the given case, a particular identification of criticism cannot be justified but only defended by adducing good reasons, which is to say arguments, in its favor. That is, what constitutes criticism may be subjected to critical evaluation. In this metatheoretical framework, it may be perfectly rational to either conjecture a new theory on the "basis" of inconsistent foundations or even to manifest the commitment to a paradigm that is so characteristic of normal science practice.

The point, with regard to criticism and consistency, is that science can be perfectly rational, even though logically anything at all could have been deduced from any set of inconsistent premises that it employs. Scientific creativity can be completely illogical, unconscious, even inconsistent. So can the assessment of theories; neither proof nor consistency need enter into acceptance of a theory. Scientific theories are defended by adducing good reasons for them, not by judging them consistent. If the inconsistency between theory and background knowledge (and competing theories) is not sufficient to warrant rejection (of either), then it is hard to see why either criticism or rationality should be identified with consistency. Both criticism and rationality can be reinterpreted, within a nonjustificational framework, such that consistency is not identified with either. Rhetoric ought to explore in detail how this can be accomplished in case law determination, where (as many rhetoricians have noted) it is uniquely focused to deal with the specifics of a given case.

Consider now the separation of dialectic and rhetoric. The Greek conception of dialectic as a means to knowledge is nothing more, nothing less, than the prototypic justificationist theory of instant rational assessment. As the quotation from the *Republic* illustrates, dialectic is taken to be an algorithm of knowledge acquisition that results in certainty, i.e., proven assertion. This infallible "method" in turn rests upon the classic justificationist conception of comprehensive rationalism, according to which a rationalist must justify all knowledge claims and hold none that are not justified. Having disposed of "method" in the guise of instant assessment procedures, we need only recall that this conception of rationality faces a crises in integrity: It is irrational (because it cannot be justified) according to its own standard. Classical dialectic, as an inductive means to proven assertion, is nonexistent. In more modern guise (stemming from Hegel and Marx), dialectic has taken on more of the character of probabilistic inductive logic, but it remains as nonexistent as its classic counterpart. But if we abandon the justificationist conception of knowledge as proven (or probable) assertion in favor of the nonjustificational notion of *warranted* assertion, the character of dialectic changes completely. This has been implicitly recognized by many philosophers—for example, Popper (1963):

> The Greek expression 'Hē dialektikē (technē)' may be translated '(the art of) the argumentative usage of language'. . . . One at least of its ancient meanings is very close to what I have described above as 'scientific method'. For it is used to describe the method of constructing explanatory theories and of the critical discussion of these theories, which includes the question whether they are able to account for empirical observations. . . [p. 313].

With this admission, however dialectic and rhetoric merge into one another, equally utilizing comparable concepts of argument and criticism. Critical appraisal of a theory (which must always be the appraisal of competing theories rather than a single theory appraised against atheoretical facts) becomes at heart a rhetorical process; it is "dialectical" only insofar as it involves competing alternatives. As contemporary rhetoricians have put it (Arnold, 1971):

> Anytime an affirmation is challenged, that action is rhetorical. . . . Whenever and wherever claims occur and those claims either are or might be challenged a situation exists which can be fully explained only if *rhetorical* explanation is provided [p. 195].

And Perelman (1971):

> The rhetorical dimension is unavoidable in every philosophical argument, in every scientific discussion which is not restricted to mere calculation but seeks to justify its elaboration or its application, and in every consideration on the principles of any discipline whatever,. . . whenever [men] act on other men by means of a discourse or are acted upon, they are engaged in an activity which is of interest to the rhetorician.
>
> Man thus appears to be an essentially rhetorical animal [p. 119].

But the point, a major focus of this section, remains: If dialectic is justificational, it is chimerical; if it is nonjustificational, it is rhetorical. Furthermore, an analogous argument holds for logic: If logic is amodal, it is *not inferential* and does not occur in science; if it occurs in science (as the theory of deducibility), it is rhetorical, a matter of the argumentative use of language. In a nonjustificational framework that acknowledges the argumentative nature of theoretical explanation and understanding, *logic and dialectic are facets of rhetoric and have no independent existence apart from the rhetorical transaction.* Rhetoric has as its domain all aspects of the argumentative mode of discourse including logic, dialectic, and the methodology of science.

From this perspective, the problem of theory choice in science, perhaps the most vexing aspect of research practice facing the methodologist, takes on a new dimension. Heretofore the major debate has concerned the adequacy of philosophical versus socio-psychological reconstructions of the scientific endeavor, and such clashes as the Kuhn–Popper–Lakatos debates have been interpreted primarily in that light. But theory choice is equally a subject for rhetorical analysis, and an adequate rhetorical theory could add much to our understanding of science as an argumentative form of discourse within a nonjustificational framework. Kuhn's recent remarks on theory choice lead straight to rhetorical analysis, as comments such as this make clear (1970c):

> Nothing about that relatively familiar thesis [that theory choice is not susceptible to logical proof] implies either that there are no good reasons for being persuaded or that those reasons are not ultimately decisive for the group. . . . If two men disagree, for example, about the relative fruitfulness of their

theories, or if they agree about that but disagree about the relative importance of fruitfulness and, say, scope in reaching a choice, neither can be convicted of a mistake. Nor is either being unscientific. ... To understand why science develops as it does, one need not unravel the details of biography and personality that lead each individual to a particular choice, though that topic has vast fascination. What one must understand, however, is the manner in which a particular set of shared values interacts with the particular experience shared by a community of specialists to ensure that most members of the group will ultimately find one set of arguments rather than another decisive [pp. 199–200].

This last sentence of Kuhn's summarizes the function of rhetoric in the understanding of science: Rhetoric can provide a framework and theory for the explanation of decisions that result from the argumentative use of discourse, in both revolutionary reconceptualization and normal science practice. In both cases, scientists face arguments (in print and in experimentation), never data. Rhetoric will be as indispensable to the understanding of science as social and cognitive psychology.

Thus it is incumbent upon methodologists to become familiar with and to utilize the resources available within the rhetorical tradition. Only a few philosophers (such as Finocchiaro, 1977) interested in science have dealt with rhetoric since Toulmin (1958), and there is a wealth of material available— including Arnold (1974), the Bitzer and Black (1971) volume, and Scott and Brock (1972)—that should be assayed for its application to science and its methodology. Among many theorists, the voluminous writings of Kenneth Burke (e.g., 1945, 1953, 1962, 1966, 1967) stand out as especially relevant, as do some of Richard McKeon (e.g.,1957, 1968); however, there is a considerable amount of justificationist conventionalism that must be purged from these works (especially in McKeon) before they can be utilized effectively.

Let us conclude this section by noting one way in which rhetoric and sociology combine to shed light on the nature and role of the audience in scientific communication. The production of scientific knowledge involves a producer interacting with an audience, if for no other reason than that argument presupposes a plurality of points of view and therefore (neglecting arguing with one's self) a community of knowers. The community structure of science has been extensively studied of late from the perspective of the sociology of science; and the work of Merton (1968, 1973), Hagstrom (1965), Mulkay (1972), Ziman (1968), and others has begun to sketch an informative picture of the scientist as a social being. But as yet there is little of consequence on the audience in science; accounts have focused upon the research community primarily in terms of its impact upon the individual scientist. The scientific community as a rhetorical audience, as an active constructor of the scientific dialogue and the meaning that it manifests, has received little attention. But consider how the research community in which the individual operates becomes a *persona* to whom the scientist must address his or her findings. In communicating results, researchers are quite literally engaged in a dialogue with the persona representing their research community. The initial process of formulating (to themselves) what they know, what they can argue for and against, involves researchers in an internal dialogue with *what they perceive to be* the point of view of their research community. Subsequent communication (from informal discussion with colleagues, through colo-quim or convention presentation, to and including publication) requires researchers to sharpen their presentation such that it will be maximally effective to the audience persona in question. In periods of Kuhnian normal science, much of the metaphysical and/or sociological paradigm finds concrete expression in views that researchers attribute to the persona they are addressing, and this persona typifies a community of "like-minded" scholars. In revolutionary periods the persona is often hostile, opaque, disinclined to listen to "reason," etc.; and the entire nature of the communication process changes accordingly.

The personae of science renders intelligible another phenomenon that historical research has disclosed to be characteristic of science: that there is enormous discrepancy between a scientist's preachment and his or her research practice. When queried about their research methods and practice, scientists usually respond that it conforms to one or another methodology that they take to be the *personification* of "good science." Thus Newton, a consummate visionary and theoretician, would utter "hypotheses non fingo" to a community of inductivist researchers in absolutely convincing fashion, because he really believed in it. Historians examining his research have found Newton to be much more speculative than he would have admitted, and one way to understand the discrepancy is to consider Newton both as a persona and also as addressing one. The ideal and the real interact in the construction of the products of science, and a rhetorical theory of personae could be enormously informative of how that interaction occurs.

INTERNAL AND EXTERNAL HISTORICAL RECONSTRUCTION AND THE RATIONALITY OF SCIENCE

There is one obvious way in which the philosopher who wishes to preserve a purely rational picture of science and its growth *from the philosophical point of view* can turn to deny the role of the psychological sciences in the explantion of these matters: to the distinction of internal and external history. *Internal* history is the "purely" scientific history of a discipline; that is, it is concerned with the factors that determine the growth of knowledge independently of external influences. *External* history is the history of factors that are relevant to progress in a domain but that are not themselves "internal." The French revolution is, for example, an external factor that must be taken into account when discussing the progress of science in France at the end of the 18th century. A rough and ready internal–external history distinction is a commonplace of virtually all histories of science, although historiographers rarely discuss the principles according to which one makes the intuitive distinction precise.

Now the theorist who wishes to preserve a purely philosophical reconstruction of the growth of science, and eschew psychological and sociological considerations *as somehow irrational*, need only proclaim that:

1. All the rationality of science lies in its (reconstructed) internal history.
2. All disturbing influences (that rule out the rationality of science from the purely philosophical point of view) are *by definition* part of external history.

Such an historian would then reconstruct the rational growth of science in a world apart, i.e., a realm of "objective" knowledge that was independent of the knowing subject. An ideal candidate for such a nonhuman realm would be Plato's conception of the "Third World," inhabited by the eternal Forms of knowledge to which the human intellect could aspire if it prepared itself in the correct manner. As a reaction to Kuhn's conception of science and its growth, both Popper (1972, 1974) and especially Lakatos (1970, 1971) have claimed that the rationality of science resides in such a Third World reconstruction. Lakatos (1971) summed up this position well:

> Each rational reconstruction produces some characteristic pattern of rational growth of scientific knowledge. But all of these *normative* reconstructions may have to be supplemented by *empirical* external theories to explain the residual non-rational factors. The history of science is always richer than its rational reconstruction. *But rational reconstruction or internal history is primary, external history only secondary, since the most important problems of external history are defined by internal history.* External history either provided non-rational explanation of the speed, locality, selectiveness, etc. of historic events *as interpreted* in terms of internal history; or, when history differs from its rational reconstruction, it provides an empirical explanation of why it differs. But the *rational* aspect of scientific growth is fully accounted for by one's logic of scientific discovery [pp. 105–106].

Note that all psychological and sociological factors are defined as external on this account and that external history is also definitionally *not rational*.

Now there is nothing wrong with a redefinition of terms, provided it is theoretically motivated. Unfortunately, there appears to be no theory motivating Lakatos's redefinition, only an attempt to evade the force of

Kuhn's criticisms of Popperian methodology. It is all very well to advance the claim that "the *rational* aspect of scientific growth is fully accounted for by one's logic of scientific discovery," but one must ask the Popperians to deliver this so-called logic—something that has not been done. Instead, Lakatos proposed to evaluate rival methodologies of science according to how much of scientific history they can reconstruct as internal—which is to say, as rational. His methodology judged a historiographic reconstruction superior to its alternatives if it reconstructs more of science as rational. (Clearly this "metacriterion" of methodologies is inadequate; one would not want to say that a methodology that reconstructed *everything* as internal history was the "best" methodology. No one claims that all factors that are properly part of the history of science are "internal" and "rational." But the point remains: The mass exodus of disgruntled Popperians to the Third World has occurred without being theoretically motivated; these theorists have yet to produce any *logic* of discovery (Weimer, 1974a, 1974b). This being so, it seems far more fruitful to study how actual human scientists (rather than denizens of the Third World) do science and how they form "scientific" concepts. Philosophy may rationally reconstruct the end products of knowledge acquisition, but it remains for the psychological sciences to explain the growth of knowledge.

RATIONALITY REVISITED:
TACIT VERSUS EXPLICIT CONCEPTIONS

One of the major themes of this essay is that the rationality of science both transcends justificationist notions of rationality and also defies analysis from a solely philosophical perspective. We have discussed these issues in many particular applications, ranging from overviewing inadequacies in received view accounts (such as the lack of firm foundations for inference, the problems of commitment, incommensurability and paradigm clashes, etc.) to noting directions for future research and corrections to redress traditional analyses (such as the psychological and sociological nature of paradigms, research programs, and theory choice, the rhetorical nature of tuition and communication, and the untenability of internal versus external analyses). But in all of this our characterization of rationality has been largely by indirection, pointing out inadequacies and suggesting new directions in which to proceed rather than attemptimg a precise specification, or explicit theory, of rationality. The reason that I have not addressed the theory of rationality directly is that speculation concerning its nature is premature; we need to study human behavior and the nature of inquiry much more fully before undertaking that task. The strongest claim that I have made is that Barley's comprehensively critical rationalism, as a conception of rationalist identity, is the only position that is tenable enough to warrant further development and criticism.

I do not mean to imply by that claim that Bartley's account has been unchallenged, or that alternatives are not continually being proposed. I do mean that criticisms of comprehensively critical rationalism seem to fall into one of three categories: First, attempts to resurrect an absolute framework of some kind which will somehow be self justifying. Trigg's (1973) thesis that the preconditions for language provide an objectivity that renders commitment objectively specifiable, and hence at least potentially justifiable, is a typical example. While such views might merit discussion as instances of the pervasive power of justificationism, they add virtually nothing to our understanding of rationality. A second class of criticisms comes from "loyalists" Popperians who have attacked Bartley as a traitor to Popper because his article on demarcation (Bartley, 1968) is critical of Popperian doctrine (see various articles in the journal *Philosophy* from the late 60's to the present). Most of these attacks retreat to one or another form of critical rationalism similar to that which Popper endorsed prior to Bartley's influence. The third class of criticism reaches a much more vital issue, one which has been repeatedly hinted at in our examination of whether or not the rationality of science transcends the limits of philosophical analysis: At issue is whether rationality must be explicit, or whether it could possibly be tacit.

An explicit conception of rationality is one which is consciously available to the individual in a form that can guide his or her behavior in given cases. Philosophers who defend explicit, "internalist" reconstructions of scientific practice, and automatically reject psycho- or sociological accounts as irrational, apparently assume that no other conception of rationality is available. I can think of little else that would explain patronizing remarks like this comment by Laudan (1977) in endorsing the "arationality" assumption:

The arationality assumption establishes a division of labor between the historian of ideas and the sociologist of knowledge; saying, in effect, that the historian of ideas, using the machinery available to him, can explain the history of thought insofar as it is rationally well-founded and that the sociologist of knowledge steps in at precisely those points where a rational analysis of the acceptance (or rejection) of an idea fails to square with the actual situation [p. 202].

Theorists (such as Lakatos and Laudan) who assume that rationality must be explicit are responsible for attempting to force not only a division of labor between philosophy and the psychological and social sciences but also a class or status separation in which philosophy, conceived as explicit and rational, receives pride of place.

But what if the rationality of science is *implicit* in its practice (rather than explicit), as Kuhn, Polanyi, and I assert? Then any division of labor would be one of convenience, and the status separation (which attempts to allocate use of the honorific term 'rational') would no longer exist. It would be very helpful if we could point to other complex phenomena which are rational in a tacit or implicit sense, not only to provide a model account of such rationality, but also to diminish the fears of traditional philosophers that the account of science I have proposed either sanctions "anything goes" or is an ad hoc response to the breakdown of justificationist rationality.

Fortunately there is such an account available, at least in rudimentary form, in the economic theorizing of F. A. Hayek (see especially Hayek, 1948, 1952a, and 1967). For much of his life Hayek has attempted to explain the rationality of complexly organized systems (such as the economic system constituted by the market place, and the individual instantiated by the nervous system) which are forced to operate, due to the knowledge and information transmission capabilities of such systems, according to principles of organization which prevent explicit analysis and defy centralized control. Thus, somewhat surprisingly, although Hayek's analysis of scientific methodology is well known for often anticipating and usually paralleling Popper's, his conception of the rationality of complex phenomena is more compatible with Kuhn's than Popper's account. Let us examine Hayek's *methodological individualism* to see the tacit dimension of its rationality and the compatibility of his views with both Bartley and Kuhn.

Consider the problem posed by attempting to utilize the marketplace, as an instantiation of the economic system, to maximal extent. Modern *collectivism*, as evidenced in socialism and attempts at collectivization and central planning, asserts that maximal efficiency can only be obtained with conscious intervention and direction from a centralized locus of control. This is the economic counterpart to the desire for explicit rationality, and it permeates the "positive" approach to economics from Saint Simon to Comte down to the postivists and socialists of the present.

But what is the economic problem that central planning and explicit control is to solve? It would appear to be that of the most efficient utilization of our resources, which in the case of the marketplace means maximal utilization of knowledge (to buy or sell). Hayek (1952a) turns this into the problem of "How that knowledge of the particular circumstances of the moment can be most effectively utilized (p. 98)." No single authority could possess enough knowledge of the particular at any time to succeed. Thus Hayek argues for the superiority of individualism over collectivism, and for the primacy of tacit over explicit rationality and control (1952a):

> A successful solution can therefore not be based on the authority dealing directly with the objective facts, but must be based on a method of utilizing the knowledge dispersed among all members of society, knowledge of which in any particular instance the central authority will usually know neither who possesses it nor whether it exists at all. It can therefore not be utilized by consciously integrating it into a coherent whole, but only through some mechanism which will delegate the particular decisions to those who possess it,

and for that purpose supply them with such information about the general situation as will enable them to make the best use of the particular circumstances of which only they know.

This is precisely the function which the various "markets" perform [p. 99].

Consider the parallels of this account of the market as a knowledge gathering and transmitting system to Kuhn's account of exemplary puzzles as the locus of the cognitive content of normal science research. In both cases the problem concerns how we can make maximal use of tacit knowledge and skill. As Hayek (1952a) said: "The problem is precisely how to extend the span of our utilization of resources beyond the span of the control of any one mind; and, therefore, how to dispense with the need of conscious control and how to provide inducements which will make the individuals do the desirable things without anyone having to tell them what to do (p. 88).

The conception of rationalism which Hayek endorses, and which he called (1967) a critical rationalism (prior, however, to Bartley, 1962), is quite antithetical to conscious planning and explicit control in complex systems such as science and the economic order (1967):

> That we should not be able fully to shape human affairs according to our wishes went much against the grain of generations which believed that by the full use of his reason man could make himself fully master of his fate. It seems, however, that this desire to make everything subject to rational control, far from achieving the maximal use of reason, is rather an abuse of reason based upon a misconception of its powers, and in the end leads to a destruction of that free interplay of many minds on which the growth of reason nourishes itself. True rational insight seems indeed to indicate that one of the most important uses is the recognition of the proper limits of rational control [p. 93].

This conception of rationality, although not addressed to the issues discussed by either Bartley or Kuhn, is quite compatible with the major aspects of their analyses. Not only does it show in what senses it is rational to work within an institutionalized system that is neither fully known to any individual nor under any single locus of control, but Hayek's analysis also discloses that even if we were aware of all the abstract principles of determination according to which a complex system such as the marketplace operates it would not enable us to be more "rational" or "in control" of the particular behaviors which constitute the system. The institutionalization of tacit knowledge structures within the social system (or the internalization of tacit knowledge within the nervous system) operates according to highly abstract rules of determination which, in an explanatory context, Hayek calls explanation of the principles involved rather than explanation of the particulars. The distinction between explanations of the principle and the particular (detailed in Hayek, 1967) supports and clarifies Polanyi's claims that our tacit knowledge of complex skills can be exhibited but never explicitly trained. But whereas Polanyi's account appeared to rely upon a form of psychological and individual intuitionism, which seemed to lead to an "anything goes" account which terrified explicit rationalists such as Lakatos, Hayek's analysis of complexly organized systems in general (not just the individual) indicates that it is simply not possible to achieve sufficiently exhaustive explanations of the particular in such systems to ever gain explicit control over them. The sort of control over complex systems (such as science) that Lakatos and the Popperians desire thus seems to be, as Hayek noted, an *abuse* of reason based upon a misconception of its powers. On the other hand, both Bartley's insistence that what counts as criticism requires thorough study in the given case and Kuhn's account of knowledge generation and transmission from exemplary puzzles are directly compatible with Hayek's account of the nature and rationality of complex phenomena, and the psychology of concept formation, inference, and expectation which I have advanced in many locations makes indispensable use of the theoretical psychology of Hayek's *The sensory order* (1952b). Since this is so, it would seem that students of science and its methodology could benefit greatly from Hayek's methodological individualism and his pioneering work on the theory of complex phenomena.

If we are ever to achieve a more complete understanding of science as an ongoing endeavor it will be necessary to abandon the explicit rationality and solely philosophical analyses that have attempted to limit, in advance of studying it thoroughly, the nature of scientific inquiry. Working within the various appproaches outlines in this chapter is the best way that I know to accomplish that goal. I hope that future research will flesh out the this programmatic sketch.

APPENDIX:
An Examination of Detail
on Selected Topics

The preceding chapters outlined aspects of the methodology of scientific research from a great viewing distance. Initially, we overviewed justificationism, especially as it relates to epistemology and the nature of science. Then our focus shifted to the development of nonjustificational philosophies. Here we were at treetop level, skimming over a maze of detail to touch upon major points at which nonjustificational approaches clash with both justificationism and themselves. The final chapters introduced what I feel are necessary correctives to philosophical and historical–sociological analyses now available, by focusing upon the indispensability of the psychological sciences and an adequate theory of rhetoric.

Now, to both complete and supplement our overview, we must descend to the forest's floor, to walk through the jungle of details necessary to back up the generalizations concerning the nature and inadequacies of the received view. Thus the next four chapters examine in detail aspects of justificationist philosophy and methodology and the manner in which that position is reflected in psychology. Once again, our presentation is simultaneously expository—in attempting to exhibit the structure of justificationist thought—and highly critical. Our intent is to examine enough contemporary and recent philosophy of science to show how justificationism treats issues and how that treatment is inadequate.

9

The Quest for a Theory of Rational Inference: The Nature of Induction, the Foundations of Knowledge, and the Rationality of Science

This chapter overviews the nature of knowledge and its acquisition, as these issues are construed by recent empiricist philosophers. It ought to be concerned wholly with problems of epistemology, but paradoxically, it is not; although it begins and ends upon epistemological issues, a large portion of this chapter discusses *logical* issues. Why should logic, specifically inductive logic, occupy a chapter on knowledge and its acquisition?

The reasons we discuss all center around a strategic shift in the problem situation that has been made by logical empiricists. Their initial concern for epistemology has been traded for the task of constructing (inductive) logical systems.

Faced with seemingly inescapable skeptical arguments from Hume, neojustificationists abandoned the classic conception of knowledge as proven assertion in favor of knowledge as probable assertion. Indeed, they joined in and reinforced the power of the skeptical argument, in so doing portraying themselves as far more sophisticated than their predecessors. But despite the new emphasis upon what Reichenbach called "the probability structure of knowledge," the neojustificationist is still a justificationist. The certainty that once resided in the *nature* of knowledge has been abandoned, to be sure; but it has reappeared, completely unchanged, in the *foundations* of (empirical) knowledge. The quest for certain knowledge has subtly been shifted to the quest for certain foundations for probable knowledge.

It is here that so-called inductive logic enters the scene: for *given* the foundations of knowledge, inductive logic is to provide an algorithm for assessing the probability of scientific hypotheses that, although based upon them, go beyond the foundations. Inductive logic is to *rationalize* our admittedly indispensable leaps beyond the "data." If such leaps can be legitimated, then science is a rational means of knowledge acquisition or, put another way, a rational *source* of knowledge. And if science is, after all, a rational source of knowledge, the sophisticated neojustificationist can afford to turn away from the Humean skeptic and go on to other constructive tasks. Whether or not the neojustificationist actually can afford to turn away is a matter for subsequent discussion; for now it suffices to mention that the problem-shift from epistemic to logical concerns merely indicates that the logical empiricist *has* in fact *ignored* the skeptic and gone upon a path (slightly primrose) of his or her own making. In this sense, logical empiricism, like its more brash, positivist predecessor, continues to serve as a reaffirmation of faith in the face of skeptical doubt.

THE "PROBLEM" OF INDUCTION

According to traditional accounts, there are two classes of claims that can be known for certain (neglecting tautologies, mathematics, and so-called a priori truths): the conclusions of valid deductive argument forms and the immediately presented data of acquaintance or experience. Deductive logic is a matter of 'empty' symbol manipulation according to rules; the content or meaning of such argument forms does not affect their validity. Deductive inference is thus independent of content; or, stated another way, valid deductions tells us nothing new, nothing not already known to the premises. Knowledge by immediate acquaintance is a problematic issue (discussed later); about the most that can be said is that we are acquainted with our own phenomenal experience. Although characterizing the nature of that experience is quite troublesome, the point to note is that our individual experience is incredibly limited. So now the problem arises: How are we to *know* things not presented to our immediate experience? Deductive inference will not help us, for we must first know the truth of the premises of deductive arguments; thus what we could deduce would be nothing more than what we already knew, i.e., were acquainted with. But in both science and everyday experience, we constantly and habitually make inferences about things we have not experienced; and life would literally be impossible unless we did. The problems of induction concern whether or not such inferences beyond the data of our immediate experience are legitimate, which means for the justificationist, *justifiable*.

Bertrand Russell (1912) introduced the problem very well quite some time ago:

> Let us take as an illustration a matter about which none of us, in fact, feel the slightest doubt. We are all convinced that the sun will rise to-morrow. Why? Is this belief a mere blind outcome of past experience, or can it be justified as a reasonable belief?...

It is obvious that if we are asked why we believe that the sun will rise to-morrow, we shall naturally answer, "Because it always has risen every day". We have a firm belief that it will rise in the future, because it has risen in the past. If we are challenged as to why we believe that it will continue to rise as heretofore, we may appeal to the laws of motion. ... The interesting doubt is as to whether the laws of motion will remain in operation until to-morrow. If this doubt is raised, we find ourselves in the same position as when the doubt about the sunrise was first raised [pp. 60–61].

But it seems that the only reason to believe that the laws of motion will remain in operation is that they have operated in our past experience. So now we can formulate the problem slightly differently: Do instances of the occurrence of something in the past afford any evidence whatsoever for its occurrence in the future? Will the future continue to behave as the past? According to Russell (1912):

If not, it becomes plain that we have no ground whatever for expecting the sun to rise to-morrow, or for expecting the bread we shall eat at our next meal not to poison us, or for any of the other scarcely conscious expectations that control our daily lives. It is to be observed that all such expectations are only *probable*; thus we have not to seek for a proof that they *must* be fulfilled, but only for some reason that they are *likely* to be fulfilled [p. 62].

Note the emphasis on probability as indispensable to the nature of inductive inference; it was assumed by all that *all inductive inferences are at best probable*. In another location, Russell was very clear on this (1927):

It is important to realize the fundamental position of probability in science. At the very best, induction and analogy only give probability. Every inference worthy of the name is inductive, therefore all inferred knowledge is at best probable [p. 285].

This is an extreme change from the classic justificationism that is characteristic of early inductive logicians; it is, in effect, a concession to Hume's skeptical arguments (its significance is discussed later).

At this point it might be objected that as yet there is no real problem; so inductive inference is merely probable, but so what? Doesn't our experience indicate that that is all we can hope for? This objection indicates that the force of Russell's (and Hume's) argument has not been perceived.

The problem, simply stated, is to *justify* probable inductive knowledge *as* knowledge. The logical problem concerns *what grounds we have as rational beings for continuing to infer* when inference can never be certain. And it was David Hume who showed that not only is inductive inference not analytically true but that it cannot be proven on the basis of experience. It is not analytic, because one can always imagine that the opposite of an inductive inference will obtain; thus there is no logical necessity connected to induction. It does no good to appeal to past successful experience with inductive inferences to justify induction, for that is to circularly use induction to justify inductive inference. Hume's skeptical conclusion is that since induction is neither analytically true nor experientially justified, it must be unjustifiable.

Whereas empiricism had gained much influence and support because of its claim to provide an unimpeachable rational authority to counter tyrannical irrational authority such as that of the Roman Catholic Church, submission to this so-called rational authority—sense experience—became for the post-Humean empiricists an irrational procedure too. And if scientific activity thus rested on illogical psychological habit, who could offer a convincing argument against a person with different habits? As Bertrand Russell put it, more strongly, if there were no answer to Hume's argument, there would be "no intellectual difference between sanity and insanity" (Russell, 1945, p. 673). This *is* the problem of induction for justificationism.

Reichenbach put the dilemma that has faced every justificationist since Hume quite clearly (1951):

> The inductive inference is unjustifiable; that is what Hume claims to be the result of his critique. The seriousness of this result must be fully realized. If Hume's thesis is true, our instrument of prediction breaks down; we have no way of anticipating the future. We have so far seen that the sun rose every morning and believe that it will rise tomorrow, but we have no proof that it will do so tomorrow. What if the rivers start to run uphill tomorrow? You think: I shall not be so foolish as to believe that. But why is such belief foolish? Because, you answer, I have never seen water run uphill, and because I have always had success with such inferences from the past to the future. There you are, a prey to the fallacy discovered by Hume; you prove induction by the use of an inductive inference. Over and again we fall into the trap; we see that induction cannot be justified, then go on making inductions and argue that we should be fools if we doubted the inductive principle.
>
> That is the dilemma of the empiricist: either he is a radical empiricist and admits no results other than analytic statements or statements derived from experience—then he cannot make inductions and must renounce any statements about the future; or he admits the inductive inference—then he has admitted a nonanalytic principle not derivable from experience and has abandoned empiricism. A radical empiricism thus arrives at the conclusion that knowledge of the future is impossible; but what is knowledge if it does not include the future? A mere report of relations observed in the past cannot be called knowledge; if knowledge is to reveal objective relations of physical objects, it must include reliable predictions. A radical empiricism, therefore, denies the possibility of knowledge [pp. 88–89].

If knowledge gained by inductive inference cannot be justified—i.e., proven to be genuine knowledge—then all science and reflective common sense reasoning will have to be scrapped (because it will be *unfounded* opinion). Our so-called knowledge will not be knowledge; it will be at best mere habit or animal belief. Science will then be an irrational endeavor that can be at best psychologically satisfying but never logically justified. Thus the Humean skeptic concludes that genuine knowledge is not possible and throws induction into the obviously disreputable hands of the psychologist. The quest of every scientific philosopher since Hume has been to avoid this specter of irrationality; that is, the quest has been for a theory of instant assessment of scientific propositions (inferences) that is *rational in the sense of being logically justified* (Note 9.1).

The history of recent empiricist philosophy is a series of attempts to either reverse the conclusion of the skeptical Humean argument or to render innocuous the victory that the skeptic has won. Both problems turn out to resemble that of squaring the circle; and as a result, the literature on the justification of induction has decreased recently. The new trend is neither to reverse the skeptic's victory nor render it Pyrrhic, but rather to ignore it altogether: "The justification of induction no longer seems to be quite the problem it used to be, because the justification, if any, is now regarded as subsidiary to and dependent on the logic of induction, rather than vice versa" (Kyburg, 1966, p. 276). Philosophers now work on what Goodman called "the new riddle of induction," the problem of *explicating* the concept of 'valid induction' (see Goodman, 1955, p. 68). Justification no longer receives much attention. In this respect, contemporary inductive logicians have forgotten Reichenbach's (1938) warning about earlier attempts that ignored justification: "It is astonishing to see how clear-minded logicians, like John Stuart Mill, or Whewell, or Boole, or Venn, in writing about the problem of induction, disregarded the bearing of Hume's objections; they did not realize that any logic of science remains a failure so long as we have no theory of induction which is not exposed to Hume's criticism (p. 342)."

But the problem of induction that has plagued the (justificationist) theory of rationality from Hume's time to the present remains that of justification. Reichenbach was almost alone among logical empiricists in having emphasized that aspect as the ultimate goal of the "theory of scientific method." Others either concede the victory to skepticism (as does Ayer) or refuse to take the problem seriously, perhaps reflecting an earlier attitude when everything for which a ready-made answer was not easily at hand became a "pseudoproblem" that arose from the incorrect use of words. No wonder that the actual work of the logical empiricists shifted from the epistemological aspects of confirmation to the logical ones; the technical puzzles awaiting solution in "inductive logic" at least held the promise of being solvable, and the creative energy of the research program had to be directed at something other than the task of self-annihilation (Note 9.2). The majority of theorists in the area implicitly echo Hintikka's (1968) sentiment when confronted with any of the obviously perplexing problems facing the inductive logician: "In this truly philosophical predicament, I am moved to ask whether part of the issue could be reduced to a more manageable technical problem [p. 144]." The insurmountable logical issue of justification has largely been replaced by the technical puzzle-solving exercise of constructing various "logics" of induction and checking them for consistency and susceptibility to paradox. What has been lost sight of by virtually all concerned (there *are* exceptions; see Salmon's position in Note 9.2) is that *even if* a suitable (i.e., consistent and nonparadoxical and applicable) logic of confirmation could be developed, the problem of justification of inductive inference would remain to be solved.

THE SHIFTING BASIS OF CERTAINTY: FROM THE NATURE OF KNOWLEDGE TO ITS FOUNDATIONS

The problem-shift in the logical empiricist treatment of instant rational assessment begins with the epistemological aspects of confirmation and ends with the purely logical aspects, having managed to ignore the methodological aspects all along the way. This shift in the research program of inductive logicians was outlined elegantly by Radnitzky (1970):

> The epistemological question par excellence "What is the nature of knowledge?" or, if you please, the task of explicating Knowledge, is replaced by the question "What does it mean that *a hypothesis h* constitutes knowledge?", which question is replaced by "What does it mean that *h* is *confirmed by e*, that *e supports h*?", which is in turn replaced by "What does it mean that *e* confirms *h* to the degree *r*?"—or that *e* makes *h* probable to degree *r*, and eventually that $c(h,e) = r$. *The final explicandum is the metric concept c.* . . . In retrospect one can now see that the above sequence of explication tasks constitutes but a *prelude* to the task of constructing an inductive logic, of *laying the foundations of an inductive logic* [pp. 96–97].

This section outlines this problem-shift in sufficient detail that one can understand how it came about and why it goes virtually unnoticed except to certain critics of logical empiricism. In order to understand the shift from the overriding problem of the justificationists—how to justify knowledge gained by induction—to the technical logical problem of constructing an inductive logic, we must examine the pattern of criticism that the neojustificationists advance against classic justificationists. A key feature is the vehemence with which the sophisticated neojustificationists attack the classical conception of knowledge as certainty. It is in this attack that the neojustificationists present the picture of being sadder than their naive predecessors (because as critical rationalists they now are forced to admit the limitations of 'rationality'; recall

Chapter 1), yet definitely wiser. They now picture themselves as having abandoned an impossible dream and come back down to reality.

Reichenbach never ceased to chide the naiveté of his Logical Positivist friends, and his attitude toward the quest for certainty clearly reflects this "sadder but wiser" attitude (1938):

> It was the intention of modern positivism to restore knowledge to absolute certainty; what was proposed with the formalistic interpretation of logic was nothing other than a resumption of the program of Descartes. The great founder of rationalism wanted to reject all knowledge which could not be considered as absolutely reliable; it was the same principle which led modern logicians to a denial of a priori principles. It is true that this principle led Descartes himself to apriorism; but this difference may be considered as a difference in the stage of historical development—his rationalistic apriorism was to perform the same function of sweeping away all untenable scientific claims as was intended by the later struggle against a priori principles. The refusal to admit any kind of material logic—i.e., any logic furnishing information about some "matter"—springs from the Cartesian source: It is the ineradicable desire of absolutely certain knowledge which stands behind both the rationalism of Descartes and the logicism of positivists [pp. 344-345].

Reichenbach's criticism of the positivistic program is to echo Hume and to show that the positivists could not escape the Humean skeptical conclusion (1938):

> The answer given to Descartes by Hume holds as well for modern positivism. There is no certainty in any knowledge about the world because knowledge of the world involves predictions of the future. The ideal of absolutely certain knowledge leads into skepticism—it is preferable to admit this than to indulge in reveries about a priori knowledge. Only a lack of intellectual radicalism could prevent the rationalists from seeing this; modern postivists should have the courage to draw this skeptical conclusion, to trace the ideal of absolute certainty to its inescapable implications [p. 345].

Reichenbach's strategy for defeating Humean skepticism is to abandon the classic conception of knowledge as proven in favor of a probabilistic interpretation. His goal is to show that inductive inference will "probably" lead to success rather than that it will be *guaranteed* to lead to success. Despite the fact that Reichenbach's justification is ultimately a failure (which is so acknowledged as such by his descendants such as Salmon, 1967), his reasoning shows very clearly the switch in emphasis from certain knowledge to certain foundations for inference. Let us pause briefly to trace the origin of the concern for foundations from the essential tenets of justificationism through to the quest for foundations in logical empiricism.

The two most central tenets of justificationism are the identification of knowledge with proof and the authoritarian basis of epistemology. Together they lead to a third: the thesis that genuine knowledge must be an outgrowth from, and directly anchored to, a foundation (specified by the rational authority). All *genuine* knowledge must be grounded upon an authority; in the last analysis, the authority chosen *is* the foundation of knowledge. Practically each so-called "new revolution" in the history of philosophy has disclosed that the reigning epistemological authority is unsatisfactory; and then a new, allegedly more satisfactory and more rational authority is proposed in its stead. "The church should be replaced by intellectual intuition, intellectual intuition by sense experience, sense experience by a particular language system. And so on. These revolutions have had a depressingly similar pattern" (Bartley, 1962, p. 106). Neglecting the church, which has never figured essentially in scientific epistemologies, we can take a brief look at traditional sources of authority to see the new and subtle twists neojustificationism has taken (mainly to *camouflage* its sources of authority).

Traditionally, the intellectualist philosopher is called a rationalist or idealist. An intellectualist, who extols intelligence above empiricism, holds that *informative* theoretical knowledge is gained by the operation of the intellect. The intellectualist admits that knowledge (of sorts) may be gained from the senses but maintains that *theoretical* knowledge is a product of the active mind (in Kant's sense) rather than of a passive one (as in Locke's *tabula rasa*). The intellectualist is an *apriorist* concerning the nature of justification of theoretical or scientific knowledge.

There are many intellectualists of note in the history of Western philosophy, any of whom may be taken as representative. With regard to the issue of foundations, however, Descartes is a convenient example (Note 9.3). The method of Cartesian doubt is motivated by the search for an *indubitable* epistemological authority. Dissatisfied with traditional forms of authority, Descartes sought, by the expedient of persistent self-doubt, to find a solid and indubitable foundation of certainty upon which to erect his philosophy. That absolutely certain bedrock beyond doubt he found in the famous, "Cogito, ergo sum." The problem with all such candidates for self-evident truth is that either they are not self-evident (to the next philosopher) or they cannot constitute a foundation of knowledge. Ayer (1956) brings out the latter failure in Descartes's attempt:

> But this certainty does not come to very much. If I start with the fact that I am doubting, I can validly draw the conclusion that I think and that I exist. That is to say, if there is such a person as myself, then there is such a person as myself, and if I think, I think. Neither does this apply only to me. It is obviously true of anyone at all that if he exists he exists and that if he thinks he thinks. What Descartes thought that he had shown was that the statements that he was

conscious, and that he existed, were somehow privileged, that, for him at least, they were evidently true in a way which distinguished them from any other statements of fact. But this by no means follows from his argument. His argument does not prove that he, or anyone, knows anything. It simply makes the logical point that one sort of statement follows from another [p. 46].

The intellectualist attempt to found knowledge upon the authority of intuition (of a priori truths or conditions of knowledge, etc.) runs afoul of the fact that different thinkers have different intuitions. What is self-evident for one is almost invariably not so for others. But if the mind cannot provide a foundation, what about the *senses*? Consider now the other major tradition of thought on foundations.

For sensationalism, the problem comes to the fact that science deals in generalities; it makes a point of leaping beyond the evidence at hand, in generalizing from past to future—from "some..." to "all..."—and in extending the scope of its explanatory systems. And scientific propositions must be *justified* to be considered genuine knowledge. Thus arises the problem situation from which stems the quest for a theory of scientific rationality. This problem has in turn *two* aspects; not only must we justify scientific inference, but we must also ground it upon an epistemological authority. *Sensationalism* is the name of the doctrine that holds that all genuine knowledge comes to us through the senses (see Agassi, 1966b). The foundation of knowledge is thus sense experience. There are two groups of sensationalists: optimistic ones—the *inductivists*—who hold that informative *theoretical* knowledge bases upon 'sensational' foundations is possible, and skeptical ones—the *conventionalists*—who hold that no theoretical knowledge is possible. The appeal of the doctrine (in either inductivist or conventionalist guise) is that it promises science a way out between the Scylla of apriorism and idealism and the Charybdis of irrationalism.

The history of sensationalist thought has been one of retreat from naive to more sophisticated versions of the doctrine. The problem for sensationalism is blatantly straightforward: *If* science utilizes theoretical knowledge, *then* sensationalism is false. That is the thrust of Hume's skeptical argument from yet another perspective. It is in the attempts to deny this obvious refutation of sensationalism, to develop a sophisticated variant of the position that equally avoids apriorism and irrationalism, that the modern search for foundations has its primary motivation and direction. The focus of modern concern has almost invariably led to the development of conventionalism at the expense of inductivism. Let us see why this is so.

The two traditional grounds for validity of theoretical knowledge are apriorism and empiricism. The desire to avoid apriorism leaves only empiricism, traditionally based upon sensationalist assumptions. Empiricism is the thesis that we gain theoretical knowledge from experience or, more correctly, that every nonatomic or protocol sentence (those that do not refer *directly* to experience) has meaning only insofar as it can be linked (directly or indirectly) to observables (experiences). But isn't the idea of an *empirical* theoretical science self-stultifying? Agassi has argued exacty that (1966b):

> If we do not go beyond sense experience we have no theoretical knowledge of the world, while if we do go beyond it the margin is not contained in sense experience, and is, thus, *a priori*.
>
> This is the logic which led thinkers to abandon empiricism in favour of apriorism or conventionalism. For according to both these views our present theoretical knowledge necessarily transcends our experience; they differ only as to the question of whether this knowledge is informative (apriorism) or not (conventionalism) [p. 7].

Perception of this dilemma has led many sophisticated methodologists to embrace conventionalism as a last resort to save a philosophy *based upon* experience.

There is a problem that we have thus far ignored but that can be bypassed no longer: Not all experience is reliable or—in justificationist terms—valid. Our senses can, and often do, lie to us. Thus we must reject any naive sensationalism (either inductivist or conventionalist) that claims that any and all experience is the basis of knowledge—that experience cannot mislead us. Now there are both strong and weak versions of "sophisticated" sensationalism that take this unreliability of the senses into account. The strong version specifies some component of experience as the reliable one. An example of strong sophisticated sensationalism is John Locke, who *postulated* 'sense data' as the pure and valid sensory experiences. Sense datum theory has had a long and honorable tradition in philosophy; and respectable names still hold the view today, despite the fact that psychology refuted the view decades ago. The weak sophisticated sensationalist claim is only that there is *some* reliable element in experience. Thus the inductivist who is aware of the unreliability of our senses can put off the problem of justification by turning to the search for reliable (valid) elements in sensory experience. This explains the great resurgence in the search for 'basic experiences,' atomic propositions, and other such 'firm' elements in sensory experience. By pursuing such a goal, despite the low promise of success, one can avoid the all but hopeless alternative task of justification. And besides, when the going gets particularly rough, induction *as a method* can always be defended by retreating to sophisticated conventionalism.

Sophisticated conventionalism easily brushes aside criticisms that are damning to either the naive conventionalist or the sophisticated inductivist. The key to the tenability of sophisticated conventionalism is the weakness of its claims: It does not claim that theoretical knowledge is derived from experience, and it also does not claim that theoretical knowledge is informative. Theoretical knowledge is thus cut off from its base and left to wither on the vine. The doctrine easily accommodates the unreliability of the senses, for all it claims is that there is sometimes knowledge in sensation but that one cannot isolate it. Thus for sophisticated sensationalism, the information that is the basis of knowledge cannot be isolated within the sensory experience. A philosophy "based" upon sense experience is thus salvaged by the sophisticated conventionalist but at an enormous cost. Science can be at best a convenient calculational fiction for such a theorists; the game of science costs very little to play, but the rewards that can be expected from playing are also very small, indeed. Thus sophisticated conventionalism is almost too sophisticated for a scientific philosopher to bear; he or she will endorse it only when the criticism is extremely severe and then only as a last-ditch measure. At all other times, the scientific philosopher will lapse into the more pleasurable (if frustrating) posture of the sophisticated inductivist and join in the puzzle-solving endeavor of the search for reliable observation reports that will constitute the firm foundation of knowledge.

It seems that the search for foundations is the only stopgap alternative that the justificationist has between Humean skepticism, apriorism, and sophisticated ("disinfected" would be better) conventionalism. None of these alternatives is as attractive as inductivism, and the bonus prize is that the inductivist *can* retreat to conventionalism if need be to avoid criticism. Indeed, the sophisticated conventionalist can always stop criticism by employing the *tu quoque* argument. When worst comes to worst one can always retreat to commitment.

It will be seen immediately that a theorist's position with regard to foundations will be governed by a combination of his or her sophistication (concerning the reliability of sensory reports) and feelings toward conventionalism. Let us examine some representative positions.

Rudolf Carnap, during his *Aufbau* stage (Carnap, 1928), was extremely naive. His program, alluded to in the scathing comment by Reichenbach, was to found certain knowledge upon certain sense data (*erlebs*). The early Carnap was, as Reichenbach alleged, Descartes in modern dress. His position is now universally employed as a straw man. Under pressure from realists such as Schlick and Feigl and conventionalists such as Reichenbach, Carnap abandoned the firm foundation of phenomena for a conventional one at the same time he abandoned verifiablility for testability (and certain knowledge for probable knowledge). As a logician, it did not bother Carnap at all to endorse conventionalism; indeed, his syntactic approach to empiricism is perhaps the most conventional philosophy that has ever paid lip service to experience.

Reichenbach, the sophisticated advocate of the probability theory of knowledge, attempted to retain both inductivism and conventionalism. That is, he believed that induction could be justified by a pragmatic or conventional argument if one acknowledged probable knowledge instead of certain knowledge. Thus he retained certain realist elements (informative theoretical knowledge, etc.) within a conventionalist framework. Feigl, who inherited the realistic position among the logical empiricists after Schlick's death, has always been a phenomenalist, seeking a genuinely firm foundation in sense data. As a realist, he has always remained an inductivist who attacks conventionalism, especially in the extreme forms in which Carnap embraced it. Thus when pressed, Feigl retreats to Reichenbach's position, seeking a pragmatic justification of induction rather than any more blatant form of conventionalism. But Feigl (1970a) still believes that the basic statements of science (although no longer experience) can be purified of theoretical contamination (as well as error) and can be made a firm foundation of knowledge (see the following section).

But the upshot of the search for foundations in logical empiricism is clear: It allows one to temporarily hold the terribly difficult problem of justification in abeyance while constructive research is directed toward articulating that part of 'the given' in experience that can be 'taken'—taken as a foundation for knowledge claims. But soon that problem will also be given up by all but the most persistent in favor of another technical puzzle that can be solved with the tools available to the research program. The change runs smoothly from justification to foundations to evidence to confirmation to articulating a metric in logical terms.

The reasoning is straightforward. Because knowledge must be justified, we will look for what supports knowledge claims. What supports knowledge claims is evidence—the evidence of the senses. What does it mean to say that a scientific hypothesis is supported by evidence? Clearly it means that the evidence e *confirms* hypothesis h to some extent. If knowledge is probable rather than certain, then "to some extent" is to be explicated in terms of the calculus of probabilities. Thus the question becomes what makes h probable to degree c on the basis of e? At this point, the logician steps in to explicate c, the concept of degree of confirmation. The task of justification has receded beyond the horizon of immediate concern. And its retreat has gone all but unnoticed to the "confirmation theorists" directly concerned. It remains for external critics of logical empiricism to call attention to it (see, e.g., Radnitzky, 1970).

One reason for the invisibility of this change in task is the shift to the probability theory of knowledge. By loudly claiming to have abandoned the untenable conception of knowledge as proven assertion, and by concentrating on the probabilistic character of inductive inferences, the logical empiricists who had worried about justification came to think that they had changed the situation from that confronting Hume. They came to think that instead of a *proof* that induction would *certainly* yield proven knowledge, all that was required was a *relative* justification that induction is "reliable" and the "best" alternative available. This leads to the idea of *pragmatic justification* of inductive inference as the procedure most likely to give reliable knowledge *if* anything does. Although the *success* of induction cannot be guaranteed in advance, its results (which are probable) are superior to any alternative method of prediction. This is Reichenbach's reasoning, discussed in Note 9.2. This line of reasoning led able logicians (e.g., Carnap) and statistician–probability theorists (e.g., Reichenbach, von Mises) to exploit technical puzzles in logic and probability at the expense of basic epistomeological isssues.

THE "FOUNDATIONS" OF EMPIRICAL KNOWLEDGE: THE "GIVEN" AND THE "TAKEN"

A surprising fact about logical empiricists is that despite obvious similarities and sympathies to realism, few genuine realists are to be found in their camp. The philosophy of the logical "-isms" is actually somewhat hostile to realism, whereas it is quite congenial to pragmatism or conventionalism. In this section we must disgress to note one reason for this hostility to realism by studying attitudes toward the given in experience.

Recall that the central problem for logical positivism was a satisfactory explication of the meaning of scientific terms; the technical puzzle to be solved at all costs became that of spelling out the mechanics of verification. That problem becomes one of asking what meaning *reduces* to. Ayer summed this up when considering the meaning of a proposition:"We are asking what are the propositions to which the proposition in question is reducible. ... These propositions are in turn reducible to others until we reach the elementary propositions which are not descriptive but ostensive " (Ayer, 1934, p. 337). The problem of what constitutes the ultimate reduction basis of "empirical" meaning, the ostensive or given in scientific experience, is the problem of the foundations of knowledge. That which is 'given' as foundational is that which is 'taken' for the construction of science. Thus solving the problem of the data base of science, i.e., of *factual reference*, is central to the program of the logical "-isms."

Factual reference may be explicated in several ways. It may be construed such that the meaning of a proposition is equivalent to *another* set of propositions. In this case, ostensive meaning is a *linguistic* reduction; and 'verification' becomes a peculiar way of speaking, for factual reference "reduces" to a matter of *definition*. Factual reference becomes a matter of words and their usage rather than of facts or, more properly, of explicating the formation rules of a language system. On the other hand, if the factual reference is construed to be a relation between propositions and nonpropositional objects (in the world), then verification becomes more literal, for meaning will be a matter of the relation of words to objects. Rather than ultimate or ostensive meaning involving logical relations between words, it will involve the relation between words and the objects of experience. The *syntactic approach* to empiricism construes meaning as a matter of linguistic equivalences, and the *experientialist approach* construes meaning as a relation between words and objects.

Under the heading of the experientialist approach belong all those attempts to provide a foundation for knowledge that tie the meaning of scientific propositions to occurrences in the world. There are two major classes of experientialists: the *realists* who relate statements to material objects and the *phenomenalists* who relate statements to (constructions based upon) sense data. Both classes of the experientialist approach endorse what may be dubbed a *correspondence approach* to meaning and truth; for both camps, meaning is a matter of *factual* (or objective) *reference*. For the realist, facts are material objects in the world; for the phenomenalist, facts are constructions out of the deliverances of sense (sense data). Let us review the difficulties that face either approach to the foundations of knowledge.

The failure of either brand of factual reference within the experientialist camp can be seen by showing its parallels to the odyssey of the verifiability theory of meaning. The devastating problem facing the quest for verification is that all verification is conventional in nature; there is no such thing as a verified-for-once-and-for-all statement (proposition), either in science or everyday life. Precisely the same problem plagues factual reference; all facts are conventionally determined, and there is no ultimate bedrock of factual truth given in ostension. There is nothing that is given absolutely, and therefore everything that is taken cannot be taken for certain. Factual reference is never absolute; it is always relative (Note 9.4). The conventional nature of factual attribution has to be incorporated into the empiricist system if it is to survive. The question comes in asking whether this can be done (Note 9.5).

The realist faces quite a problem in incorporating factual relativity into a scientific empiricism. Granting that meaning and factual reference must have a conventional element, the ultimate arbiter must always remain experience. But how can this be maintained if *experiencing* always involves conceptual structures and contents that are a priori in the sense that they precede experience and determine its very nature?

There simply has never been a satisfactory answer to this dilemma. The distinction between strong (or conclusive) and weak (or "in principle") verifiability failed to save the essence of verificationism. If there are no ultimate verifiers, then the problems of the *tu quoque* haunt the verificationist; if there are no ultimate facts, that same dilemma haunts the realist who interprets scientific meaning, factual status, and truth in terms of a correspondence between statements and material objects. Because the relation between statements and objects-in-the-world cannot be specified conclusively or unambiguously, the theorist who wishes to endorse a realistic position seemingly has only a retreat to commitment available to defend realism. Defenses of the correspondence theory of truth (and meaning) were few and far between in the logical "-isms" (Note 9.6).

The seemingly insurmountable difficulty facing the realist is to reconcile the uncertainty and conventionality of factual reference, which everyone in one way or another admitted, with the idea that meaning and truth are a matter of correspondence between statements and objective states of affairs. If factual attribution is not certain, not absolute, then how can any correspondence obtain between statements and *objective* states of affairs? Factual relativity destroys the objectivity and externality of the "objects" to which statements are to correspond. If there is no firm factual basis, then correspondence is purely conventional. If correspondence is conventional, then the coherence theory of truth reigns by default. The meaning of a scientific statement becomes a matter of its *use*—a matter of correctly explicating the formation and transformation rules of the language in which it occurs. Reality, as an external object, is then unnecessary for the determination of the meaning of a 'scientific' concept. Once it is admitted that the protocol statements of science are determined by *conventions* (be they theories or decisions of the scientific community), it is all but impossible to retain a realistic basis for science, for the objectivity and neutrality of the external world is lost to conventional determination. *Primary* meaning can no longer reside in the firm factual basis that is independent of theoretical involvement, with theoretical constructions having secondary or derived meaning. The protocol statements of science have lost their privileged position (Note 9.7). Against this the realist like Schlick could only repeat his gentle warning (1935):

> If anyone should tell me that I believe in the truth of science ultimately because it has been adopted "by the scientists of my culture circle," I should—smile at him. I do have trust in those good fellows, but that is only because I found them to be trustworthy wherever I was able to test their enunciations. I assure you most emphatically that I should *not* call the system of science true if I found its consequences incompatible with my own observations of nature, and the fact that it is adopted by the whole of mankind and taught in all the universities would make no impression on me... the *only ultimate* reason why I accept any proposition as true is to be found in those simple experiences which may be regarded as the final steps of comparison between a statement and a fact [p. 69].

But gentle warnings receive little attention in a brash movement. Both phenomenalists and syntactic empiricists argued against the realism that Schlick championed but for different reasons. The phenomenalist championed an alternative approach to factual reference that was based upon experience, and that position is worth mentioning. Actually there are two representative classes of phenomenalistic treatments of factual reference—one a naive version championed by Carnap (1928), the other a more sophisticated position defended for a time by Ayer (1940). Let us consider them in turn.

Carnap's motivation in the *Aufbau* was to found knowledge upon a certain basis. His concern was with the justification of scientific knowledge claims (1928):

> This requirement for justification and conclusive foundation of each thesis will eliminate all speculative and poetic work from philosophy. As soon as we began to take seriously the requirement of scientific strictness, the necessary result was that all of metaphysics was banished from philosophy, since its theses cannot be rationally justified. It must be possible to give a rational foundation for each scientific thesis [xvii].

In order to effect the justification of our knowledge, Carnap embarked upon a program of the rational reconstruction of scientific concepts to show that they could be conclusively and unambiguously grounded in the immediately given. Speaking retrospectively, Carnap noted (1928):

> I wanted to attempt, for the first time, the actual formulation of a conceptual system of the indicated sort; that is to say, I was going to choose, to begin with, some simple basic concepts, for instance sensory qualities and relations, which are present in the raw material of experience; then I was going to formulate on this basis further definitions for concepts of various kinds [p. vi].

Carnap proposed to analyze reality with the aid of a theory of relations developed in the then new logic of Frege and Whitehead and Russell.

The naiveté of Carnap's attempt at a constructional system adequate to reconstruct all of scientific knowledge (Note 9.8) rests upon two of his assumptions—first, that a phenomenalistic basis is adequate to the task; and second, that such a basis is in any sense "firm" and certain. Let us consider these issues in reverse order.

Carnap was argued out of the certainty he attached to the constructional basis of erlebs by Neurath. Neurath argued for the position of sentence positivism—that sentences (such as those in the system of science) can be compared only with other sentences, never with reality *per se*, which is totally inexpressible. Sentences in science are to be verified in terms of protocol sentences, as discussed earlier. Neurath's protocol sentences contain reference to acts of perception. Neurath handled this perceptual component behavioristically; his protocols ascribe such acts to "publically observable" persons, e.g., 'Otto,' not to the 'I' of subjectivism and solipsism. It is through Neurath's emphasis that Carnap allied the logical "-isms" so completely with behaviorism (see Carnap, 1959).

But Carnap, like Schlick, thought that an *element* at least of certainty had to be retained at the basis of science. He defined protocol sentences (1937) as those which 'refer to the given, and describe directly given experience or phenomena' or as 'statements needing no justification and serving as the foundation for the remaining statements of science' (see Carnap, 1937). But the impersonality of the foundational protocols remains as Neurath indicated: Although they record experiences, no protocol sentence specifies an observer. Their certainty is in a sense due to their subjectless status as mere records of experience. Now the question comes to this: How can protocol sentences serve as a foundation for the sentences that constitute science?

Carnap argues that there is a language into which both the protocol sentences and all the sentences of science can be *translated* and that that language, following Neurath's physicalism, is the language system of physics. According to Passmore (1966):

> Carnap argues that this fundamental language is the language of physics, in which 'a definite value or range of values of a coefficient of physical state' is attached to 'a specific set of coordinates'. All the propositions of science, he is confident, can be formulated in this language; the problem for him is whether the same is true of 'protocol statements', those 'records of direct experience' upon which scientific statements rest. Science is impossible, on Carnap's view, unless protocol statements are thus translatable [p. 377].

By translating every protocol statement into statements about the status of 'my' (percipient) body, we can establish that they have the same meaning, where by meaning Carnap understands logical equivalence (equipollence). A demonstration that a protocol such as "red, here now" is logically equivalent to a psychological statement such as "the body S is now seeing red" is sufficient, Carnap thought, to build science upon a basis of protocols.

Carnap came to regard Neurath's criticism of his view that the protocols are certain (because of the conjectural nature of all factual attribution) as merely a quibble over different methods of constructing the language of science. Carnap, holding protocols to be certain, claimed that they were *outside* the language of science and only translatable into it, whereas Neurath held that protocols were within the language of science. This difference Carnap felt was of no consequence, because both he and Neurath agreed that the physicalistic language was the correct one for the reconstruction of science. Thus certainty characterized the basis of Carnap's constructional system from the *Aufbau* through to his syntactic physicalism, but the phenomenalism gradually faded out of his thinking. As Reichenbach noted, Carnap never abandoned his quest for certainty; he was literally Descartes in modern dress.

The reason that Carnap abandoned the phenomenalistic basis in favor of the physicalistic one was spelled out in "Testability and meaning" (1936–1937). Essentially, he came to realize that the more abstract, theoretical terms of science could not be introduced upon the basis of explicit definitions. The method of reduction sentences can introduce these concepts, Carnap held, but the assertion that all scientific terms are translatable into sense data statements must be abandoned (Note 9.10).

Ayer's phenomenalism was somewhat more sophisticated in that the conventional element present in it was acknowledged from the outset. For Ayer, the dispute between realists and "sense datum" theorists is metaphysical —no observations can settle it. Therefore, if we are not to lapse into metaphysics, all we can do is give reasons for a preference in one or the other and let it go at that. Since we can talk consistently and meaningfully about reality in either 'sense datum' or 'material object' terms, we have only to decide which is more convenient.

Ayer's preference was for a restricted, or linguistic, phenomenalism. It is best formulated thusly: Everyday sentences about material objects can be translated into sentences that refer exclusively to sense data. This translation is to hold even for hypotheticals and conditionals such as are found in science. The beauty of a sense datum formulation is that sense data per se are firm and incorrigible. Consider the distinction between 'real' and 'illusory' experience: Perceiving an object is never certain, for the possibility of illusion always exists. Yet one cannot, Ayer maintained, question the having of a sense datum; sense data are an indubitable given.

The problem, of course, is that this 'given' cannot be 'taken' very far. For one thing, Ayer was careful to point out that no set of sense data entail a material object: "It must be clear that what the statement that material things consist of sense data must be understood to designate is not a factual but a linguistic relationship" (Ayer, 1940, p. 232). And a purely linguistic convention of translatability is not sufficient to establish the truth value of any material object statements. But Ayer felt that all that could reasonably be asked of the phenomenalist is that he or she formulate the sufficient conditions for material object discourse in purely sensory terms rather than attempt to provide necessary conditions (see Ayer, 1954, p. 164). In a sense, Ayer was aware of the objections to phenomenalism that Waismann raised (see Note 9.9). All we are entitled to say is that sense datum statements never "precisely specify" a material object; the open texture of objects prevents us from ever analyzing a statement about, say, a table into a set of statements about sense data. Once again, the given is there for all to glory in, but it cannot be taken. Ayer later (1956) argued against his earlier phenomenalism in this manner:

If the phenomenalist is right, the existence of a physical object of a certain sort must be a sufficient condition for the occurrence, in the appropriate circumstances, of certain sense-data; there must, in short, be a deductive step from descriptions of physical reality to descriptions of possible, if not actual, appearances. And conversely, the occurrence of the sense-data must be a sufficient condition for the existence of the physical object; there must be a deductive step from descriptions of actual, or at any rate possible, appearances to descriptions of physical reality. The decisive objection to phenomenalism is that neither of these requirements can be satisfied [pp. 124–125].

So much, then, for early approaches to experientialist foundations. The most charitable thing to say about these attempts is that they are inadequate. The inescapable tension between the quest for certainty and epistemological authority, and the realization of the conventional and theoretical determination of scientific statements, were never resolved (Note 9.10).

More recently, the realist wing of the "experientialist" camp has modified its views in response to *external* criticism (from nonjustificational perspectives) as well as in response to internal criticism. Let us see how Feigl has attempted to find a new foundation for knowledge in the empirical constants and laws of science.

The quest for the given in experience is a quest for stability in the face of change and uncertainty. The arguments against the given from the conceptual nature of facts are that it is "theory contaminated" and therefore subject to the same change, uncertainty, and conjectural status that was to be avoided. The counterargument that has motivated the defender of the given all along is that unless there is stability and relative certainty *somewhere* at the foundations of knowledge, the entire (justificationist) system of science collapses into capricious ruins. For example, as we see in Chapter 10, the claim is made that unless there is a stable observation language *uncontaminated* by theory, the idea of testing in science cannot be defended. But if the stability that is to be the basis of scientific practice *and* its subsequent progress does not reside in either the given in experience or the facts based upon experience, where could it be? Obviously it must be in the next step "upward" from experience, in *the basic empirical constants and laws* of science.

Precisely this view has recently been put forward by Feigl, in defense of what is now termed the orthodox view of science and its theories. Although not denying the revolutionary changes that often occur in scientific *theory*, Feigl asks where these theoretical changes affect the "facts" that constitute the impressive body of scientific laws. His answer is that they (scientific laws and constants) are virtually unaffected by revolutions in theory and that it is in the empirical generalizations of science—the scientific "laws"—that the locus of stability and relative security is to be found, rather than in 'the given.' Thus the "testing ground" of theory is no longer 'the given' but rather the empirical laws of nature; the firm foundation of knowledge is now one giant step upward from experience. Feigl's (1970a) thesis is: "Epistemologically, I suggest, it is the domain of the elementary, rather directly testable empirical laws (instead of the "given," be it conceived as sense data or as perceptual

Gestalten) that is the testing ground to which we should refer in the rational reconstruction of the confirming or disconfirming evidence for scientific theories [p. 9].

Fiegl thinks that the nonjustificational theorists have *misled* their readers and (perhaps) unintentionally condoned skepticism and subjectivism (1970a):

> Dazzled by the (indeed) radical changes ("revolutions") in the theoretical "superstructure" of the sciences, various scholars (especially Michael Polanyi, P. K. Feyerabend, N. R. Hanson, Thomas Kuhn) have, I believe (each in his different way), misled their readers by stressing the dependence of science upon "passionate commitment" to theoretical presuppositions, the relativity of conceptual frameworks or even of their perceptual bases; they have contributed to the current vogue of skepticism and subjectivism [p. 7].

Feigl's justificational realism is, however, in sharp constrast to the conventionalistic and instrumentalistic interpretations of some of his fellow logical empiricists. As a good *empiricist*, Feigl is willing to abandon 'theory' for 'fact' in searching for the basis of science and its progress, which he takes to be the *testing* of theories (1970a):

> Theories *are* "superstructures" in the sense that we usually have more possibilities of choice in regard to them that we have on the level of empirical or experimental laws. Just consider the thousands of "empirical" constants in physics and chemistry. While, of course, each of them may be subject to correction (in some cases—as, for example, in regard to the isotopes—very radical revisions), on the whole, and by and large, these constants—and the empirical laws in which they figure so pivotally—represent the most precise and the most reliable knowledge mankind has yet attained. Philosophers of science (and I am not excluding myself) have very understandably been fascinated by, and have focused their prime attention upon, the *theories*. But theories come and go, whereas most empirical laws seem here to stay! Of course, there are many theories that have been very well established (until further notice!) by impressive lines of converging evidence, often from qualitatively quite heterogeneous areas of empirical evidence. Naturally, such theories are of the greatest interest also to the philospher of science. All I am urging is that we should not be blinded by the shift in theories to the hard core of empirical regularities in the light of which the validity of theories must be appraised. ... I still see in the empircal laws (deterministic or stochastic, as the case may be) the major objectively (or, if you prefer, intersubjectively) certifiable content of the sciences (natural and social!) [pp. 7–8].

Thus if the *objectivity* of science is to be preserved from subjective contamination and obscurantism, we must not be misled by the new "radical" revolutionaries but rather must recognize the autonomy of empirical laws and physical constants. For, Feigl claimed, the method of science, which allows it to continue to increase its body of knowledge *despite* revolutions in theory, was correctly described long ago by Reichenbach (1938) as the successive testing *and securing* of its knowledge claims. Feigl thinks there are many cases of "facts" described and *secured* despite changes in theory (1970a):

> It is simply not true that all empirical knowledge is "contaminated" by theories. Among the countless examples that are ready at hand, let me mention just a very few: The phenomenon of the Brownian motion can be *described* independently of the explanations given by Einstein and Smoluchowski in 1905. The chemical laws of constant and multiple proportions (i.e., of compounding weights) can be formulated without the atomic theory for which, of course, they formed the primary evidence nearly 200 years ago (Dalton!). The laws of the propagation, reflection, and refraction of light (as in geometrical optics) can be formulated quite independently of any theory regarding the nature of light (particles, waves, or "wavicles"!). The speeds of chemical reactions as dependent on concentrations, temperature, etc., can be asserted without reference to any micro-theory: etc., etc. [p. 8].

In sum, theories come and go, but empirical laws seem to stay. Thus there is a bedrock of objectivity in the *descriptive* codification of fact as opposed to either 'the given' in experience or theoretical *explanation*. The search for objectivity and intersubjectivity must be relocated at the level of empirical laws. The question now becomes "What price must be paid for this objectivity?" Feigl, at least, finds whatever concessions are necessary a small price to pay in return for a realistic justificationism. One of the costs of this position should not go unnoticed, however; theoretical *explanation* and *understanding* are now second-class citizens of diminished importance in comparison to *descriptions* of phenomena. That which is real and hard are the empirical phenomena; theories are ephemeral—if not calculation devices, then still more conventional than real. And this is a very strange kind of "realism"; it embraces an inductivism with respect to facts and a conventionalism for theories. It attempts to combine the best of (what Feigl perceived to be) two basic insights into science and its progress: the inductive methodology of knowledge acquisition (for the collection of laws and descriptive constants), which seems to retain a realistic picture of science; and the instrumentalist and conventionalist contention that theories come and go in science in a manner that is somehow different from the collection of "facts." Feigl's justificational realism thus combines the classic empiricist methodology of inductivism for facts with the conventionalism of Reichenbach and Carnap for theories. As such, it is an interesting halfway house between the sophisticated inductivism of Bacon and Mill and the sophisticated conventionalism of Duhem and Meyerson (Note 9.11).

But halfway houses are never popular, and the majority of logical empiricists would shun Feigl's position for a purer form of conventionalism.

These theorists would attempt to retain inductive methodology, as the cornerstone of empiricism, but would willingly abandon the last vestiges of realism in favor of "nothing but" conventionalism. The syntactic approach to empiricism initially developed chiefly by Neurath, Carnap, and Reichenbach epitomizes this "sophisticated" conventionalism. This position, as we shall now see, takes the ultimate step with regard to foundations; it declares them necessary to science but *purely* conventional in character. The realist could never solve the problem of how the meaning of *a* statement, which is not the external object, involves a relation to *the* object; the conventional element simply destroyed ultimate factual reference. It turns out that all we can conclusively prescribe are the rules for assigning (conventional) symbols to objects; beyond the assignment of a symbol, we cannot show how the symbol relates to the object. Why not, then, explicate the meaning of scientific concepts *solely* in the syntactical domain of symbols and their manipulation and abandon factual reference completely? The syntactic approach to empiricism, the ultimate epistemological conventionalism of the logical "—isms," does exactly this.

Carnap's thought in the mid-thirties is representative of the syntactic approach to foundations. His book, *The logical syntax of language* (1937), and the essay, "Testability and meaning" (1936–1937), led to *physicalism* as a purely conventional doctrine. Under pressure from several directions, Carnap took a giant step "up" from empirical foundations, a great deal farther than the halfway house of empirical constants and laws to which Feigl much more recently retreated. Carnap the logician abandoned empiricism entirely and looked to the language of science, in the nature of its logical syntax, as the source of certainty upon which to "found" knowledge. Syntactic conventions in the language thus become the "firm foundation" for empirical knowledge—*if* one can be sure that one has the *correct* language for science. But what is the language of science? Here Carnap bowed to Neurath and adopted, purely by convention, the thesis of physicalism, which asserts that the necessary and sufficient language for science is the "physical" language: "The thesis of physicalism maintains that the physical language is a universal language of science" (Carnap, 1937, p. 320).

Any language, including the "physical thing" one, is a convention. Carnap no longer asks how factual reference is to be specified in the sense of "tied down" to empirical reality; instead, he asks: "What consequences will ensue if we construct a language (such as factual language) in this or that way" (Carnap, 1937, p. 46)? The task is to construct protocol sentences that can serve the purpose of science, not to tie protocols to reality. As Turner (1967) put it:

> There is no effort in *The Logical Syntax of Language* to show what is the nature of the relation of protocol propositions to fact, other than to allude to the

requirement that a syntactical system must have its formation rules. Ironically, the problem of factual reference is regarded as a pseudo-problem. ... All relations are those between propositions. Thus they are matters of logic. No reference is made to the ineluctable relation of proposition to fact, none is made to the verification of an hypothesis in terms of facts, nor to meaning as a method of verification [pp. 133–134].

Thus we have a firm foundation in the syntactic formation rules of a language that seems to "solve" many of the nasty problems plaguing logical empiricism—factual reference, meaningfulness, etc. The only problem is that the solution is a convention that ignores those problems entirely. But that had of course been anticipated by Carnap and even taken as a strong point of the system. Consider his principle of tolerance: "*It is not our business to set up prohibitions, but to arrive at conventions*" (Carnap, 1937, p. 51). Compare that to Popper's definition of (empirical) content as the class of statements *forbidden* by a theory, and it will be obvious how far from "reality" this empiricism has come.

Not surprisingly, Carnap did not adduce empirical evidence in favor of physicalism (Note 9.12). Instead, it was defended pragmatically by attempting to use the approach in the logical reconstruction of science. Thus it is in defense of physicalism that the program of the unity of science was spawned; the motivation for reductionism is to show that the physical thing language is indeed sufficient for all of science (Note 9.13). At this point, the coherence theory of truth replaced the realist's correspondence theory, and the attempt to explicate truth was virtually abandoned until Tarski's (1944) semantic conception became available (at which point the *semantic* conception replaced the earlier *syntactic* conception of truth). Likewise, testability was replacing verifiability (due to the dispositional nature of all "observation" predicates), and here the positivists actually learned something from Popper—the conventional nature of testing. In all cases, pragmatism, conventionalism, and logic merged to produce agreement favoring physicalism, but no justification of it was ever attempted. Having moved into a glass house, the physicalists wisely decided not to throw stones. If empirical meaning is construed as a problem in the formation of language, the thesis of sensationalism is automatically abandoned; and nothing is left but conventionalism. Thus it is not surprising that the search for foundations has all but ceased in the last 30 years (except for Feigl's forays) and that constructive effort has been directed to tasks that seemed to show more promise of success. Justificationists have gone on to confirmation theory even though it is *without foundations* of the sort that must be presupposed if it is to be a rational source of knowledge. Genuine theoretical knowledge no longer exists for the empiricists; sensationalism has come and gone, leaving only conventionalism.

CONFIRMATION THEORY: PROMISE AND PROBLEMS

If one grants the inescapability of conventionalism in justificationist approaches to science, the present state of the art in confirmation theory becomes more understandable. Contemporary confirmation theory is no longer inductivist (or sensationalist) at heart; it is, instead, just one more aspect of conventionalism. And if it is conventional, then the old riddle of induction concerning justification may easily be abandoned in favor of Goodman's new riddle of explicating what an inductive inference is—or better what an inductive "logic" looks like. This has enabled the logical empiricists and their current descendants to abandon epistemology for the "firmer" realm of pure logic. In this manner, the logical or mathematical aspects of confirmation receive considerable attention but at the expense of all but total neglect of the epistemological and methodological problems that precede and run parallel to them (Note 9.14).

The chief task of that "inductive logic" is to replace the deductive concept of formal implication by a continuum of degrees of implication, the limiting case of which is the original notion of (deductive) logical implication. Thus implication is to be explicated as a metrical concept that can be based upon the calculus of probability. As Radnitzky (1970) put it:

> Inductive logic is *a theory of partial or total implication*, a mathematical probability theory interpreted in such a way that Probability is interpreted not as a frequency, nor as a subjective estimate or rational degree of belief, but as a metrical logical relation. Hence degree-of-confirmation statements (if true) are analytic. What logical empiricists have to offer in this field is not a theory of confirmation, but *a logic of probability as a logic of gradual implication* [p. 98].

The promise of this inductive logic is that Carnap, in *The continuum of inductive methods* (1952) was able to survey an indefinite number of "inductive methods." The problem however, is that in order to be of use to the scientist, the nasty methodological and epistemological problems have to be solved (or satisfactorily bypassed). It is clear that inductive logicians intend that their logical tools, polished to such brilliance in the mathematical realm, should be of use in science. For example, Carnap (1952):

> In view of the multiplicity of inductive methods, the scientist who wants to apply a method is compelled to make a choice. Now the main point is that the scientist should be given, as a means for his choice, not simply the list of those inductive methods which have been proposed or considered so far but *a systematic survey of all possible inductive methods* [p. 7].

In order to be of use in actual science, however, degree of confirmation statements cannot remain purely logical (and analytic) statements; the idea that such statements were of use to science could arise only in a framework that, like physicalism, substituted the logico-linquistic task of reconstructing the language of science for the process of doing scientific research. The situation has not been changed from Radnitzky's dour comment (1970):

> As regards the stylization of specimens of confirmation patterns or of statistical explanations from the history of science it is clear that the field of application of the inductive logics so far available is very limited. Inductive logic as we know it today cannot be applied to such patterns *unless* these patterns can be transcribed into IL (formalized) and *unless* they can be metricized, i.e., they *cannot* be applied to intensional contexts, *nor* to historiographic hypotheses, *nor* even to say, the gravitational hypothesis [p. 102]!

How might one move from logic to its application, from inductive logic to confirmation theory, and then finally to scientific practice? The usual moves involve "interpreting" degree of confirmation statements in such a manner that they relate to knowledge or belief (ignoring the insoluble problem of justification of induction all the while, of course). Thus we find considerable discussion of rational betting quotients, degrees of belief, personal probabilities, etc. This explains one recent phenomenon in the literature of inductive logic: the almost universal replacement of relative frequency models of probability by Bayesian and personalist interpretations (Note 9.15). This sleight of hand at least makes it look as if confirmation theory were relevant to science.

Another recent twist to the literature is a response to Popper's contention that probability has nothing to do with the empirical content of scientific propositions. Numerous writers have (often vehemently) denied Popper's contention or proposed an interpretation of "degree of confirmation" that can be allied with probability. Many of these evasion attempts are transparent failures. For example, Hesse (1975):

> Much confusion has arisen in this debate from failure to recognize that there are many different explicata closely connected in ordinary discourse with the concept of confirmation, but not all behaving in the same way. Among others, the notions of *acceptability* of hypotheses, *desirable risk* in action, *utilities, power, content, expectation of truth* or *success*, and *support* by evidence have all entered the discussion. . . . I shall, therefore, concentrate here on the notion of confirmation or support of hypotheses by evidence, and begin by adopting the personalist interpretation of confirmation as *degree of rational belief* in hypotheses or predictions relative to evidence [pp. 51–52].

Hesse apparently feels that all she must do is identify confirmation with personalist degree of rational belief and all will be well. But not only must one argue persuasively for that identification; one must then show how personalist degree of rational belief is utilized in actual scientific practice and (assuming that science yields valid knowledge) how it evades Hume's problem of the justification of induction. I, at least, am unable to see anything but hand waving toward the first problem in attempts such as Hesse's, but such attempts are beginning to clog the literature.

Hesse, indeed, is a very enlightened confirmation theorist; she is an advocate of factual relativity, having argued that what must be developed is an inductive logic of *theories*; and she is an outspoken critic of H–D methodology (see Hesse, 1970). Her arguments along these latter lines are worth mention, for they effectively incorporate much of Kuhn's conception of learning from exemplary puzzle solutions and psychology of concept formation into the received view. Hesse attempts to account for what constrains the pattern of our inference when a theory explains certain evidence (e_1) and predicts more evidence (e_2), to develop a confirmation theory based upon the relation of analogy between e_1 and e_2. Arguing against the usual H–D account, she says (1970): "We are no longer concerned with a dubious inductive inference from e_1 up to t [the theory] and down to e_2, but with a direct analogical inference from e_1 to e_2 [p. 170]." Her thesis is that the use of models in theories "provides examples of inference in which we need stronger logical relations between e_1 and e_2 than can be included in the usual deductivist scheme [p. 170]." Theories must receive their support from material analogies supplied by external models; they cannot be pulled up by their own bootstraps. According to Hesse (1970):

> Though deductivism represents our existing knowledge. . . , it does not explicate the kinds of inference to prediction that we normally find justifiable. And these inferences ought not to be dismissed to the context of discovery or heuristics or psychology or history, but ought to be seen as part of the content of theories as we state them [p. 180].

Hesse is avant-garde with respect to recognizing problems that are not often seen in the received view tradition, but unfortunately she has few solutions to offer. One will look in vain for an account of what a "direct analogical inference" is and for when an inference is "justifiable." Also, to anyone familiar with the material in Chapters 7 and 8, it is fairly easy to predict in what directions her account will move in the future. This is because the once internally motivated research program in confirmation theory has lost its sense of direction and now responds to the external stimulus of criticism from nonjustificational approaches. Hesse and the other "daring innovators" in confirmation are now guided by external criticism. The positive research program is now almost entirely negative—a never-ending attempt to "catch up" and address problems that are given their focus and import by external critics of the received view. Thus, although there are numerous responses to Lakatos's (1968a) critical overview of inductive logic in the last decade, none has been more than a partial response, addressing one or another issue in "me too" fashion.

WHITHER RATIONALITY?

If one grants that confirmation theory is succeeding in technical puzzle solving in the mathematical domain of probability but not in the foundational issues that such puzzle solution presupposes, one can then ask whether or not the practice of science is rational for the confirmation theorist; is it, that is, a legitimate or justified source of knowledge? The answer was presaged in the discussion of sensationalism and conventionalism with regard to foundations. The sophisticated inductivist is by definition a conventionalist who has retreated to commitment in the certainty of the probability calculus. This conventionalism, however, shows itself only when the theorist is challenged; as soon as the challenge passes, inductivism will again be adopted. Thus inductive logicians embody a curious quality of self-deception; to use Bartley's (1962) turn of phrase, they go about "limping before the lame." It is as if they believe in the beneficence of the noble lie—that although they know that the research program is impossibly difficult, they must at least appear to be working upon it, in order to protect the masses who would otherwise toil upon the task of science in vain. But although the limping before the lame is obvious from an external perspective, it is quite clear that it is not seen at all from within. Within the research program, it is merely one more occasion for the sophisticated justificationist to appear "sadder but wiser." The quotations from Ayer, Russell, and Turner in earlier chapters apply here with the same force; the only rationality within justificationism is irrational, embraced rather than justified, retreated into rather than secured by argument, a matter—in Russell's phrase—of theft rather than honest toil.

CONFIRMATION IN A NONJUSTIFICATIONAL FRAMEWORK

One may ask if it is possible to discuss the role of positive evidence as confirmation of a conjectural hypothesis when one is not engaged in the attempt to justify it. The answer is yes, and the work of Grover Maxwell (1975) provides one instance of a nonjustificational approach to confirmation. Maxwell is willing to abandon both empiricism (in the theory of confirmation) and justificational epistemologies (1975):

> Neither the general assumption that we have (and shall continue to have) knowledge (or even true belief) nor specific knowledge claims about the world can be justified in the strong sense that has preoccupied empiricists.... *We must discard the question* How are our knowledge claims to be justified? *They cannot be justified at all in the sense required by those who usually ask the question* [p. 132].

What Maxwell is concerned with is the context of constraint that determines what conditions would have to be fulfilled *if* our contingent and fallible conjectures were ever to constitute significant knowledge. *If we have knowledge at all* (and Maxwell repeatedly warns that we cannot guarantee, or justify, that we do), then it must be the case that: "The theories and hypotheses that humans propose (i.e., the guessess or knowledge claims that they make) to meet problem situations and account for data or 'evidence' at hand must be true (or reasonably 'close to the truth') a relatively great portion of the time, given the number of false though *otherwise adequate* possibilities that always exist" (Maxwell, 1975, p. 133). Maxwell then assembles the major ingredients in a *contingent* theory of confirmation utilizing the Bayesian prior and posterior notions of personal probability *in conjunction with* a relative frequency interpretation of the nature of probability.

We need not detail Maxwell's proposals; the important thing to note is that many aspects of "confirmation" can be addressed in nonjustificational terms; and on that note—plus the plea for more thorough study of the scientist along the lines indicated in Mahoney (1976) (to ascertain whether or not scientists actually do reason according to Bayes's theorem)—we can end this chapter.

CHAPTER NOTES

Note 9.1. One often sees reference to the *principle* of induction. For example: "The principle of induction expresses the increase of the probability of inductions in dependence upon the accumulation of factual evidence" (Feigl, 1934, p. 297). It is the so-called principle of induction, according to which we are all assumed to act, that requires justification; the justification of induction is a justification of the principle of induction. Stated generally, the principle of induction holds (Russell, 1912):

> (a) When a thing of a certain sort A has been found to be associated with a thing of a certain other sort B, and has never been found dissociated from a thing of the sort B, the greater the number of cases in which A and B have been associated, the greater is the probability that they will be associated in a fresh case in which one of them is known to be present;
> (b) Under the same circumstances, a sufficient number of cases of association will make the probability of a fresh association nearly a certainty, and will make it approach certainty without limit [p. 66].

Note 9.2. A brief enumeration of the standard attempts to justify induction may prove helpful. An excellent overview of the most common approaches is Salmon's (1967) monograph, *The foundations of scientific inference.* Salmon considered eight major classes of attempts to deal with justification.

1. Justifications of induction by inductive methods. Some theorists have attempted to construct self-supporting or self-justifying inductive procedures, i.e., to construct inductive justifications of induction that are not susceptible to Hume's charge that they are circular. The foremost exponent of this approach is Max Black (1954, 1962). Black freely admits that he is not concerned to justify all induction "from scratch" but only to justify *particular* inductive procedures by showing that a self-supporting argument can be constructed. Thus he solves the problem of justification that Hume raised by *abandoning* it. As Black stated, "Anybody who thinks he has good grounds for condemning all inductive arguments will also condemn inductive arguments in support of inductive rules" (Black, 1954, p. 206). As Salmon noted, such attempts to justify particular inductions rather than induction *per se* simply beg the question at issue, which is, after all, to justify induction *as a policy.*

2. Arguments from the complexity of scientific inference. Everyone knows that science does not proceed by simple induction by enumeration, and something like the hypothetico–deductive method is more in keeping with actual practice. One could then say that the *logic* of science is entirely deductive and that the (allegedly inductive) generation of hypotheses or premises is *not* a logical matter. This would obviate the problem of justifying induction by dispensing with it as far as the logic of science is concerned. Salmon argued against such positions thusly (1967):

> The whole trouble with saying that the hypothetico-deductive method renders the logic of science entirely deductive is that we are attempting to establish a *premise* of the deduction, not the conclusion. Deduction is an indispensable part of the logic of the hypothetico-deductive method, but it is not the only part. There is a fundamental and important sense in which the hypothesis must be regarded as a conclusion instead of a premise. Hypotheses (later perhaps called "theories" or "laws") are among the *results* of scientific investigation; science aims at establishing general statements about the world. Scientific prediction and explanation require such generalizations. While we are concerned with the status of the general hypothesis—whether we should accept it or reject it—the hypothesis must be treated as a conclusion to be supported by evidence, not as a premise lending support to other conclusions. The inference *from* observational evidence *to* hypothesis is surely not deductive [p. 19].

3. "Deductivism." Salmon discussed one particularly influential variant of the second argument form under the heading of deductivism, which he attributed to Popper. According to Salmon, Popper agrees that science is, overall, not strictly deductive but ampliative in character. Salmon (1967) sees Popper as shifting the problem from hypothesis generation to that of support or confirmation:

> As long as the hypothetico-deductive method is regarded as a method for supporting scientific hypotheses, it cannot succeed in making science thoroughly deductive. Popper realizes this, so in arguing that deduction is the sole mode of inference in science he rejects the hypothetico-deductive method as a means for confirming scientific hypotheses. He asserts that induction plays no role whatever in science; indeed, he maintains that there is no such thing as correct inductive inference. Inductive logic is, according to Popper, a complete delusion [p. 21].

Salmon then claims that Popper *rejects* the H–D method as it is usually characterized and accepts only the logic of *modus tollens* for science. He then discusses the naive falsificationism of *The logic of scientifc discovery*.

Salmon's argument against Popper's position is that if science is not to be sterile, there must be an ampliative inference procedure somewhere, to provide the new, informative content. Salmon sees Popper smuggling induction back into science in the concept of corroboration: "If science is to amount to more than a mere collection of our observations and various reformulations thereof, it must embody some other methods besides observation and deduction" (Salmon, 1967, p. 24).

Salmon's conclusion is that Popper is actually playing the same game as those who try to justify induction (1967):

> I am not arguing that Popper's method is incorrect. I am not even arguing that Popper has failed in his attempt to justify this method. I do claim that Popper is engaged in the same task as many inductivists—namely, the task of providing some sort of justification for a mode of nondemonstrative inference. This enterprise, if successful, *is* a justification of induction [p. 27].

4. Justifications that deduce induction from synthetic a priori principles. Under this heading Salmon discussed the rationalistic tradition, culminating in the work of Kant, which claims that there are synthetic a priori truths that human reason can grasp. The synthetic a priori approach would, if successful, provide a valid answer to Hume's problem (Salmon, 1967):

> The doctrine that there are synthetic a priori truths is, as I explained above, tantamount to the view that there are necessarily truth-preserving ampliative inferences. If we could find a *bona fide* demonstrative ampliative inference we would have a solution to Hume's problem of the ground of inference from the observed to the unobserved. This solution could be presented in either of two ways. First, one could assert that there are factual propositions that can be

established by pure reason—without the aid of empirical evidence—and that these synthetic a priori propositions, in conjuction with premises established by observation, make it possible to deduce (nonampliatively) conclusions pertaining to unobserved matters of fact. Second, one could claim that these synthetic a priori propositions, although not added as premises to ampliative inferences to render them nonampliative, do instead provide a warrant for genuinely ampliative inferences from the observed to the unobserved [pp. 27–28].

The difficulty with all alleged cases of a priori truths is that what is "obviously" and "necessarily" an a priori truth to one philosopher never convinces another, who sees it as an a posteriori (or synthetic, or empirical) claim. Although not ruling out the approach "*a priori*," Salmon concludes that the burden of proof remains with the proponent of the synthetic a priori, who has yet to deliver anything that will withstand critical scrutiny.

5. *The principle of uniformity in nature.*   The synthetic a priori approach shifts the focus of the attempt at justification toward the *presuppositions* of inductive inference. If certain presuppositions can be shown to be fulfilled, then induction as a policy would be justified automatically. Hume himself, despite his arguments to the effect that we cannot prove nature to be uniform—i.e., we cannot prove that the present and future will be like the past—seems to have felt that if nature could be shown to be uniform, then induction would be acceptable—i.e., justified. Indeed Kant followed this Humean suggestion by attempting to establish a principle of uniformity in nature—that of the principle of universal causation—as a synthetic a priori truth. In more recent times, John M. Keynes's (1952) famous "postulate of limited independent variety" is an attempt to show that nature is indeed uniform in such a manner that induction becomes a justifiable policy. Thus there is a venerable tradition of justification attempts based upon the presupposition of the (or a) uniformity in nature.

Salmon argued that even if nature could somehow be shown to be uniform, it would not provide an adequate basis for the justification of induction. The problem is that we cannot specify a principle of uniformity that is informative enough about how and when the future resembles the past. Salmon wrote (1967):

The most that a principle of uniformity of nature could say is that there are some uniformities that persist into the future; if it stated that every regularity observed to hold within the scope of our experience also holds universally, it would be patently false. We are left with the problem of finding a sound basis for distinguishing between mere coincidence and genuine causal regularity [pp. 42–43].

It is perfectly conceivable that we generalize only on the basis of coincidence and never on causal regularity; such a principle of uniformity gives no direction in the crucial problem of identifying prior causes and genuine causal regularity. Salmon concluded that it could not, therefore, serve to justify induction as a policy.

6. *Postulates of scientific inference.*   If synthetic a priori truths are not satisfactory, why not look for other presuppositions that, if accepted, would render inductive method acceptable? The foremost exponent of the attempt to justify induction by postulating assumptions or presuppositions to "scientific method" is Bertrand Russell (especially 1948). To justify induction we need a postulate (or set of postulates) that is a sufficient condition for the correctness of induction. The problem is that we should not assume postulates that are false, and we should not assume more than are absolutely necessary. The search is therefore for a minimal sufficient set that are not false. Russell believed that he had found such a set in the five postulates he discussed in the last part of *Human knowledge* (1948). But the problem now arises: Why should we accept Russell's set of postulates when there are indefinitely many potentially available?

Salmon put the problem this way (1967):

> Russell writes as if we have a simple choice between accepting his postulates (or some suitable modification thereof) and embracing solipsism of the moment. The situation is not that simple. We have a choice between accepting Russell's postulates and a wide variety of other conflicting postulates. We cannot pretend to know, except by inductive reasoning, which ones are true. We cannot use inductive inference to establish one set of postulates in preference to the others on pain of circularity. The most we can hope to establish is a series of conditional statements of the form, "If postulates set *P* holds, then inductive method *M* will work (at least decently often)." We cannot hope to show the unconditional utility of any method. Such a result can hardly be said to do justice to the method of science. In astronomy we predict an eclipse unconditionally. We do not say, either explicitly or implicitly, "If Russell's five postulates hold, then the sun's disc will be obscured by the moon at a specified time from a particular vantage point." From the postulational standpoint, however, the most we can assert is the conditional. Science, as a result, would be empty [p. 47].

Salmon was suspicious of the whole approach on the further grounds that the admission of *any* unjustified (and unjustifiable) postulates is "tantamount to making scientific method a matter of faith [p. 48]."

7. *Probabilistic approaches to inductive 'truth.'*   The neojustificationist has completely repudiated the earlier quest for certain knowledge and accepted the much weaker goal of merely probable knowledge. To the vast

majority of contemporary philosophers, this all but solves the problem of justification automatically. As Salmon formulated it (1967):

> Hume's search for a justification of induction, it might be continued, was fundamentally misconceived. He tried to find a way of proving that inductive inferences with true premises would have *true* conclusions. He properly failed to find any such justification precisely because it is the function of *deduction* to prove the truth of conclusions, given true premises. Induction has a different function. An inductive inference with true premises establishes its conclusions as *probable*. No wonder Hume failed to find a justification of induction. He was trying to make induction into deduction, and he succeeded only in proving the platitude that induction is not deduction. If we want to justify induction, we must show that inductive inferences establish their conclusions as probable, not as true [p. 48].

But what meaning should we attach to "probable"? If the straightforward interpretation in terms of relative frequency is used, Hume's argument is still devastating; not only can we not justify the truth of every conclusion from true inductive premises, but we cannot justify *any* conclusion from true premises. Thus we must look elsewhere for a new interpretation of "probable." One influential approach identifies probability with degree of rational belief. To say a statement is probable in this sense effects a problem-shift: It means that the statement is supported by evidence. Now, so the linguistic analyst claims, the problem of induction can be dissolved (Salmon, 1967):

> But, so the argument goes, if a statement is the conclusion of an inductive inference with true premises, it *is* supported by evidence—by inductive evidence—this is part of what it *means* to be supported by evidence. The very concept of evidence depends upon the nature of induction, and it becomes incoherent if we try to divorce the two. Trivially, then, the conclusion of an inductive inference is probable under this concept of probability. To ask, with Hume, if we should accept inductive conclusions is tantamount to asking if we should fashion our beliefs in terms of the evidence, and this, in turn, is tantamount to asking whether we should be rational. In this way we arrive at an "ordinary language dissolution" of the problem of induction [p. 49].

The problem with this dissolution is that whether an inference is valid or not depends on the correctness of the rule of inference according to which it was performed. Thus what constitutes evidential support in induction is inextricably bound up with the correctness of inductive rules of inference. This failure of the attempted dissolution has led to a distinct problem-shift, for there is now a bustling research program whose goal is to explicate the concept of inductive evidence. Salmon, always out to tackle the classic problem of justification, grudgingly admits that this is a worthwhile program (1967):

The problem of induction can now be reformulated as a problem about evidence. What rules ought we to adopt to determine the nature of inductive evidence? What rules provide suitable concepts of inductive evidence? If we take the customary inductive rules to define the concept of inductive evidence, have we adopted a proper concept of evidence? Would the adoption of some alternative inductive rules provide a more suitable concept of evidence? These are genuine questions which need to be answered [p. 51].

But in any event, all this shift accomplishes is a relocation, rather than a resolution, of Hume's problem.

8. Reichenbach's pragmatic justification.   An ingenious approach developed by Reichenbach attempts to vindicate (rather than validate) induction by showing that it is superior to any alternative method of prediction. Reichenbach adduced arguments to the effect that if *anything* will yield valid conclusions, then the inductive "method" will also—i.e., that if any method works, induction works.

Salmon's melancholy conclusion is that this approach, although the most promising, is still inadequate (1967):

Unlike many authors who have sought a justification of induction, Reichenbach does not try to prove the truth of any synthetic proposition. He recognizes that the problem concerns the justification of a rule, and rules are neither true nor false. Hence, he tries to show that the adoption of a standard inductive rule is practically useful in the attempt to learn about and deal with the unobserved. He maintains that this can be shown even though we cannot prove the truth of the assertion that inductive methods will lead to predictive success. This pragmatic aspect is, it seems to me, the source of the fertility of Reichenbach's approach. Even though his argument does not constitute an adequate justification of induction, it seems to me to provide a valid core from which we may attempt to develop a more satisfactory justification [pp. 53–54].

The conclusion of his monograph reflects the same chastened attitude of the "sadder but wiser" neojustificationist that has been mentioned in Chapter 3:

The extensive examination of the foundations of scientific inference reveals, however, that neither induction by enumeration nor any comparable method has yet been satisfactorily justified. We cannot claim to have a well-established method for ascertaining fundamental probabilities. Hume's problem of the justification of induction remains at the foundations of scientific inference to plague those who are interested in such foundational studies [p. 132].

Note 9.3.   Perhaps the firmest foundation for knowledge ever proposed by a Western thinker (excepting various deities) was the immortal soul of

Plato. In order to avoid the paradoxes that we cannot know anything unless we are already acquainted with it and that we cannot learn anything *new* from prior learning, Plato proposed the doctrine of *Anamnesis* (or, recollections). According to his formulation, all that passes for learning is but remembering, the remembering of the immortal soul (Sesonske & Fleming, 1965):

> The soul, then, as being immortal, and having been born again many times, and having seen all things that exist, whether in this world or in the world below, has knowledge of them all; and it is no wonder that she should be able to call to rememberance all that she ever knew about virtue, and about everything; for as all nature is a kind, and the soul has learned all things, there is no difficulty in her eliciting or as men say learning, out of a single recollection all the rest, if a man is strenuous and does not faint; for all enquiry and all learning is but recollection [p. 17].

Since the soul knows *everything*, it is the most authoritative foundation for human knowledge ever proposed.

Note 9.4.   The traditional statement of factual relativity is in terms of the conventional determination of basic statements, as though it is a matter of decision on the part of the scientific community (see Popper, 1959, especially section 30). As we saw in Chapter 3, however, there is far more to factual relativity than just convention and decision. But for now the point is that the given in experience is not certain or firm in the sense of being independent of theory and convention. This effectively prevents the experientialist from "founding" scientific concept formation upon a basis of certainty in the deliverances of sense.

Note 9.5.   The classic statements of realism in logical positivism simply do not acknowledge this conventional element but present instead a "conclusive" approach to meaning, verification, and truth. Consider this statement by Schlick (1959):

> It is the first step of any philosophizing, and the foundation of all reflection, to see that it is simply impossible to give the meaning of any statement except by describing the fact which must exist if the statement is to be true. If it does not exist then the statement is false. The meaning of a proposition consists, obviously, in this alone, that it expresses a definite state of affairs. And this state of affairs must be pointed out in order to give the meaning of the proposition. ... In order to find the meaning of a proposition, we must transform it by successive definitions until finally only such words occur in it as can no longer be defined, but whose meanings can only be directly pointed out. The criterion of the truth or falsity of the proposition then lies in the fact that under definite conditions (given in the definition) certain data are present, or

not present. ....The statement of the conditions under which a proposition is true is *the same* as the statement of its meaning, and not something different.

And these "*conditions*," we have already seen, must finally be discoverable in the given. Different conditions mean differences in the given. The *meaning* of every proposition is finally to be determined by the given, and by nothing else [pp. 86–87].

Bringing conventionalism and factual relativity into this absolutist conception of meaning and truth appears to be an impossible task. Once conventionalism is acknowledged, realism is abandoned as untenable.

Note 9.6. A discussion of truth may seem out of place in a chapter ostensibly concerned with the nature of knowledge and its acquisition, but it will indicate how the conventionalism of the logical "-isms" led to the abandonment of the problem of factual reference. The correspondence theory, which explicates truth as a matter of statements being related in a particular manner—i.e., corresponding—to objects, is the position most naturally assumed by the realist. For the realist, believing in the existence of an external world that is "pretty much" as science discloses it to be, the scientific warrant of a proposition is its correspondence with the "facts." Now if one takes correspondence to be unproblematic, then the problem is to explicate the "facts" that are at the basis of science. In this framework, there is a direct relationship between the problem of the empirical basis of science on one hand and meaning and truth on the other.

Indeed, for the realist Schlick the entire problem of the empirical basis of science arises only because it is related to the criterion of truth (1934):

> The end [reason for choosing given protocol statements] can be no other than that of science itself, namely, that of affording a *true* description of the facts. For us it is self-evident that the problem of the basis of knowledge is nothing other than the question of the criterion of truth. Surely the reason for bringing in the term "protocol statement" in the first place was that it should serve to mark out certain statements by the truth of which the truth of all other statements comes to be measured, as by a measuring rod [p. 213].

The problem for the realist becomes that of reconciling the shifting nature of the basis with the correspondence interpretation of truth.

Schlick accomplished this task by first criticizing the coherence theory, which explicates truth as agreement with the accepted body of statements, and then defending the correspondence theory. His criticism (1934) of the coherence view is that the mere absence of contradiction is not sufficient to warrant the application of truth in the physical or material realm:

> The criterion of truth cannot be compatibility with any statements whatever, but agreement is required with certain exceptional statements which are not

chosen arbitrarily at all. In other words, the criterion of absence of contradiction does not by itself suffice for material truth. It is, rather, entirely a matter of compatibility with very special peculiar statements. And for this compatibility there is no reason not to use—indeed I consider there is every justification for using—the good old expression "agreement with reality."

The astounding error of the "coherence theory" can be explained only by the fact that its defenders and expositors were thinking only of such statements as actually occur in science, and took them as their only examples. Under these conditions the relation of non-contradiction was in fact sufficient, but only because these statements are of a very special character. They have, that is, in a certain sense (to be explained presently)' their "origin" in observation statements, "from experience" [p. 215].

Then Schlick returned to the protocol statements of one's own immediate experience, seeking a formulation according to which they can be the ultimate grounds of all knowledge *without* being "absolutely certain" or "incorrigible." It is at this point that critics feel he failed to make a convincing case.

Schlick claimed that "protocol statements" such as "M. S. perceived blue on the nth of April 1934 at such a time and place" are hypotheses; whereas observation statements or, as he preferred confirmation statements like "Blue here now" are only the occasions for the subsequent utterance of a protocol statement. Schlick saw in confirmation statements an absolute psychological certainty or rather, a finality (1934):

The function of the statements about the immediately experienced itself lies in the immediate present. Indeed we saw that they have so to speak no duration, that the moment they are gone one has at one's disposal in their place inscriptions, or memory traces, that can play only the role of hypotheses and thereby lack ultimate certainty. One cannot build any logically tenable structure upon the confirmations, for they are gone the moment one begins to construct. If they stand at the beginning of the process of cognition they are logically of no use. Quite otherwise however if they stand at the end; they bring verification (or also falsification) to completion, and in the moment of their occurrence they have already fulfilled their duty. Logically nothing more depends on them, no conclusions are drawn from them. They constitute an absolute end. . . . In them science as it were achieves its goal; it is for their sake that it exists. The question hidden behind the problem of the absolutely certain basis of knowledge is, as it were, that of the legitimacy of this satisfaction with which verification fills us [pp. 222, 223].

Thus Schlick was willing to grant that the protocol sentences of science that Neurath and Carnap were discussing are not certain and are not the basis of knowledge. Instead he located the certainty upon which knowledge is to rest in the finality of the observational confirmation that constitutes the essence of verification in science. The "unshakable" point of contact between knowledge and reality comes in the joy of confirmation or the disappointment of falsification.

Not many other logical positivists were willing to confuse truth with confirmation in this manner, nor were they willing to acknowledge any certainty in statements such as "Blue here now." Most abandoned the correspondence theory as being even less tenable than the coherence theory, which was at least in a *prima facie* manner compatible with a shifting basis. The correspondence theory (or picture theory of meaning and truth), which had earlier been so suggestively put forward by Wittgenstein's *Tractatus* (1922), was all but abandoned with the shift from verifiability to testability and with the introduction of conventionalistic physicalism in place of realism.

Another theorist who upheld the correspondence theory was A. J. Ayer (1936). But Ayer's positive arguments are all directed against the coherence theory. He argued against Neurath, Hempel, and Carnap that basic statements cannot be distinguished by solely conventional designation, but rather that they require agreement with the 'given' and that their validity will likewise depend on agreement or correspondence between the basic propositions and the experiences that verify them. But Ayer had no positive theory of correspondence at all, and his only discussion of correspondence theories is critical, directed at rejecting incorrect formulations such as picture or map analogies. Thus, in effect, he is no better off than Schlick. Because the advocates of correspondence could do little more than criticize coherence, while the coherence theorists could at least begin to explicate truth and meaning, it is not surprising that coherence reigned "by default" in the philosophy of the logical "-isms."

Note 9.7. The consequences of this demotion in status of protocol statements was beautifully summed up by Ayer (1959) in his reflection upon logical positivism:

> The view that they were included in "the physical language" took away from elementary, or, as Neurath and Carnap called them, "protocol," statements their privileged position. They were no longer thought to be incorrigible. Their truth, like that of any other physical statements, was always open to question. But, more than this, they lost even their judicial status. If a protocol-statement conflicted with a statement of a higher order, such as a scientific hypothesis, one or other of them would have to be abandoned, but it need not necessarily be the scientific hypothesis: in certain circumstances it might be more convenient to reject the protocol-statement instead.
>
> As can be seen from his paper on the foundation of knowledge (Über das Fundament der Erkenntnis") Schlick found this conclusion unacceptable. He argued that to treat the reports of observation, which was what protocol-statements were supposed to be, in this cavalier fashion, was to put scientific hypotheses, and indeed all would-be empirical statements, outside the control of fact. Neurath and Carnap, however, were not impressed by this argument.

They had decided by this time that it was metaphysical to talk of comparing statements with facts. For what could this "comparison" be if not a logical relation? And the only thing to which a statement could stand in any logical relation was another statement. Consequently, they were led to adopt a coherence theory of truth [p. 20].

This comment ties together the manner in which the difficulties of realism stem from the lack of a firm factual basis for science and lead inevitably to the problems of meaning and truth, where a use theory replaces a correspondence theory of truth. Those theorists who remained realists (like Schlick, Ayer, and Feigl) did so largely for Schlick's reasoning that the syntactic approach to "empiricism" actually heralded a return to rationalistic and dogmatic formulations that ignored the link between science and experience. For such theorists, science without an experiential basis was simply inconceivable.

Note 9.8.   The constructional system Carnap developed added a few terms to the vocabulary of the philosophy of science. Foremost among them is the *erleb*. Erlebs are the ground elements of experience; they are the "full momentary cross sections of the total stream of experience"(Goodman, 1951, p. 116). A psychophysical method is needed to analyze the subjectless erlebs into their basic constituents. The procedure involves treating the phenomenal *quale* as the basic ingredient of physical science: This is the phenomenalism of the system. We sort the objects of experience into quality classes of qualia from the primitive relation, recognition of similarity. This procedure effectively begs the question of how abstract entities are formed, but that was of little consequence to Carnap; he admitted a Platonic realism with regard to universals. There are various sorting rules imposed upon erlebs that determine whether they are identical, part-similar, near-place, etc.

The problem faced by such a system is the old bugaboo of solipsism: How do we get from subjectless erlebs to the scientific observer's own private experiences at the "basis" of the protocols of science? Carnap had no answer; he embraced a methodological solipsism. The only thing to do is conventionally treat science as if it disclosed a real world and to act as if there really is a public world. The inability to offer anything other than a conventional reply to solipsism was as damaging to the *Aufbau* as any of its myriad flaws.

Note 9.9.   The phenomenalist approach to foundations in the logical "-isms" was criticized in a novel and effective manner by an ex-member, Friedrich Waismann. Waismann began in the early thirties as a disciple of Wittgenstein-the-mathematician. From his study of foundations of mathematics, Waismann arrived at a conventionalism that was definitive of his philosophy, even in his later days at Oxford during the heyday of ordinary language analysis.

For Waismann mathematics rests upon nothing but its conventions; it does not begin from necessary truths; its propositions are *neither* true nor false. The proper role for the philosophy of mathematics is simply to describe arithmetic rather than to provide a foundation for it. The propositions of arithmetic are only compatible or incompatible with initial conventions, nothing more; we could easily imagine different arithmetics, with different conventions. But conventionalism is only the first half of Waismann's philosophical orientation; and emphasis on the "open texture" of concepts is the other half.

The great virtue of language is that it leaves room to say the unexpected and unconventional; i.e., it leaves room for us to formulate novel concepts. Even definitions themselves, although the most precise specifications of how to use concepts that we possess, always have an open texture. And this openness is not regrettable, as the ordinary language analysts claim—something to be overcome with more precise analyses, to be removed by an ideally precise language. The openness of our concepts is their great virtue to Waismann, for this feature allows our knowledge to grow and enables us to incorporate new ideas within our already existing terminology. If our concepts were precisely specified and fixed in advance, as the ordinary language analyst would have it, then science would be sterile and incapable of growth.

The fundamental objection to the phenomenalistic approach to factual reference, according to Waismann, is that terms about "material objects" have an inherently open texture, an essential incompleteness, that cannot be captured by any collection of sense datum statements, no matter how large. That is, phenomenalistic reduction is always to a finite population of sense data, yet material objects refer legitimately to infinitely large domains of such sense data. As Passmore (1966) states:

> If, then, we try to set out a collection of sense-datum statements which are sufficient and necessary to establish the truth of, say, the material-object statement 'that is a cat', we shall immediately be met with objections of the following sort: 'Suppose all these conditions were fulfilled, but the thing you have described as a cat were suddenly to develop into a creature of enormous size, what would you say then?' To these questions, Waismann thinks, there is no definite answer, just because 'cat' has an 'open texture'. We do not know what we should say; there is nothing to compel us to say that the suddenly-gigantic creature is or is not a cat. It is not just through somebody's oversight, Waismann argues, that the concept 'cat' lacks definite boundaries: the fact is that we can never know all about an empirical object, can never give a complete description of it. There is always the chance that it will turn out to have quite unexpected qualities [p. 463].

And in saying this, Waismann wanted to go much further than just abandoning conclusive verifiability; he held that an empirical proposition does not even entail *any* specific observation statements. Like Quine,

Waismann endorsed the Duhemian thesis concerning falsifiability and argued that no empirical proposition can be refuted by the evidence of observation statements. A conflict between an 'empirical' scientific statement and the 'facts' is never sufficient to overthrow the "scientific" statement. Science is totally disconnected from its alleged empirical basis (see Chapter 3).

Waismann's criticism of phenomenalism is thus just one facet in his combination of skepticism and conventionalism. The emphasis on open texture was quite novel in the logical "-isms," for most of its practitioners agreed with the ordinary language analysts that such imprecision was a vice rather than a virtue. It remained for critics of the movement such as Popper to call attention to the futility of symbolic precision and for later writers such as Pap to emphasize the open texture of concepts.

To provide some closure on Waismann's "Duhemian thesis" concerning falsifiability, we may digress to note that he also provided a novel justificationist solution to this problem. Supplementing his view that all we may say is that an experience "speaks in favor" or "speaks against" a proposition rather than proving or disproving it, Waismann held that the traditional logical relations such as contradiction, apply only to statements formulated at the same *level* of language—at the same language stratum. Waismann's justificationism comes out clearly in his view that within a given language stratum, propositions may come into conflict and contradict one another and may be conclusively proved or disproved. The logical relations between different strata, however, are sufficiently loose to prohibit proof or disproof. The Duhemian thesis holds only in virtue of the fact that science operates at many strata at once. By this distinction, Waismann was able to maintain both Duhemian skepticism and some positive conceptions of justificationism in seeming harmony.

Note 9.10.   The "language" of science is an interesting notion, but are its basic entities or units of analysis *sentences, statements, propositions,* or something else? There has been considerable divergence of opinion on this matter. We can illustrate this by considering the contrasting views of Schlick and Ayer.

Schlick differentiated between sentences and propositions. All propositions are meaningful (in virtue of the methods of their verification), but *only* those sentences which express propositions are meaningful. "What is the meaning of a proposition?" is a question that cannot legitimately occur; the only possibility of not understanding a proposition is not to hear it *as such.* Schlick wrote (1936):

> If we adopt this terminology we can now easily get rid of our paradox by saying that we cannot inquire after the meaning of a proposition, but can ask about the meaning of a sentence, and that this amounts to asking, 'What

proposition does the sentence stand for?' And this question is answered either by a proposition in a language with which we are already perfectly familiar; or by indicating the logical rules which will make a proposition out of the sentence, i.e., will tell us exactly in what circumstances the sentence is to be *used* [pp. 146–147].

Ayer adds yet a third concept to the list: the statement. He defined 'sentence' as a grammatically significant set of words and 'statement' as what such symbols express. 'Propositions' are a subclass of statements, specifically those that are expressed in literally meaningful sentences. According to Ayer, sentences are now literally meaningful, and statements are verifiable (1946):

> I propose that any form of words that is grammatically significant shall be held to constitute a sentence, and that every indicative sentence, whether it is literally meaningful or not, shall be regarded as expressing a statement. Furthermore, any two sentences which are mutually translatable will be said to express the same statement. The word "proposition," on the other hand, will be reserved for what is expressed by sentences which are literally meaningful. Thus the class of propositions becomes, in this usage, a sub-class of the class of statements, and one way of describing the use of the principle of verification would be to say that it provided a means of determining when an indicative sentence expressed a proposition, or, in other words, of distinguishing the statements that belonged to the class of propositions from those that did not [p. 8].

Whether this complication of terminology is a help or hindrance depends on the memory capacity of the reader and his or her tolerance for the issues it allegedly clarifies.

Note 9.11. Indeed, this position Feigl endorses bears remarkable similarity to the revolutionary conventionalism of Pierre Duhem, as propounded in *The aim and structure of physical theory* (1954). Duhem, protagonist of the view that no theory may be conclusively disproved by an experimental refutation, claimed that theories may still be rejected when they conflict with scientific "good sense" and that despite the fact that no theory can be refuted by facts, we would find it "childish and unreasonable" for a physicist "to maintain obstinately at any cost, at the price of continual repairs and many tangled-up stays, the worm-eaten columns of a building tottering in every part, when by razing these columns it would be possible to construct a simple, elegant, and solid system" (Duhem, 1954, p. 217) Thus Duhem admitted that theory can be overthrown. It is his acknowledgment of the revolutionary nature of science, coupled with his insistence that simplicity and good sense are the criteria detemining overthrow, that make him a revolutionary conventionalist. But that is only part of the picture; although theories come and go, and although facts can be refuted by a theory, Duhem argued that we should prefer those changes in the total body of science that leave intact the most experimental laws. Discussing alternatives in a conflict of theory with *established* fact, Duhem reasoned thusly (1954):

> By taking the first alternative we should be obliged to destroy from top to bottom a very vast theoretical system which represents in a most satisfactory manner a very extensive and complex set of experimental laws. The second alternative, on the other hand, does not make us lose anything of the terrain already conquered by physical theory; in addition, it has succeeded in so large a number of cases that we can bank with interest on a new success [p. 211].

The congruence of this position with Feigl's views is so obvious as to require no further comment. But what Feigl appears not to be willing to accept is Duhem's admonition against always accepting such laws, which occurs on the very next page (Duhem, 1954):

> Indeed, we must really guard ourselves against believing forever warranted those hypotheses which have become universally adopted conventions, and whose certainty seems to break through experimental contradiction by throwing the latter back on more doubtful assumptions. The history of physics show us that very often the human mind has been led to overthrow such principles completely, though they have been regarded by common consent for centuries as inviolable axioms, and to rebuild its physical theories on new hypotheses [p. 212].

Note 9.12.   Turner (1967) is not as consistent as Carnap in this regard; he attempts to buttress physicalism with factual defenses rather than conventionalistic apologies. "What is the defense of an 'empiricism' which stipulates that the physical language, its syntax and laws, determines the character of its data language? If we could ascertain that the state of a theory detemines the observational data, then indeed we would have pragmatic support for adopting the syntactic approach of physicalism [p. 137]." Thus Turner, in a novel twist, utilizes the empirical phenomenon of factual relativity to argue for physicalism—that is, uses factual relativity to support conventionalism instead of inductivism.

Not surprisingly, the argument is fallacious; factual relativity argues *against* inductivism and foundations, to be sure, but it does not argue *for* physicalism. Carnap was at least a consistent conventionalist on this point; Turner, like most others, vacillates between conventionalism and inductivism.

Note 9.13.   The unity of science movement, in its various forms such as unity of language of science (physicalism) and the unity of theory and ontology (reductionism), is a focal point in logical empiricism and is usually one of the first things to receive a critical overview (e.g., Radnitzky, 1970). Space limitations prevent our addressing it in this volume. Nonetheless, it is worth emphasizing that one can easily overview justificationist philosophies (and logical empiricism in particular) without giving unity of science phenomena undue attention. What I would emphasize is that physicalism leads straight to the unity of science movements but not necessarily vice versa; had it not been for the search for unified foundations for knowledge in the language of science, there would have been little motivation for unity of science (other than conscious emulation of the French Encyclopedists; see Radnitzky).

Note 9.14.   The literature on inductive logic and confirmation theory is enormous; hence we cannot even begin to survey it. We can only skim one or two points in the work of theorists who are still "old fashioned" enough to admit that foundational issues still exist and that the research program is in fact being challenged. The majority of articles in the literature are normal science oriented, technical puzzle-solving endeavors that, although they have enormous reference lists and cite much contemporary history, are all but unintelligible within a few years of their publication. It would be a waste of time to cite representative examples, let alone build up enough confirmation lore to criticize it at its own level of analysis. The whole purpose of this book is to make it obvious why one need not criticize it in detail; and if that alienates those theorists whose life work consists in the spinning out of these works of trivia, I am personally sorry but intellectually totally unsympathetic.

Note 9.15.   One common argument for Bayesian inference is a perceived inadequacy of H–D methodology. For instance, Salmon (1975): "I am inclined to agree with a wide variety of authors who held that something akin to a Bayesian schema must be involved in the confirmation of scientific hypotheses. If this is correct, it is entirely possible to have positive hypothetico–deductive test results that do not confirm the hypothesis (i.e., that do not add anything to its degree of confirmation on prior evidence) [p. 35]." The problem is that not all evidence compatible with a hypothesis is taken as confirmatory of it. The Bayesian schema provides *one way* to acknowledge this, because it talks about *prior* "probabilities" of hypotheses; and in such cases the new evidence would not change the prior probability of a hypothesis into a higher posterior probability. What appears to be involved is that the Bayesian prior–posterior dichotomization at least allows one to admit that science does not start with a Lockean blank slate (i.e., zero prior probability) and proceed to "confirmation" in posterior probabilities greater than zero, but is rather a matter of increasing an already substantial "prior" probability. Thus the motivation for Bayesian approaches is to deal with the context of constraint that limits our inferences and allows us to ignore "irrelevant" evidence even when it is "logically" confirmatory—thus the increased discussion of the topic of *relevance* in confirmation (as in Salmon's 1975 essay).

What the justificationists have not yet realized is that there are other ways to deal with the questions of relevance and the context of constraint (e.g., Weimer, 1975) and that there are *non*justificational uses of Bayesian techniques (e.g., Maxwell, 1975).

10 The Nature of Theories and Explanations

Despite specific controversies, there has been striking uniformity in the accounts of the nature of theory and explanation put forth by received view theorists. Surprisingly little has changed in the transition from logical positivism to logical empiricism, and essentially the same interpretation is shared by other scientifically oriented philosophers such as pragmatists, instrumentalists, logical reconstructionists, and even ascientific linguistic analysts. Indeed this account seems to be shared by all who pay heed to the principle of empiricism. Thus we refer to the views portrayed in this chapter as the *empiricist account of theories and explanations.*

These are three tasks before us in this chapter. Two are purely expository in nature: We must lay out the "orthodox" or "standard account" of theory and explanation, and we must see how these positions have expanded or been modified as a result of *internal* criticism, i.e., criticism advanced by empiricist-oriented philosophers who operate within the justificationist framework. The third task is both expository and interpretive in nature: to show how standard accounts of theory and explanation stem from and dovetail within the justificationist metatheory. Speaking critically of the standard account, it will be seen that when explored more fully, most modifications and emendations made by received view theorists as concessions to internal criticism actually go against the grain of the principle of empiricism and (some) core features of justificationism. That is, when explored more fully, it becomes obvious that these internal criticisms are also *external* criticisms of the approach that generated them. Sophisticated justificationism merges almost imperceptibly into skepticism; it comes within a hair's breadth of repudiating itself. But that is to get ahead of our presentation. Let us begin by exploring the received view's account of the nature of theories.

THE ORTHODOX VIEW OF THEORIES

The analysis of theory is central to traditional philosophy, as Suppe's introduction to the mammoth compendium, *The structure of scientific theories* (1974), indicated:

> If any problem in the philosophy of science can justifiably be claimed the most central or important, it is that of the nature or structure of scientific theories. For theories are the vehicle of scientific knowledge, and one way or another become involved in most aspects of the scientific enterprise. . . . It is only a slight exaggeration to claim that a philosophy of science is little more than an analysis of theories and their roles in the scientific enterprise. A philosophy of science's analysis of the structure of theories is thus its keystone; and should that analysis of theories prove inadequate, that inadequacy is likely to extend to its account of the remaining aspects of the scientific enterprise and the knowledge it provides. At the very least, it calls for a reassessment of its entire account of scientific knowledge [p. 3].

This chapter traces the orthodox accounts of theory in sufficient detail to show that Suppe's remarks, although representative of "common knowledge" in current philosophy, are quite wrong. We shall see that all the problematic issues of theory and explanation are passed back to confirmation theory by justificationist philosophy and that "theory" is in no sense the keystone in the understanding of science. Indeed, it will become clear that theories, according to the received view accounts, cannot be "vehicles" of scientific knowledge at all. Suppe is correct, however, in the claim that the inadequacy of the account of theory reflects back upon other aspects of the justificationist account of the scientific enterprise. Let us begin to make this claim by explaining the orthodox view. Except for purposes of conceptual analysis, it is impossible to completely separate the received view conceptions of theory and explanation. Both involve the same concepts, and the "theory" of explanation differs from the "theory" of theory primarily in emphasis rather than substance. Thus, which one we examine first is largely a matter of expository convenience. Although it could easily and appropriately be done the other way round, we first sketch the received view account of theories, beginning with their formal structure and ending with their role in science.

There are four *components* of a scientific theory that virtually everyone acknowledges. The classic account of these structural components stems from N. R. Campbell (1920, 1921). Campbell distinguished hypotheses, models, and dictionaries in scientific theories. Subsequent accounts have added a fourth component by splitting "hypothesis" into a set of axioms or postulates on one hand and a calculus or logical syntax (a language) on the other. The *hypothesis* of a theory is what we would normally think is all there is to a theory; it is the "theoretical" formulation that states the relationships between the entities with which the theory deals. But in well-developed theories at least, there is more to the theory than just a set of basic axioms (what would be traditionally called hypotheses); these axioms have consequences that can be derived from them by logical operations within the language in which they are embedded. And each *theorem* that can be derived from the axioms of a factual theory is in itself a separate, empirically testable, hypothesis. (Theories are thus "bigger" than hypotheses, because they are interrelated clusters of hypotheses. They are interrelated hypotheses in the sense that all *follow from* an initial postulate or axiom set.) As an example of an axiom in a theoretical system, consider the $F = ma$ relationship postulated by Newton. Stated as an axiom, $F = ma$ states a relationship holding between forces, masses, and accelerations (never mind what these terms *mean*; that is a problem discussed later). But this axiom, when manipulated by appropriate mathematical procedures (within the "calculus' of the theory), can be transformed into different expressions of the same fundamental relationship; and separate theorems can thus be derived from it. For example, if the problem area for application of the theory is that of freely falling bodies, the original $F = ma$ must be transformed to $mg = m \, (d^2 s / dt^2)$. Each new class of problems in science requires the application of a "new" formalism; and each formalism will be a transformation of the original one—i.e., a theorem derived from the postulate set by application of formation and transformation rules supplied by the calculus.

But what does a theorem (or even an axiom) in a theoretical language *mean*? How are we to tell what things in the real world constitute F's, or m's, or a's? The standard account makes a very sharp separation between the hypothesis (postulates and calculus)—which is *devoid* of primary meaning (uninterpreted)—and observations—which are the *source* of primary meaning (and interpretation). What a theoretical statement such as $F = ma$ means can only be ascertained by observations of particular forces, masses, and accelerations. The meaning of theoretical terms seeps upward from observation and experience. Theoretical terms are second-class citizens in the sense that their meaning is *derived* from the primary meaning of observational terms. Reality is that which is observable and particular and concrete; primary meaning and existence are found at this observational level. Theoretical terms, being abstract and generalized and often unobservable, can gain their meaning and ontological status only insofar as they can be tied down, or anchored to, the primary meaning and existence of real particulars in the observational realm. This tying down, or bridging of ontological and semantic barriers, is the job of Campbell's dictionary

(Carnap's term, "correspondence rules," is much closer to the point and has almost universal currency today). Correspondence rules provide the bridge that renders theoretical terms intelligible by linking them ontologically and semantically to observation.

The fourth class of components, models, is the most controversial part of a theory that the received view account distinguishes. Campbell's initial motivation for including models as components of a theory is clear. A "fruitful" axiom set, one sufficiently large and flexible to provide a "good" theory, will potentially be able to generate an indefinite number of theorems. By ingenious manipulation of formation and transformation rules of the language in which it is embedded, a nearly endless supply of testable consequences can be generated from a theory. But science does not advance rapidly by the painstaking grinding out of theorems. What is needed for more rapid advance is a source of insight, a model or an analogy, that will tell the theorist where to go to get a supply of theorems. Campbell looked upon concrete models as indispensable to the theory in two related senses: First, they provide a semantic interpretation for certain theoretical terms and thus facilitate understanding of the theory; second, they provide a source of extensions of the theoretical system to new and unexplored domains (by suggesting new theorems). The controversy in the literature surrounding models and analogies concerns their indispensability, as part of the cognitive component, to a theory. This controversy is sufficiently important to warrant separate discussion later. This issue cannot be answered without considering the dynamic aspects of theories in science, i.e., their role and functioning within the scientific enterprise.

But these four structural components are all there is to a theory on standard accounts (Note 10.1). After overviewing these components, many treatments go on to discussion of the nature and desirability of axiomatization of scientific theories. Axiomatization is merely a formal statement of the hypothesis in sufficiently rigorous detail to spell out all the theorems that are entailed by the axiom set and calculus. As such, axiomatization is only concerned with the formal unity or consistency of theories; it is not necessary for their use in scientific practice, and indeed few theories have ever been successfully axiomatized. Nevertheless, it remains a goal of traditional analysis to axiomatize scientific theories (Note 10.2). But the topic of axiomization, dealing with the purely formal and semantically uninterpreted side of theories, emphasizes their *conventional* nature. If theories are conventional in so many respects, what exactly is the status of theoretical entities?

Theories are second-class citizens both semantically and ontologically. The formal structure of a theory is purely conventional in character; any meaning that a theoretical term in the factual sciences has must be given to it by its relationship to the primary language of science, the experiential–observational language. Thus realistic interpretation of theoretical terms requires one to link them to observation-level entities. If this cannot be done on a systematic basis, the "natural" interpretation will be that theoretical entities are indeed merely conventional in character. A flirtation with instrumentalism will be the all but inevitable result. But if theoretical terms are only conventional, then it ought to be possible to eliminate them from the body of science. The motivation for doing so would be straightforward; one would hardly want science to be conventional in character, and it would be reasonable for an empiricist to try to avoid that conclusion. But whichever way a justificationist turns at this choice point, the result is not entirely satisfying. Received view theorists themselves have shown that theoretical terms *cannot* be reduced to observational ones but can at best be given a partial interpretation in observational terms. Thus the empiricist approach to realism has rough sledding; one must show how theoretical terms can be simultaneously "real" and "nonempirical." But conventionalism fares no better; the attempt to dispense with theoretical terms fails *for the same reasons*, and so they cannot be solely conventional either. The conclusion seems to be that theoretical terms are indispensable to science *and* nonempirical. Needless to say, this is most distressing to empiricists, yet they have led themselves to this conclusion by exploring the consequences of the "ultimate" empiricist philosophy—the logical "-isms." Let us see how this conclusion obtains.

An indispensable part of the orthodox view of theories is a conception of *levels of explanation*. The first requirement one would impose upon genuine explanation would rule out self-explanation; no event can explain itself. An explanation must utilize premises of a greater degree of generality than that which is to be explained. Thus it requires lawlike generalizations to explain facts. But what can explain laws? The unanimous answer is "theories." As we see in detail in the next section, explanation is said to consist in subsumption of whatever is to be explained under higher order (more inclusive and comprehensive) principles. To explain facts, one must have laws; to explain laws, one must have a theory; to explain a theory, one must have a more inclusive theory. The rough hierarchy of explanatory generality that results is shown in Fig. 10.1.

This diagram makes obvious the distinction between *lower level* explanation, or *explanation by instantiation*, and *higher level*, or *theoretical*, explanation. Explanation by instantiation occurs when a law subsumes a fact. That elm tree shed its leaves, because *all* elm trees (being deciduous) shed their

Theories	Nonexplained Explainers
Laws	Explained Explainers
Facts	Explained Nonexplainers

FIG. 10.1.

leaves. This procedure in effect *classifies* facts to be explained; it says that *this* particular is a member of a *class* of particulars, *all of which* have some characteristic. Such explanation merely subsumes a particular under a general regularity (classification) that is stated in the form of a lawlike generalization. At this level, explanation is "nothing but" classification and description.

But there is "something more" possible; we can have a theoretical explanation that tells us *why* some particular law holds to the extent that it does. Theories are said to be integrated complexes of laws, and the individual laws within a theory are deductive implications of the postulate set. Now undeniably it is more "cognitively satisfying" (whatever that means) to have theoretical explanation than just an explanation by instantiation. Indeed, the lower level explanatory pattern is circular; "Why did X behave in that manner?" is "explained" by responding, "Because all X's do that." This latter explanation is satisfying from a psychological perspective only when we did not know beforehand what the law states; i.e., it is satisfying only when the law statement is extended to cover cases not contemplated in the initial law formulation. But we still want to know why *this* law holds and not another. Only a theory can answer that question for us.

But now we face a problem; how can it be that science strives after theoretical explanations, and how can it be that we find them *more* satisfying than lower level explanations when the meaning and ontological status of theoretical terms is supposed to be derivative from experiential–observational ones? Why should one engage in theory construction *at all*? Let us put this problem in the form of the theoretician's dilemma. Hempel's (1965) formulation of the problem cannot be improved upon:

> The conclusion suggested by these arguments might be called the *paradox of theorizing*. It asserts that if the terms and the general principles of a scientific theory serve their purpose, i.e., if they establish definite connections among observable phenomena, then they can be dispensed with since any chain of laws and interpretative statements establishing such a connection should then be replaceable by a law which directly links observational antecedents to observational consequents.
>
> By adding to this crucial thesis two further statements which are obviously true, we obtain the premises for an argument in the classical form of a dilemma:

>> If the terms and principles of a theory serve their purpose they are unnecessary, as just pointed out; and if they do not serve their purpose they are surely unnecessary. But given any theory, its terms and principles either serve their purpose or they do not. Hence the terms and principles of any theory are unnecessary.

> This argument, whose conclusion accords well with the views of extreme methodological behaviorists in psychology, will be called the *theoretician's dilemma* [p. 186].

In trying to avoid the theoreticians's dilemma, Hempel argued for two related point, a slight liberalization must be acknowledged to have occurred. The "observational" occurrences; second, that the paradox can arise only if an overly restrictive interpretation of the purpose of theory in science is presupposed. The first topic is treated later; suffice it to say that the upward seepage doctrine of the received view will be but a shadow of its former self by the time Hempel and Carnap are through with it. With regard to the second point, a slight liberalization must be acknowledged to have occurred. The empiricist and positivist *ideal* of the language of science being the *observational* language has been abandoned. *All knowledge in science cannot be a deliverance of sense* (for the reasons detailed later); and *for that reason*, the function of theory is far more important than had heretofore been acknowledged. Theories are now absolutely indispensable to scientific understanding. Hempel's conclusion regarding the theoretician's dilemma requires this admission but does not spell it out very clearly (1965):

> Our argument, the theoretician's dilemma, took it to be the sole purpose of a theory to establish deductive connections among observation sentences. If this were the case, theoretical terms would indeed be unnecessary. But if it is recognized that a satisfactory theory should provide possibilities also for inductive explanatory and predictive use and that it should achieve systematic economy and heuristic fertility, then it is clear that theoretical formulations cannot be replaced by expressions in terms of observables only; the theoretician's dilemma, with its conclusion to the contrary, is seen to rest on a false premise [p. 222].

All the force of this conclusion, which goes against the grain of received view ideals, is hidden in the "false premise." But the import of that "false" premise's being false is that the language of science is not the empirical language. The purpose of theory is not to explain by integrating generalizations that are empirical in character. There is indeed a fundamental difference between explanations that are theoretical in character and those that are only subsumptions under laws.

The only reason one could have for wanting to avoid theory in science would be an infatuation with a doctrine such as sensationalistic empiricism. If it is assumed that all knowledge really *is* a deliverance of sense, and further, that such deliverances of sense *are* observations, then theories—to be genuine knowledge—must *reduce* to observations. That is, it must be possible to translate theoretical terms into (conjunctions of) statements about observations, or they will not be meaningful (empirically significant, etc.). Only if some *sharp* break is made between the authoritative foundation of knowledge (the observation language concepts) and the theoretical components of science will it make sense to say that theories are second-class citizens. (A second proposition intimately related to the idea that observation is "safer" than theory is the idea that the sole *goal* of theory construction is the production of codified and systematized information. Theories are then second-class, because their sole function is to organize information.)

But if this separation of problematic and unproblematic concepts and propositions is made, and if the thesis that theories are derivative from observations (or whatever is "unproblematic") is accepted, then two things follow. First, it ought to be possible to replace each theoretical term in a theory by the observations that constitute its meaning and ontological status; second, it ought to be possible to deduce observational outcomes from a theory. In fact, neither of these things can be done. We saw in Chapter 3 that no theoretical proposition is deductively linked to observation (i.e., perception); here we see that theoretical terms cannot be explicitly defined in (or by means of) observation terms. That is, it cannot be either: (a) that *the* ideal language of science is the empirical or observation language; or (b) that *the* sole function of theoretical terms is to organize observational data.

There are two techniques commonly referred to when the replacement of theoretical terms is under discussion. One is the technical device of the *Ramsey Sentence*, stemming from the work of Frank P. Ramsey (1931). Ramsey's method transforms a theory into a huge "sentence" by treating theoretical terms as existentially quantified variables, so that the only extralogical constants that appear belong to the observational vocabulary. This procedure, although it allows talk of the observational truth or falsity of theories (because theoretical terms are existentially quantified), does not entirely eliminate reference to theoretical terms. It merely substitutes variables for constants and thus transforms, rather than eliminates, theoretical terms.

The other technique for theory replacement by observational terms is due to William Craig (1956). Craig's paper is entitled "Replacement of auxiliary expressions," and it emphasizes the standard account of theories and the sharp break between theoretical (T. L.) and observational (O. L.) languages (indeed, calling theoretical terms *auxiliary* expressions demonstrates the approach). What Craig's theorem demonstrates is that for any theory T employing both theoretical and non-theoretical terms (i.e., previously understood terms), there is an axiomatized system T^* that uses only the nontheoretical terms of T and yet is functionally equivalent to T. That is, T^* effects exactly the same deductive connections as T among the sentences in the nontheoretical vocabulary. Mario Bunge (1967, Vol. 1) simultaneously demonstrates this technique and shows its futility:

> A slightly modified version of the best available technique (W. Craig's) for theory demolition runs as follows. Take a theory proper, i.e., a hypothetico-deductive system T that cannot fail to contain theoretical concepts. Derive and collect all the lowest-level theorems, i.e., those which can be confronted with

empirical information. (Pretend that no auxiliary theories are needed to this end.) Next replace in them every theoretical term by the corresponding empirical expression. For example, if one of the theorems is about a light *ray* (nonempirical) falling on a *plane* (nonempirical) at a definite *angle* α, (nonempirical), translate it into a statement concerning a narrow light *beam* falling on an *interface* at an angle *interval* $[\alpha - \xi, \alpha + \xi]$, where ξ is the experimental error. That is, take every "net result" t of the theory and translate it into a statement t^* couched in the experimenter's language, just as you would proceed if, instead of rebuilding the theory, you were to test it (Craig's original procedure assumes the Carnap–Braithwaite–Hempel doctrine that (i) every theory contains purely observational predicates alongside the theoretical ones, and (ii) by sheer deduction within a theory one can obtain purely observational statements t^*, i.e., theorems in which only observational predicates occur. These assumptions have not been made here because (i) is unrealistic and (ii) is false: the very universe of discourse of a theory is a more or less idealized model of the real thing, and even the most modest theorem refers to a member of the universe or basic set of the theory.) Now handle these observation statements t^* as the building blocks of a mock theory T^* free from allegedly unsafe concepts ("auxiliary expressions"), hence acceptable to anti-theoretically biased philosophers: see Fig. 8.4. More precisely, take as axioms of the new "theory" T^* the conjunctions $t^* \& t^* \& \ldots \& t^*$ of the theorems of T translated into an empirical language. If the original theory T is rich enough there will be infinitely many theorems with one empirical translation each. Moreover, if T contains at least one continuous magnitude, such as length, the set $\{t\}$ of theorems will be nondenumerably infinite; but the set $\{t^*\}$ of its possible translations into empirical terms will be denumerably infinite because measurement yields only fractionary numbers, which are denumerable. . . .

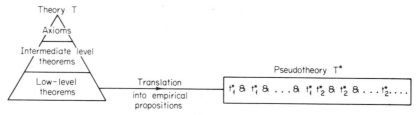

FIG. 8.4.   The theory demolition technique. The case of a theory without continuous variables has been illustrated.

Anyhow, the expurgated "theory" T^* will contain infinitely many axioms. This infinite (and pointless) formal complexity will overcompensate its epistemological poverty [pp. 461–463].

It becomes obvious at this point that Craig's theorem and the procedure it envisages *cannot substitute for the construction of scientific theories*; that is, theories can only be demolished *after* they have been constructed (by other means). Bunge's conclusion (1967, Vol. 1) is that "this theory demolition technique, then, far from proving that theoretical concepts and nonobservational hypotheses and theories are dispensable, actually fires a coup de grace at every attempt to trivialize science by shaving off its transempirical concepts and hypotheses [p. 463]." Further, Bunge lists three strikes against utilizing Craig's procedure: First, T^* is not a genuine theory at all, because it does not allow for the deduction of new observational consequences; second, T^* cannot apply to the *model* of the theory, because the model does not characteristically refer to observables but rather to empirically inaccessible entities; and third, because T^* presupposes T, it cannot possibly be built directly out of "data": T^* cannot be induced from facts.

Indeed, both Craig's replacement procedure and the Ramsey Sentence procedure were stillborn as theory construction procedures. They are purely technical devices that can reduce a theory to observational consequences (usually an infinitude of such consequences, in which case "reduce" must be understood in a most peculiar manner) only after the fact. One must first have a theory, and then one can apply these procedures; but neither procedure can generate anything, let alone a theory. One is led to wonder, then, why anyone would bother to be concerned with these devices (as other than fascinating technical tours de force).

One reason for their very existence (and subsequent discussion) has to do with the old problem of empirical significance. If it is taken as a goal of science that all its terms be "empirically significant," then these procedures provide— albeit in an ex post facto manner—for the assignment of empirical significance to theoretical terms. In this regard, it is not surprising that Hempel, who wrote the obituary notice for criteria of empirical significance, should examine theory replacement techniques in connection with the theoretician's dilemma and find them wanting, *either* as procedures to replace theoretical terms *or* as procedures to give them empirical significance. But the motivation for entertaining these devices as either a means of replacement or as generating meaning (i.e., empirical significance) stems from the thesis of empiricism underlying the logical "-isms." Once the futility of these procedures is acknowledged, it becomes clear that the thesis of empiricism cannot be maintained. One can save the received view account of theories (and the sharp separation between antecedent, unproblematical languages and subsequent, theoretical languages) to be sure but the empiricism that motivated that conception will be lost in the process.

The nose can be preserved, but only at the expense of cutting it off from the face that supported it!

But the received view theorists who have so painstakingly argued themselves into acknowledging the indispensability of theoretical terms (and their only partial specification in observational terms) do not see that these "acknowledgments" cut against the grain of the framework in which they operate. They are very sophisticated with regard to certain points and readily admit that certain "liberalizations" must be made in order to preserve anything like the received view account. But they do not for a moment ask whether the "liberalizations" actually made are compatible with the framework that generated the initial account; it is assumed implicitly that these liberalizations are refinements rather than refutations. Yet from an external perspective, it is hard to see how any of these changes could be refinements. It is impossible for theoretical terms to be both derivative (either ontologically or semantically) and simultaneously indispensable (i.e., nonderivative). It is impossible for the hypothesis of a theory to be uninterpreted if the meaning of theoretical terms is not completely specified in observational terms. Likewise, if explanations are answers to "why?" questions, then lower level explanations cannot be explanations, because they do not address the "why?" of occurrences. And yet all these imcompatible assertions stem from the liberalization of the received view account by it own proponents.

Granting these problems concerning the interpretation of theoretical terms, however, puts us in a position to understand why models are such controversial items in received view accounts. It turns out that many theorists have attempted to save the essentials of the received view account, while acknowledging the liberalizations made, by packing all the surplus meaning and ontological status that theories must possess into the model of the theory (Note 10.3).

Now we can see why virtually all received view theorists except out-and-out conventionalists argue in favor of the indispensability of models as part of the "cognitive content" or meaning of a scientific theory. This is because the theory *must* provide some "meaning" (and, if one is a realist, ontological status) for its terms in addition to that which manages to "seep up" from the observational level. *If theories did not have some source of surplus meaning over observations, then all explanations would be circular.* Thus to avoid circularity in theoretical understanding, we must have a source of surplus meaning. Models are regarded as indispensable, because they can provide such a source of "new" meaning (and even ontological import).

Wartofsky's textbook (1968) makes this line of reasoning very clear:

> In the deductive model, the "theories" are higher-level laws, and the terms in such laws are theoretical terms. But these are reducible to empirical terms, by the reduction of theories to their empirical consequences—say, empirical laws–and these are the ones which contain the "direct observation terms" or the "basic terms" by means of which, however indirectly, the theory may be said to refer to experience or experiment. The question of the asymmetry of explanation arises here, however; i.e., if T explains L, and L explains O, we cannot in turn also say that O explains L and L explains T. Yet if we say that the explanation of a statement containing a theoretical item like *the charge on an electron* is by means of its reduction in terms either of the observation-

statements concerning pointer readings in a laboratory or of the operations of measurement, then we cannot in turn claim that the theory explains (by means of laws deducible from it) the pointer-reading statements. That is, we cannot have it both ways, on pain of circularity.

But what is the difference between a theoretical model and a law [pp. 279–280]?

The question Wartofsky asks has already presaged his conclusion. By referring to theories *as models*, he has set the stage for declaring models indispensable to theory. This is his conclusion (1968):

Theories are models which are taken *either* as imaginary constructs or as conjectures about the real nature of things. We may characterize the alternative views on the epistemological and ontological uses of theories as (1) *Realist*: Theories constitute knowledge of the way things are, and thus are warranted approximations to reality, tested both by the empirical test of their consequences and by the systematicity of the theory. (2) *Constructivist*: Theories (and theoretical entities) are imaginary or ideal constructs, or models of a mechanical sort which are known *not* to be true but which function to aid the imagination, or as economical representations of a system of laws [pp. 286–287].

Wartofsky himself winds up favoring the realist view on the basis of an examination of actual scientific practice. He feels that models and analogies are necessary to interpret the purely formal structure of a scientific theory. But this conclusion can be reached by consideration of the topics discussed in the interpretation of theoretical terms without ever looking at "actual scientific practice." If theories have the formal structure outlined earlier, and if the liberalizations acknowledged there are made, then models must be declared to be indispensable, because they are the only component of a theory that could have the properties that those liberalizations require.

Discussions of the static aspects of theory lead, by consideration of problematic issues involved, into the dynamic aspects of how a theory is to be used. Theories, in order to be worth their scientific "weight," must be sources of scientific knowledge claims. But within the confines of an authoritarian epistemology, any putative scientific hypothesis must be *validated* before it can be accepted as a genuine knowledge claim. Thus we must consider how theories are *tested* according to the received view account.

On this issue there is a considerable uniformity of opinion, and the upshot of this uniformity is that theories per se are not tested at all. Instead, the unit of analysis with which science deals when it tests or validates scientific knowledge claims is the particular consequence (theorem, or hypothesis in the non-Campbell sense) of a theory. Theories *per se* are examined only indirectly, as the sum total of particular hypotheses tested individually. There are virtually no chapters on "the testing of theories" in standard philosophy of science texts, but there are many on "hypothesis testing" or "experimental design." Within received view accounts, there are only two topics discussed in relation to the assessment of scientific theories: first, criteria of "good" theories such as simplicity, comprehensiveness, testability, etc.; second, the usual chapter or section on "constructing" good hypotheses and "testing" them. Virtually no thought is given to discussion of criteria of scientific adequacy; everyone seems to pay lip service to the usual standbys, and the only lively discussion occurs when one theorist attempts to add a new criterion to the list or extol the virtues of one over the others (as did Turner, 1967, with reductionism in psychology).

The topic of hypothesis testing, however, usually emphasizes the construction of testable hypotheses, i.e., testable in the sense of clearly specifying observational outcomes resulting from clearly outlined experimental manipulations. Everyone admits that hypothesis testing, when the results are favorable to the hypothesis, is tentative; the hypothesis is accepted only "until further notice." This is because everyone realizes that the "logic" of hypothesis testing is fallacious; it is an instance of affirming the consequent. Yet at the same time, most theories endorse Reichenbach's and Feigl's attitude (mentioned in Chapter 9) that once tested and confirmed, the hypothesis is *secured*. Just exactly how a *tentative* hypothesis can be *secured* has never been made very clear, and we have seen how the quest for certainty at the foundations of knowledge led theorists higher and higher "up" from the deliverances of sense. But these problems of testing are familiar from the discussion of instant assessment in Chapter 9, and there is no need to reiterate them here (Note 10.5).

This cursory overview of received view thought on the structure and function of theories in science is admittedly quite incomplete. Nevertheless, when combined with the views discussed in Chapter 9, a reasonably coherent picture emerges. One should, for instance, be able to anticipate the response that received view theorists would make to certain forms of criticism. By examining in detail the positions of two received view theorists in the next section, we can begin to flesh out the bare bones of the account of theories thus far presented.

AN EXAMINATION OF DETAIL:
FEIGL AND HEMPEL ON THE DEFENSE AND
REFINEMENT OF THE ORTHODOX VIEW OF
THEORIES

Herbert Feigl and Carl Hempel have lucidly and succinctly appraised a number of key features of the received view account of theories. Whereas Feigl has concentrated on defending the reasoning behind the orthodox account, Hempel has incorporated a number of criticisms into the formulation of a *neo-orthodox* position that he sees as a necessary refinement of earlier views. By pausing to examine these two positions, we can gain some understanding of what motivates received view theorists and what they consider essential to the nature of theories in science. Let us consider Feigl's defense first.

Feigl begins by reiterating Reichenbach's distinction between the contexts of justification and discovery, admonishing that the orthodox view of theories is a reconstruction of their logical structure in the context of justification. Thus all criticism of the orthodox view from the standpoint of its inadequacies in the actual practice of research, in the context of discovery, are admitted at the outset but dismissed as resting upon an incorrect conception of what the orthodox view is designed to do. Feigl (1970b) summarizes the standard account:

> In the picturesque but illuminating elucidations used, e.g., by Schlick, Carnap, Hempel, and Margenau, the "pure calculus," i.e., the uninterpreted postulate system, "floats" or "hovers" freely above the plane of empirical facts. It is only through the "connecting links," i.e., the "coordinative definitions" (Reichenbach's terms, roughly synonymous with the "correspondence rules" of Margenau and Carnap, or the "epistemic correlations" of Northrop, and only related to but not strictly identical with Bridgman's "operational definitions"), that the postulate system acquires empirical meaning. A simple diagram (actually greatly oversimplified!) will illustrate the logical situation. As the diagram indicates, the basic theoretical concepts (primitives) are implicitly defined by the postulates in which they occur. These primitives (O), or more usually derived concepts (△) explicitly defined in terms of them are then linked ("coordinated") by correspondence rules to concepts (□) referring to items of observation, e.g., in the physical sciences usually fairly directly measurable quantities like mass, temperature, and light intensity. These empirical concepts are in turn "operationally defined," i.e., by a specification of the rules of observation, measurement, experimentation, or statistical design which determine and delimit their applicability and application [pp. 5-6].

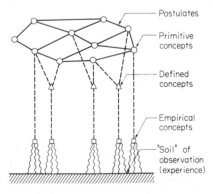

Diagram from Feigl, 1970b, p. 6.

Crucial to this account is a distinction between the theoretical "language" and the language of observation. Theoretical terms gain partial interpretation in virtue of their particular location in the nomological network that constitutes the theory (i.e., are accorded implicit definition by their position in the theoretical language), but a far more important definition of their meaning is due to "upward seepage" from the empirical concepts of the observational level. Feigl wrote (1970b):

> In view of the "orthodox" logical analysis of scientific theories it is generally held that the concepts ("primitives") in the postulates, as well as the postulates themselves, can be given no more than a partial interpretation. This presupposes a sharp distinction between the language of observation (observational language; O. L.) and the language of theories (theoretical language; T. L.). It is asserted that the O. L. is fully understood. . . . Terms like "electromagnetic field," "neutron," "neutrino," and "spin" are understood only partially, i.e., with the help of postulates, explicit definitions, correspondence rules, and operational definitions. In the picturesque description of our diagram, it was said that there is an "upward seepage" of meaning from the observational terms to the theoretical concepts [p. 7].

Feigl mentioned three classes of criticisms that have been directed at the orthodox view: a first class directed against the notion of "partial interpretation" via upward seepage of meaning; a second class of criticisms directed at the logic of explanation and assessment of theories; and a final class of objections based upon the monolithic nature of theories. His response to theses criticisms, although brief, is characteristic of received view theorists. With regard to criticisms of the first class, such as those of Feyerabend (1962, 1965b), Feigl can only assert that empiricism is preferable to rationalism (1970b):

> He maintains that theories are tested against each other. If this were so, which I do not concede, then even the most liberal empiricism would have to be abandoned in favor of a, to me, highly questionable form of rationalism. But Feyerabend's construal of the history of scientific theories seems to me rather extravagant [p. 8]!

Concerning the second class of criticisms, Feigl maintains that it is obviously wise to separate the validation of derivations from a theory from the assessment of the theory's empirical adequacy. Then he adds (1970b): "But ever since the analyses of scientific explanation given on the basis of *statistical* postulates, especially by C. G. Hempel, we have known how to explicate nondeductive derivations, which are actually the *rule* rather than the exception in recent science [p. 9]." We shall see the import of this claim more fully in the discussion that follows. The third class of criticisms have to do with Duhem's and Quine's contention that theories are tested only globally and that particular hypotheses cannot be tested independently. Feigl explicates this contention in terms of the problematic nature of auxiliary hypotheses involved in testing. His response (1970b):

> A closer look at the actual history and procedures of scientific research, however, indicates that the auxiliary hypotheses, etc., have usually been "secured" by previous confirmation (or corroboration). And while, of course, even the best established hypotheses are in principle kept open for revision, it would be foolish to call them into doubt when some other more "risky" hypotheses are under critical scrutiny [p. 10].

Feigl concludes his discussion with some comments on levels of explanation, a topic he introduced into the literature somewhat earlier (Feigl, 1945). Though not wanting to abandon or modify the essentials of the orthodox view of theories, Feigl admits that recent criticism (especially by Feyerabend) has shown that his picture of levels of explanation needs some "emendations." Feigl's initial conception had distinguished a "low" level of singular statements of fact, a higher level of empirical laws, and a still higher level of theories. The progress of science consists largely in constructing ever higher level theories, so that the ratio of facts "covered" to postulates required increases with higher, more comprehensive theories. Feigl admits (1970b) that:

> The plausibility of the level-structure model has been, however, drastically affected by Feyerabend's criticisms. He pointed out quite some years ago that there is hardly an example which illustrates strict deducibility of the lower from the higher levels, even in theories with 100 percent deterministic lawlike postulates. The simple reason is that in straightforward deductive inference there can be no concepts in the conclusion that are not present in the premises and definitions. Most of us thought that definitions, or else bridge laws, would accomplish the job. In fact, however, the lower levels which (historically) usually precede, in their formulation, the construction of the higher levels are, as a rule, incisively revised in the light of the higher level theory.... The conceptual frameworks of the theories of different levels are so radically different as to exclude any deductive relationships. Only if bridge laws help in defining the lower level concepts can the derivation be rendered deductive [pp. 12, 13].

But in keeping with his new approach to the foundations of knowledge (see Chapter 9), Feigl continues to require an observational language that is *uncontaminated, at least by the theory under test.* This is a slight change from previous formulations (such as Carnap's), which required a *neutral* observation language uncontaminated by theory in any sense. Now Feigl is willing to admit theoretical contamination in the language of observation, but he insists that testing in science requires that the theory under test not affect its relevant observation language. He continues (1970b):

> In disagreement with Feyerabend, I remain convinced that in the testing of a new theory, the relevant observation language must not be contaminated by the theory; nor need there be a competing alternative theory. If he contends that in most concerns of empirical testing there are presuppositions of a pervasive theoretical character, I would argue that those pervasive presuppositions, for example regarding the relative permanence of the laboratory instruments, of the experimental records, are "theoretical" only from a deep epistemological point of view and are not called into question when, for example, we try to decide experimentally between rival theories in the physical, biological, or social sciences [p. 13].

This slight change in the distinction between the T. L. and O. L. provides a transition to Hempel's "refinements" of the orthodox view. Hempel likewise insists upon a sharp separation of languages, but in the neo-orthodox account they are the theoretical language and the *antecedent language*. This antecedent language is antecedent to the theory language but *may* be theoretical in nature (Hempel, 1970):

> The antecedently examined phenomena for which a theory is to account have often been conceived as being described, or at least describable, by means of an observational vocabulary, i.e., a set of terms standing for particular individuals or for general attributes which, under suitable conditions, are accessible to "direct observation" by human observers. But this conception has been found inadequate on several important counts.
>
> The distinction I have suggested between theoretical and antecedent vocabulary hinges on no such assumption. The terms of the antecedent vocabulary need not, and indeed should not, generally be conceived as observational in the narrow sense just adumbrated, for the antecedent vocabulary of a given theory will often contain terms which were originally introduced in the context of an earlier theory, and which are not observational in a narrow intuitive sense [pp. 143–144].

By this slight shift in the characterization of the two languages of theory, Hempel seems to avoid the sort of criticism that Feyerabend advanced against the orthodox view as he, Feigl, and Carnap had earlier formulated it.

Another slight change that Hempel introduces concerns the bridge laws of the standard account. On Hempel's new view, bridge laws are a part of the class of sentences asserted by the theory. One problem in the standard account was that correspondence rules were neither fish nor fowl, for they did not fit neatly into either the theoretical or observational language.

Hempel finds a number of criticisms of the orthodox view to have merit. Considering the idea that theoretical terms are given an "implicit meaning" by their place in the ramified network of the axiomatization, he says (1970):

In what sense can an uninterpreted axiomatization be said to "bring out the meanings" of the primitive terms? The postulates of a formalized theory are often said to constitute "implicit definitions" of the primitives, requiring the latter to stand for kinds of entities and relations which jointly satisfy the postulates. If axiomatization is to be viewed as somehow *defining* the primitives, then, it is logically more satisfactory to construe axiomatization, with Suppes, as yielding an explicit definition of a higher order set-theoretical predicate. In either case, the formalized theory is then viewed in effect as dealing with just such kinds of entities and relations as make the postulates true.... But it is not plausible at all to hold that the primitive terms of an axiomatized theory in empirical science must be understood to stand for entities and attributes of which the postulates, and hence also the theorems, are true; for on this construal, the truth of the axiomatized theory would be guaranteed a priori, without any need for empirical study [pp. 150–151].

A related point concerns the theoretical language as an *uninterpreted* calculus. Hempel (1970) finds that the internal principles (the new term for the postulates and calculus) of the theory actually "employ not only 'new' theoretical concepts but also 'old,' or pre-theoretical, ones that are characterized in terms of the antecedent vocabulary [p. 153]." This leads to another reformulation (1970):

The internal principles of a theory   and hence also the corresponding calculus C—have to be viewed, in general, as containing pre-theoretical terms in addition to those of the theoretical vocabulary. Accordingly, the conjoined postulates of C would form an expression of the type $(t_1, t_2, \ldots, p_1, p_2, \ldots, p_m)$, where the t's again correspond to "new" theoretical terms, while the p's are pre-theoretical, previously understood ones. Consequently, the theoretical calculus that the standard conception associates with a theory is not, as a rule, a totally uninterpreted system containing, apart from logical and mathematical symbols, only new theoretical terms [p. 153].

For similar reasons, Hempel now joins the rank of theorists who declare models to be an indispensable component of the theory rather than a mere aid to theorizing.

But Hempel is not willing to "give in" to the views of nonjustificational theorists concerning the changes that occur in the "meanings" of theoretical terms both in the process of explanation and during the reduction of one theory to another. For example Hempel rejects Feyerabend's meaning dependence thesis as a terminological issue that cannot be resolved due to the vagueness of the meaning of meaning (1970):

This question has received much attention in recent years in the debate over the ideas of Feyerabend, Kuhn, and some others concerning theoretical change in science and the theory-dependence of the meanings of scientific terms. As the debate has shown, however, a satisfactory resolution of the issue would require a more adequate theory of the notion of sameness of meaning than seems yet to be at hand [pp. 155–156].

Returning to the specifications of the meaning of theoretical terms, Hempel acknowledges their "open texture" (in Pap's sense; see Pap, 1958, 1962). The problem then arises (at least for the orthodox view) as to how one can understand theoretical terms *at all*. If their "implicit specification" in terms of the network is not of any help, and if the upward seepage doctrine is only partially correct, then there appear to be problems (Hempel, 1970):

> The very relaxation of the requirements for the introduction of new scientific terms gave rise to such questions as whether we can claim to understand such partially interpreted terms; whether the sentences containing them can count as significant assertions or can be regarded at best as an effective, but inherently meaningless, machinery for inferring significant statements, couched in fully understood terms, from other such statements; and whether reliance on incompletely interpreted theoretical terms could be entirely avoided in science [p. 163].

Hempel's answer to this problem is to say that we learn the meanings of such terms in "other" ways (1970):

> But this way of looking at the issue presupposes that we cannot come to understand new theoretical terms except by way of sentences specifying their meanings with the help of previously understood terms; and surely this notion is untenable. We come to understand new terms, we learn how to use them properly, in many ways besides definition: from instances of their use in particular contexts, from paraphrases that can make no claim to being definitions, and so forth. The internal principles and bridge principles of a theory, apart from systematically characterizing its content, no doubt offer the learner the most important access to an "understanding" of its expressions, including terms as well as sentences [p. 163].

But this is all Hempel has to say on this issue; no specification of how this understanding can come about is ever given, and no comment is offered on whether or not such understanding is compatible with either the orthodox or Hempel's neo-orthodox position on theories. Having raised this point, Hempel says nothing more; the article ends on this issue.

CONCEPT FORMATION AND THE LIMITS OF THE ORTHODOX VIEW OF THEORIES

The various liberalizations in the orthodox view of theories may be seen from either an internal perspective, in which case they are "necessary refinements" of the empiricist approach to justificationism; or they may be viewed from an external perspective, in which case they are arguments against the framework that generated them. In this section we must examine the problem of concept formation as it arises in logical empiricism from an external perspective, in order to see how the various liberalizations have prevented theories from forming concepts as the received view claims they must. The conclusion we reach here parallels that reached in Chapter 9; by successively liberalizing aspects of the orthodox view, the logical empiricists have reached a point at which no further maneuvering is possible. Their approach is at a dead end, having exhausted the resources it has allowed itself. We can see this in broad overview by examining the effect of the liberalization of the upward seepage doctrine of meaning upon scientific concept formation.

The initial sharp separation between theoretical and observational languages, in combination with the upward seepage doctrine of meaning, provided a straightforward answer to the problem of how scientific concepts are formed. So long as this sharp separation could be maintained, concept formation in empirical science was a matter of *definition*—the definition of theoretical concepts in terms of observational occurrences. (We are not yet concerned with the supposed interpretation of theoretical terms supplied by their position in the nomological network of a theory.) But it soon became obvious that not all theoretical terms are explicitly definable in terms of observations. There was upward seepage of meaning, but it was not enough; only a partial interpretation could be thus supplied. At this point, theoretical terms were said to be "partially interpreted" by observational statements and also "implicitly specified" by their location in the nomological network. There were two sources of meaning that could be counted on to make theoretical concepts testable and meaningful. But the recent liberalizations that Hempel made have abandoned both of these sources of meaning without specifying what is to replace them.

The location of a theoretical term within the nomological network can indeed provide some systematization, but it is hard to see (as Hempel persuasively argues) how the postulates of the uninterpreted calculus can provide "implicit definitions" that are meaningful. The problem is analogous to that of specifying "where the meanings are" in a dictionary. There are no meanings in a dictionary, only alternative verbalizations. In order to use a dictionary, one must *already know* the meanings of terms, at least those terms in which the alternative verbalizations are couched. What one learns in using a dictionary is certain structural relations between terms (e.g., synonymy, antonymy, relations of paraphrase, etc.), but the only meanings that are learned are those that depend on our already knowing the meaning of other terms. Thus there is systematization in abundance in a dictionary, but no meanings at all. Dictionaries are meaningful, but they contain only alternative verbalizations, not meanings. Hempel's arguments against implicit definition by the structural properties of the nomological network are alternative ways of making this point that dictionaries, indeed definitions themselves, are conveyers of meaning from another source rather than sources per se.

But human beings who speak a natural language are obviously in possession of meanings as well as words and sentences. How do native speakers of a language get the meanings they attach to their terms? The traditional empiricist answer has been that sense experience is the ultimate source of meaning (as well as knowledge) and that, in the last analysis, meaning becomes a matter of ostensive definition. For the empiricist, experience (at least some) is inherently meaningful. If this approach is applied to theories, the upward seepage doctrine results. The meaning of theoretical terms must be found, in the last analysis, in the experiences that human beings undergo.

But the new liberalization, distinguishing antecedent and theoretical languages in science, cuts against the grain of the empiricist approach to meaning. For in order to evade Feyerabend's criticisms, Hempel was forced to acknowledge that observation is theoretical in nature. Now the theoretical terms of science get their meaning from (are defined in terms of) theoretical terms. But theoretical terms, on Hempel's account, can only provide systematization for other theoretical terms. Thus the new liberalization faces the empiricist account of theories with the prospect of an infinite regress with regard to specification of meaning. The specification of theoretical terms is now by means of other theoretical terms, and one never reaches an observational bedrock of meaning.

But Hempel's account ends at this point. He rests his case on the truism that we can come to understand the meaning of theoretical terms "in many ways besides definition." This is of course true, as a matter of empirical fact. But one must ask what the acknowledgment of this fact does to the empiricist account of theories. The answer is that at one stroke, it simultaneously destroys the residual empiricism in the empiricist account of theories and also turns the problems of meaning in science over to the cognitive psychologist. It destroys the empiricism in the orthodox account, because there has been *no* positive proposal advanced for how theoretical terms *do* acquire meaning (except from other theoretical terms) (Note 10.5). It throw the problems of meaning back to the psycholinguist and cognitive psychologist by default; if anyone can tell us how scientific concepts are formed, how they acquire meaning, etc., it ought to be the (Utopian) psychologist. The maneuver space remaining within philosophy has vanished. Hempel's account ends with the admission that definition is not the answer, because it has no place else to go.

To conclude this overview of the nature of theories, let us mention two themes that recur in subsequent discussion. First, as we shall see in the discussion that follows, the problems that arise with regard to the nature of explanation are strikingly parallel to those facing the orthodox account of theories. Once again we shall see liberalizations shrink a maneuver space to zero and an entire research program abandoned until work in another research program has progressed sufficiently to solve the problems of the first program. Just as an adequate account of theories awaits development in the psychology of concept formation, so the problems of explanation await the development of a viable confirmation theory. Second, with regard to the *function* of theories in science, it should not be surprising that theories (on the received view account of what theories are) play little if any real role in the actual practice of science. As we saw in Chapter 8, the problems of the empiricist account of theories are devastating only for the received view metatheory that generated them; the real problems lie elsewhere. But that is to get ahead of our account. Consider now the nature of explanation.

EXPLANATION AS SUBSUMPTION: THE "COVERING LAW" APPROACH

The *logical* analysis of explanation presents few problems to the received view theorist. For if one neglects the *psychological* aspects of what is involved in coming to understand a logically well-formed explanation *as an explanation*, it is only necessary to realize that in its ideal form an explanation *must* transmit the assurance of its premises to that which is being explained. This constraint alone is sufficient to *guarantee* that, logically speaking, explanation must consist of logical deduction; no other form of inference transmits truth from premises to conclusion. To explain is to deduce the explanandum (that which is to be explained) from a conjunction of statements that constitute the premises of a logical argument. The explanandum is *subsumed* under the premises—shown to follow from them as a deductive consequence.

But if explanation is to be deduction, what are the premises from which the explanandum is deduced? These premises always consist of statements of two kinds: first, scientific generalizations that have the status of *laws* or *theories*; second, statements of initial or boundary conditions referring to particulars of the specific situation. The generalizations "explain" certain *classes* of phenomena, and the boundary or initial conditions specifiy that the explanandum in question *is* a member of such a class of phenomena. This is all there is to the classic account of *explanation as subsumption under covering laws*. Defenders of the covering law model of explanation maintain that it is the necessary and sufficient logical reconstruction of all kinds of explanation in science (fully deterministic or only statistical), of all singular statements, regardless of whether they refer to singular events or laws or even theories. But explanation as deduction is an *ideal*, which cannot be achieved in most cases. But that gets ahead of explicating the classic model. The classic account of explanation stems from the work of Karl Popper in the 1930s. "To give a *causal explanation* of an event means to deduce a statement which describes it, using as premises... one or more *universal laws,* together with certain singular statements, the *initial conditions*" (Popper, 1959, p. 59). But Popper was more concerned with a defense of hypothetico–deductive *methodology* (against *inductive* methodology) than with explanation per se. It is Carl Hempel (1945, 1962, 1965, 1966) who is most responsible for the systematization, elaboration, and defense of the "covering law" approach to explanation. Let us outline Hempel's account of deductive explanation (or, as he now calls it, deductive–nomological [D–N] explanation) and the posture it takes on some problematic issues.

The classic presentation of the covering-law model is found in Hempel and Oppenheim (1948). According to that account, an explanandum, which may be anything singular whatever—be it fact, law, or theory—is explained when it can be shown that the explanandum follows (logically) as a particular instance of a general case described in the explanans (Note 10.6). The explanans consists of two classes of statements: general laws that describe relationships holding for all classes of events of specified kinds, and statements of boundary or initial state conditions that relate to the particular explanandum under consideration. Taken together, the statements of the explanans enable one to deduce the explanandum as a particular instantiation of the general case that they describe. The logical schema of such explanation by subsumption to covering laws is summarized in Fig. 10.2. The "logical conditions" for the adequacy of an explanation that these authors proposed are (1965):

(R1) The explanandum must be a logical consequence of the explanans; in other words, the explanandum must be logically deducible from the information contained in the explanans; for otherwise, the explanans would not constitute adequate grounds for the explanandum.

(R2) The explanans must contain general laws, and these must actually be required for the derivation of the explanandum. We shall not make it a necessary condition for a sound explanation, however, that the explanans must contain at least one statement which is not a law; for, to mention just one reason, we would surely want to consider as an explanation the derivation of the general regularities governing the motion of double stars from the laws of celestial mechanics, even though all the statements in the explanans are general laws.

(R3) The explanans must have empirical content; i.e., it must be capable, at least in principle, of test by experiment or observation. This condition is implicit in (R1); for since the explanandum is assumed to describe some empirical

FIG. 10.2.   (After Hempel, 1962, p. 100.)

phenomenon, it follows from (R1) that the explanans entails at least one consequence of empirical character, and this fact confers upon it testability and empirical content. But the point deserves special mention because, as will be seen in section 4, certain arguments which have been offered as explanations in the natural and in the social sciences violate this requirement.

(R4) The sentences constituting the explanans must be true [pp. 247–248].

Most authors who have commented on these conditions of adequacy find (R4) the most puzzling. (R1) merely reiterates the deductive nature of explanation; (R2) avoids circularity by prohibiting particulars from "explaining" particulars; and (R3) requires testability as a hallmark of "scientific" explanation. But (R4) presents serious problems for the meaning of theoretical terms; if they are contentless in themselves (as we have seen earlier), then how can they be "true?" For example, if a theory postulates hypothetical constructs, how can an explanation utilizing them be valid unless they are not hypothetical but real existents?

But these questions never occupy much space in discussions of scientific explanation. Rather, there are only two topics that receive attention: First, potential exceptional cases must be shown to fit the deductive–subsumption model; and second, the key concept of *scientific law* or *lawfulness* must be explicated. We discuss the nature of laws later. Let us consider now the first class of problems. One recurring topic in the literature is whether or not history, as a discipline that allegedly deals with a unique and unrepeatable subject matter, can be made to fit into the covering-law model; are historical "explanations" legitimate, i.e., are they deductive–subsumptive? Hempel has persistently answered "yes" (see, e.g., Hempel, 1965).

Another problematic issue upon which Hempel takes a definite stand centers around the *symmetry between explanation, prediction, and retrodiction*. Within the D–N model, the only difference between these concepts concerns the temporal valance of the explanans. That is, predictions are explanations of events (i.e., deductions of events) that will in the future occur, and retrodictions are predictions of events that did occur in the past. The logical mechanism involved in all cases is deduction, and the deduction occurs within the framework of the covering-law model. This reasoning is often extended to other domains. For example, the classic account of reduction (due to Nagel, 1961) claims that the mechanism involved is logical deduction according to the covering-law model, and thus a further symmetry is established between reduction and explanation. Reduction, for Nagel, *is* explanation, and both *are* deduction.

Considerable literature has been devoted to a further problematic issue: the applicability of the covering-law account of explanation to *statistical explanations*. Hempel (1962) devoted a long monograph to similarities and differences between explanations with deterministic, universal laws and those with statistical, or probabilistic laws, in the explanans. The upshot of his discussion has been the considerable weakening of the requirement that explanation be logical deduction. Let us see how this is so.

The shift from certainty to near certainty with regard to nature of knowledge has been explored in detail in Chapter 9. There we saw the impossible "Euclidean dream" of proven knowledge claims abandoned for claims that were instead "probable." The classic conception of explanation has more recently undergone a similar shift as a result of the realization of the all-pervasive presence of statistical laws in scientific theories. The deterministic covering-law model deduces its conclusion (the explanandum) with certainty. But one cannot be "certain" of a conclusion if the laws that constitute the premises of an explanatory argument are statistical rather than deterministic. We can see this by noting that explanations literally are *arguments*: They argue for the validity of a conclusion. In a covering-law explanation with a deterministic law statement, the argument is conclusive. Assume a law statement to the effect that "all F's are G's." Further assume that an instance of F is at hand. This being so, one can conclude that this instance is also (an instance of) G. Consider Fig. 10.3.

In such a reasoning (pattern of inference), one can be *certain* that this instance X is a G: It is deductively certified. But consider what happens in moving to an argument with a statistical or probabilistic law statement in the explanans. Such a statistical law could be formulated as "Almost all F's are G's." With such a law as a premise, we cannot be certain that something which is F is also G (Note 10.7). According to Hempel, we have to abandon deductive logic at this point and rely on inductive logic in its stead. In a long essay, Hempel (1962) set himself the task of "refining" the Hempel–Oppenheim model by explicating the similarities and differences betweeen deductive explanations involving deterministic law statements and inductive explanations involving statistical laws. In essence, his conclusion was that his earlier, strictly deductive, covering-law–subsumption approach must be seen as a *limiting case of a family of explanatory arguments, the key features of which is that they all consitute evidential reasonings.* In the limiting case, the deductive pattern of evidential reasoning certifies the conclusion (as Fig. 10.3 illustrates). However, in nearly all other cases (Note 10.8) in which the law statements are probabilistic rather than 100 percent deterministic, *near certainty* is all that we can argue for. According to Hempel, Fig. 10.4 schematizes the statistical inference explanatory argument form. With this "liberalization," replacing "certainty" by "almost certainty," probabilistic inductive logic has entered into explanation; and the latter is now no longer

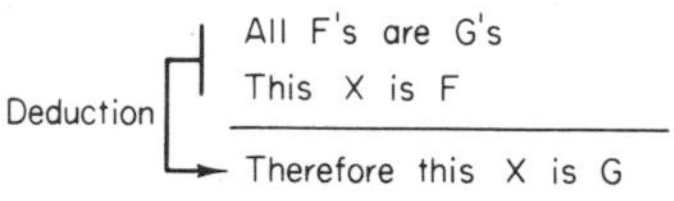

FIG. 10.3.   (After Hempel, 1962, p.125.)

Induction

Almost all F's are G's

This X is an F

Therefore *almost certainly* this X is also G

FIG. 10.4.   (After Hempel, 1962, p. 125.)

exclusively deductive. Now, *instead of the (deductive) logic of explanation, we have the inductive logic of evidential reasonings.* "The near certainty here invoked is sometimes referred to as (high) probability;... The probabilities referred to here are logical or inductive probabilities,... " (Hempel, 1962, pp. 134–135). The concern has shifted to explicating the nature of confirming evidence (the inductive logician's task) from the earlier task of analyzing the "logic" of explanation (Note 10.9). With hindsight, the only question is why it took so long for the shift to occur; one wonders why neojustificationists were content to accept the classic justificationist picture of explanation for so long when they had abandoned the classic method of inference so much earlier (Note 10.10).

What has changed in this liberalization of the nature of explanation is only its logic; the conception of explanation as subsumption of particulars under general laws has not changed at all. A prevalent opinion is that this sort of liberalization "is fatal... only if we assume that science must predict and explain individual events. A law is nonetheless a law because it expresses a probability relationship" (Turner, 1967, p. 282).

The neojustificationist twist that the admission of statistical law statements brings to the 'logic' of explanation can easily be documented. Consider this statement by Rescher (1970) concerning explanation in the light of the neojustificationist conception of inference outlined in Chapter 9.

> In general, a potentially explanatory argument can fall into one of two categories. It may be either *deductive* (D-explanation), or *probabilistic* (P-explanation). With a deductive explanation, the explanatory premises would, if true, provide *conclusive* evidence for the conclusion, constituting a *totally sufficient* guarantee of the explanatory conclusion. With a probabilistic explanation, the explanatory premises do not provide a guarantee of the conclusion, but merely render it relatively likely, and so endow it with a relatively substantial (conditional) probability, say, one in excess of one half, or perhaps some other specified value k in the interval $0.5 < k < 1$ [p. 37].

Because such "explanations" are not conclusive, we must now shift our emphasis from a logic of explanation to a *logic of evidence* to be able to assess the adequacy of various patterns of evidential reasonings. Rescher (1970) would have us believe that:

> The central and fundamental fact of the theory of evidence is that one statement may constitute evidence for another which goes beyond it in content. This feature fundamentally differentiates the concept of *evidence* from that of

deductive *entailment:* the comparative weakness of the former embodying its very reason for being. A true statement may legitimately provide evidence for a falsehood; a statement may constitute evidence for each of several incompatible statements [p. 93].

According to Rescher, there is a fundamental *methodological* contrast between deductive theoretical systems and inductive or probabilistic ones, where there is a legitimate "slippage" between evidence and conclusion. This contrast leads to a distinction between *error* and *mistake* (Rescher, 1970):

> Thus in domains in which one operates with evidence proper, leaving behind the secure ground of proof, the possibility of error must be accepted. Indeed in such fields a valid distinction may be drawn between *error* (drawing a conclusion, which, though false, actually derives from a soundly conducted inquiry) and *mistake* (falsehood owing to a fallacy in the inquiry) [p. 94].

This line of reasoning serves to reinforce Hempel's earlier abandonment of the requirement for true premises in the explanans; just as it is no longer required of a putative scientific statement that it be proven true in order to be acceptable, it is no longer necessary that an explanatory argument utilize premises that are proven true. The acceptability of scientific statements (and explanations) is no longer tied to "the facts." Rescher goes on (1970):

> In such a sphere in which the cutting edge of the evidence concept is less keen, legitimate disagreement can arise regarding the truth of statements in the face of argument regarding the evidential basis for these statements. Despite agreement on "the facts" different constructions or interpretations can be placed upon them—particularly if the scope of discussion is speculative, i.e., on a level at several removes in generality and abstraction from "the facts." In a context of this sort, the common requirement that a statement agrees with "the facts" ceases to be an effectual criterion of validity, because a significant area of assertion lies beyond the discriminatory power of this criterion [pp. 94–95] [Note 10.11].

THE NATURE AND ROLE OF LAWS IN EXPLANATION

The orthodox view of theories, being reasonably clear-cut and tightly knit, passes all problematic issues on to the topic of scientific explanation. And even with the liberalization of explanation to include both induction and deduction in its logic, the process is still that of subsumption under laws. Thus by successively "passing the buck" on problematic issues, we arrive at a point where an explication of the nature and function of law statements in science is fundamental to an understanding of both scientific explanations and theories. The nature and role of laws of nature is thus *the* major topic of discussion in most in-depth coverages of "scientific explanation." Thus it is not surprising that a full-length book by Nicholas Rescher (1970) entitled *Scientific explanation* admits in a footnote and in prefatory remarks that its main topic is the nature and use of laws in science.

Perhaps the basic problem in the received view account centers around two related issues concerning law statements: their universality and their necessity. Law statements *function* in explanations in much the manner that axioms function in a (formalized) theory—as the "first principles" from which everything else follows. But axioms or postulates are merely taken for granted for the purposes for which they are used; they have no a priori validity that can be invoked in their defense. Similarly, a law of nature, being a contingent, empirical proposition (or at least translatable into one), has no a priori validity. But now the problem arises: How can law statements, which are contingent rather than a priori, have the degree of generality and necessity that we demand of them? On virtually every analysis, law statements are universally quantified and unrestricted in scope. They are meant to apply every-where, every-when. To claim law status for a statement such as "all swans are white" is to authorize inferences about swans never seen by anyone, such as those in past ages and those yet unborn, which far transcend the experience of any observer or indeed the entire human race. How can law statements have such universality, and how can they necessitate that unexamined cases conform to a given specification?

Today it is universally recognized that the strict inductivist answer, according to which laws are merely generalizations built up from experiences, is wrong. Although the laws of nature are empirical, they are *not* experiential; laws embody knowledge that transcends experience. Virtually everyone would agree with Rescher's (1970) contention that:

> An empirical generalization is not to be viewed as fully adequate for explanatory purposes until it can lay claim to the status of a law. Now a law is not just a summary statement of observed regularities-to-date, it claims to deal with a universal regularity purporting to describe how things inevitably are: how the processes at work in the world must invariably work, how things have to happen in nature. Such a claim has to be based upon a stronger foundation than any mere observed-regularity-to-date [p. 15].

Now this very fact of the universality of laws leads to the other problem: their *nomic necessity*. Laws cannot be accidental generalizations; in some sense, they claim that something *must* be the way it is. A *definitive* characteristic of laws is that they manifest *nomic necessity* and *hypothetical force*. According to Rescher (1970):

This nomic necessity manifests itself most strikingly in the context of hypothetical suppositions, especially counterfactual hypotheses. In accepting "All A's are B's" ("All spiders are eight-legged") as a law, we have to be prepared to accept the conditional "If x were an A, then x would be a B." (If this beetle were a spider—which it isn't—, then it would have eight legs.) It is pre-eminently this element of hypothetical force that distinguishes a genuinely lawful generalization from an accidental generalization like "All coins in my pocket weigh less than one quarter ounce." For we would not be prepared to accept the conditional "If this Venetian florin were a coin in my pocket, then it would weigh less than one quarter ounce [pp. 98–99].

It is at this point that the problem of counterfactual conditionals enters in; laws commit one to making statements about "what *would* be the case *if*" certain conditions obtained. That is, if we have a law statement to the effect that "all X's *have to be* Y's," then we are *committed* to given assent to the statement "all X's and Y's and further if Z (which is't an X) were an X, then Z *would* be a Y." It is this contrafactual conditional implication that constitutes the hypothetical force of a law.

The problem for the empiricist thus reappears: The evidential basis for a law is insufficient not only to account for its universality but also to underwrite its hypothetical force. Further, this is a problem that induction cannot solve. Rescher put this clearly (1970):

> It is obvious that this basis will be *deductively insufficient* because the evidence inevitably relates to a limited group of cases while the applicability of the law is unrestricted. Moreover the evidential basis will also be *inductively insufficient*. For inductive procedures are designed to warrant the step from observed to unobserved cases, whereas a law—whose very lawfulness arrogates to it nomological necessity and counterfactual force—not only takes this inductive step from observed to unobserved cases, but also takes the added step from actual to hypothetical cases. The inductive justification of hypothetical force would have to take the form "has always been applicable to counterfactual cases." And the premise for such an induction will obviously always be unavailable. The evidential foundation for generalization is thus affected by a double insufficiency, not only in the *deductive* mode, but also *inductively* (at any rate as long as induction is construed along usual and standard lines) [p. 106].

Lawfulness is thus not discovered in the evidence at all; rather, it is supplied by the theorist. Lawfulness, as Rescher argues (1970), *is a matter of imputation. "Lawfulness is the product of the well-founded imputation to empirical generalizations of nomic necessity and hypothetical forces* [p. 110]."

Thus lawfulness is a matter of the epistemic status of a generalization rather than its syntactic form or semantic content. As Rescher put it, it is not a matter of what the generalization *says* but rather *how it is used.* And science "uses" laws to explain (1970):

A science is not a catalogue of observed regularities. It requires a certain *rational architectonic,* relating a variety of empirical generalizations in a rational structure that exhibits their conceptual relevance and their explanatory interconnections. A well-established generalization qualifies as a *scientific law* (in the proper sense of the term) only when it finds its theoretical home within some scientific discipline or branch of science [p. 111].

Let us pause to take stock. We began by noting that problems of the nature and function of scientific *theories* are transferred, by the received view account, to the problems of explanation. Then it was noted that explanation sooner or later devolves to the problem of explicating the nature and functioning of laws. "The explanatory uses of laws is not just a *de facto* actual feature of scientific explanation: it is absolutely indispensable. Only a subsumption-under laws procedure can achieve the aims that scientific explanation sets for itself: without this recourse to laws, *scientific* explanation would be impossible" [Rescher, 1970, p. 12]). Now we have explicated the nature of laws and found that they are not experiential and indeed that induction cannot be their basis. Instead we have looked at the hypothetical force of laws and decided that the key to lawfulness is in how universal generalizations are used in science. But how *are* laws used in science? Clearly their function is in explanation. Explanation is subsumption under covering laws. But laws are to be understood as explaining phenomena. We have come full circle, and we are as far away from an understanding of explanation as ever.

At this point, the uneasiness that results from understanding the implications of the preceding paragraph must be hidden somewhere. The usual ploy is to abandon the problems of explanation for those of confirmation theory, for—since explanation is now the logic of evidential reasonings—nothing pertaining to lawfulness can be clarified until we know what is involved in "evidential reasoning." This at least puts off the discomfort, for if one is totally immersed in confirmation theory, it will not be noticed that inductive 'logic' cannot underwrite lawfulness—as Rescher so clearly indicated in the quotation above. Or, with Rescher, one can claim that lawfulness, even though an imputation upon the data, is at least partially evidentially based. Then the time-consuming task of explicating "well-founded imputation" in terms of the logic of evidence will put off the problem. Indeed, it will even be possible to transfer the problem *back* to scientific theory, by splitting "well-foundedness" into an evidential reasoning component and a 'theoretical context' component (Rescher, 1970):

It is necessary and proper to distinguish between being *in fact* committed to accepting a generalization as a "law" of more or less fundamental status upon the one hand, and being *properly* or *warrantedly* commited [sic] to it, upon the other.... To be justified this decision must be based upon a rational warrant. It must have a grounding in (1) the *empirical evidence* for the generalization at issue in the law and (2) the *theoretical context* of the generalization. Such grounding is required to provide the necessary *warrant* to justify an imputation of lawfulness [pp. 109–110].

By this procedure, one can hold that a scientific law is warranted not only by its evidential basis but also and ultimately by its place in the nomological network, i.e., the "general architechtonic of our knowledge about the world" (Rescher, 1970, p. 108). Thus instead of a concilience of inductions constituting the edifice of science, Rescher postulates a consilience of laws; like Feigl's account, Rescher's moves the essence of science a giant step upward from observation as a basis.

Beyond its evidence, a law's warrant resides in its location and coherence within the body of science, and this leads Rescher to a neo-Kantian idealistic conception of the nature of laws (1970):

> Our view of the matter agrees with Hume's that lawfulness is not an observable characteristic of nature, and it agrees with Kant that it is a matter of man's projection. But we do not regard this projection as the result of the (in suitable circumstances) inevitable working of the epistemological faculty-structure of the human mind. Rather, we regard it as a matter of *warranted decision,* a deliberate man-made imputation effected in the setting of a particular conceptual scheme regarding the nature of explanatory understanding. We thus arrive at a position that is Kantian with a difference. Kant finds the source of lawfulness in the way in which the mind inherently works. We find its source in the conceptual apparatus that we in fact deploy for explanatory purposes: As we see it, lawfulness demands an imputational step made in the context of a certain concept of explanation [pp. 113–114].

It is only slightly ironic to note that a (not very) qualified idealism is now the basis of the traditionally empiricist account of explanation.

But even granting this conception of lawfulness, one can ask where we are with respect to understanding explanation. Rescher had no answer beyond suggesting that there are limits to explanation (construed on the covering-law model) that are more restrictive than those upon "scientific understanding" (Note 10.12). Rescher does, however, suggest a rather "daring" reconceptualization of the task of science *away from explanation* (as the received view conceives it) *to the search for laws.* "The root task of science ought thus to be thought of as a fundamentally descriptive one: the search for the laws that delineate the functioning of natural processes.... The key thing in scientific understanding is the capacity to exploit a *knowledge of laws* to structure our understanding of the past and to guide our expectations for the future (Rescher, 1970, pp. 133–135). But how understanding and the search for laws differ from explanation and the subsumption of particulars is never made clear, nor is any consideration given to whether Rescher's new liberalization is a refinement or a refutation of the received view that generated it. Rescher's account ends without touching these issues just as Hempel's liberalization of theories ended without answering its most fundamental questions. Laws are still a highly problematic issue for the received view (Note 10.13); and in consequence, so are explanations and theories. The same holds for causality, as we now see.

Discussions of explanation regularly mention causal explanations. Indeed, the classic Hempel–Oppenheim schema provides, so its authors claim, an analysis of causal explanation. But what is causality, and what are causal laws? Further, how are we to understand the frequent claims that modern physics has "overthrown" the concept of causality? The problem of causality for the empiricist begins (and, in a sense ends) where Hume left it. Hume saw no causal connection in nature and decided that all there is to causality is regular succession plus our animal belief. Since then, the empiricist tradition has continually tried to translate causality into the problem of understanding causal explanations and to handle the latter in terms of covering laws. To say that "A causes B" is rendered as "B is a logical implication of the law statement that 'covers' A". The concept of causality is thus *explicated away* by being translated into explanation by deterministic covering laws. The concept of cause has become identified with a certain kind of lawfulness: deterministic lawfulness.

One approach to explicating away causality relies upon the pragmatic function of explanation to allay our curiosity. Causal explanations are *satisfying* in a psychological sense, the way covering-law explanations are satisfying in a formal or logical sense. (But why are formal explanations at all satsfying? Theorists who take this approach regularly refer to covering-law explanations as "cognitively satisfying" [e.g., Turner, 1967, p. 271], but somehow we are never told what this means.) We are admonished (Turner, 1967) to bear up stoically in the nether regions of Humean skepticism:

> There is nothing compelling about contiguity. The satisfaction of explanation arises from habit-established perceptual expectancies. Thus the finest grained phenomenal conformities are described more than they are "explained." There is the uneasy feeling the world need not oblige us by conforming to our descriptions and that if an observation violates our principles or our laws, the solecism will rest with us and not with the event.
>
> For the radical empiricist, the end of the odyssey is Humean skepticism. Indeed, explanation and causal analysis can penetrate no further than the inevitable barriers of contiguity. We are often told that correlation does not mean causation, but as good Humeans, we can discount the argument by introducing certain space and time provisos with respect to stipulating the antecedents and consequents in a causal sequence. Correlation may not be causation; but causation is correlation unless, of course, we leave the domain of pure empirics—in which case it would be as well that we drop the language of causality altogether [p. 271].

For theorists in this tradition, causality remains "nothing but" lawfulness. Rescher (1970) puts this reasoning well:

> The idea of a *cause* is correlative with that of a causal law. One can speak of "causes" only where cause–effect relationships are held to be operative, and to hold this is to invoke the workings of causal laws. The step from the operative causes to the caused results cannot be made without the mediation of causal laws. Causal laws thus provide the indispensable setting within which the notion of cause–effect can be deployed and without which the idea of causality would remain inapplicable. The ideas of causality, of causal laws, and of causal explanations are inseparably intertwined correlatives: Each can be brought to bear only where the others are applicable [p. 123].

To Rescher, the principle of causality—i.e., the assertion that every event has a cause—is only intelligible as an empirical hypothesis about the nature of scientific laws. Such a hypothesis would assert that all laws are deterministic and that all explanations are deductive in character. Thus he rejects the principle of causality on the grounds that the "stochastic revolution" in physics has falsified it (Rescher, 1970):

> One of the central themes of modern physics relates to the existence of *random* events represented by such irreducibly stochastic processes as radioactive decay. In these contexts there are specific events—such as the decay of an unstable atom of some very heavy element—which, according to the standard view of currently accepted scientific theories, take place without the operation of any "causes," and with respect to which causal explanations cannot be given. Indeed, as we saw in the discussion of probabilistic discrete state systems, there can be natural systems whose history includes *not a single caused occurrence;* that is, none of whose states is "caused" by its preceding states in the sense of causality specified at the outset [pp. 125–126].

But Rescher saw no reason to despair the overthrow of causality, for on his account the earlier task of science as a search for causes (in response to our "why?" questions) ought to be replaced by a search for the lawfulness of occurrences. Rescher took the fundamental aspect of scientific understanding to be the subsumption of events to lawfulness. We understand nature when the laws of its functioning are at hand, not when we have isolated causes (Rescher, 1970):

> As we observed at the outset, causes are correlative with causal laws, and what is crucial here is not the *causality* but the *legality*. It is, after all, the discovery of the laws of things, regardless of whether they turn out to be universal or probabilistic, that provides a criterion of success in scientific inquiry. Even those natural systems, in the examples from modern, indeterministic physics, in which no caused occurrences take place at all are rigidly governed by specifiable

laws, laws to be sure of the probabilistic rather than universalistic type. This yields the important lesson that the fundamental factor in scientific understanding will be a grasp not necessarily of the *causes* but of the *laws* of things. Thus the appropriate "regulative principle," it would seem, is not so much the Principle of Causality ("All events have causes") but a *Principle of Legality* ("All events are law-governed") [p. 129].

In overview, Rescher took the Humean approach to causality as "nothing but" constant conjunction of events as a correct analysis of the concept (Note 10.14). He then assimilated the problem of causality to that of covering-law subsumption; and on the basis of stochastic, indeterministic systems, he concluded that not all events are causally related. Then he concluded that the root task of science ought to be the search for laws that govern the functioning of natural processes rather than the search for causes. Such a total replacement of the traditional concept of causality is quite in keeping with Hempel's liberalization of covering-law systematization, and the new approach to cause abandons the old conception just as effectively as the new approach to explanation based upon induction abandons the primacy of the old deductive conception. The concluding remarks of Hempel's (1962) liberalization essay drew the parallel explicitly:

R. von Mises holds that people will gradually come to be satisfied by causal statements of this kind: "It is *because* the die was loaded that the 'six' shows more frequently (but we do not know what the next number will be); or, *Because* the vacuum was heightened and the voltage increased, the radiation became more intense (but we do not know the precise number of scintillations that will occur in the next minute)." This passage clearly refers to statistical explanation in the sense considered in the present essay; it sets forth what might be called a statistical–probabilistic concept of "because," in contradistinction to a strictly deterministic one, which would correspond to deductive–nomological explanation [p. 166].

Thus to the question, "Where is causality in the received view account?", the answer is, "Nowhere." To discuss causality at all you must abandon the received view account, or at least its empiricism.

A FOOTNOTE ON METHOD: THE HYPOTHETICO–DEDUCTIVE PATTERN OF INFERENCE

A topic that any chapter on theories and explanation in science would be remiss in not mentioning is the nature and role of so-called hypothetico-deductive (H–D) method in science. We must see how and why logical reconstructions of the nature of theory and explanation, advanced in the spirit of studies in Reichenbach's context of justification, have been carried over into studies in the context of discovery.

An emphasis on *actual* scientific practice has never been characteristic of the logical "-isms"; these theorists tend to reconstruct a stage of scientific thought after the fact and thus operate in a "deep freeze" (to use Feigl's turn of phrase) that is quite removed from the scientist. Thus, not surprisingly, they spend time "justifying" why they do these ex post facto analyses and in advancing claims concerning what can be learned from such analyses (recall Feigl's defense earlier). The concern for actual practice and the claim that the H–D method reflects actual scientific practice, initially were exclusively Popper's. In countering the trend toward inductive logic with the claim that the logic of science—deductive logic—is the *only* logic, and in realizing that there is no factual basis upon which theories are built, Popper argued persuasively for the H–D method in the *Logik der Forschung*.

This argument caught on in the logical "-isms" for a number of reasons. One important reason was Carnap's analysis of actual scientific practice with regard to the introduction of "abstract" and "theoretical" terms in science. Carnap (1936–1937) argued persuasively that the theoretical calculus is, as Popper had claimed, actually constructed "floating in the air" far above the plane of empirical phenomena that it is intended to explain. Thus Carnap gave powerful support to Popper's contention that the generation of a scientific theory is initially a conjecture. A second reason that these theorists endorsed Popper's "method" was that it squared with their understanding of the logic of explanation. The classic covering-law or subsumption-under-law model clearly admitted the centrality of deductive logic in scientific explanation. Indeed, Hempel's analyses of explanation in the 1940s pick up where Popper left off in 1934, and Popper is often cited as a pioneer in the study of the logic of explanation.

This familiarity with the H–D method that Popper initially proposed as a critical alternative to "inductive method" has led many neojustificationists to assume that there is really no alternative to the H–D method and that it is "really" an inductive methodology. Turner (1967) provides an example of both attitudes. On his view, the H–D method amounts to nothing more than deducing a testable consequence from a theory and then looking for evidence to "confirm" the hypothesis (1967):

> Mention of the hypothetico–deductive method should not, however, lead one to assume that a deductivist procedure (in the sense of Popper) is invariably being invoked. The contrary is often the case. The hypothetico–deductive method is utilized to generate positive tests of the theory; i.e., experimental hypotheses are generated by the theory for given experimental conditions. If the experimental hypothesis is confirmed, then such confirmation is considered as support for the theory. But this involves the strategy of verifiability. Accordingly then, this, the customary use of the hypothetico–deductive

method, exemplifies inductivism and not deductivism, as mere words may incline us to think [p. 149].

Somewhat later, in arguing against conclusive falsification in science, Turner admits that this method is indispensable to science (1967): "The foregoing is not to argue that the inconclusiveness of experiment in the deductivist schema disqualifies in any substantial way hypothetico–deductive methodology as an instrument of inference and scientific construction. Quite the contrary, formalized theories being what they are, there is no alternative to this methodology [p. 224]." The reason Turner feels that the H–D method (which, remember, is nothing but a method of grinding out testable hypotheses) is indispensable is that there is no logic, or algorithm, of scientific discovery.

Thus with the realization that there is no firm foundation from which inference can automatically lead to theory, sophisticated neojustificationists came to adopt, as part of their own methodology, a procedure that Popper had initially used to argue against justificationist inductive methodology.

CHAPTER NOTES

Note 10.1   An excellent overview of the structure and function of theories is found in Bunge (1967, Vol. I). First Bunge defines an abstract theory:

> An *abstract theory* is a deductive system of schemata (propositional functions) in which only uninterpreted (abstract) symbols occur, such as the reference class U of nondescript elements $x, y, \ldots$ and the binary operation $°$ in an algebra $A + <U, °>$. The initial assumptions or axioms of an abstract theory may not contain free individual variables; universal and existential formulas will qualify as members of such a theory as long as the nature of the individual variables and the meaning of the predicates are left unspecified.... Abstract theories are meaningless [p. 413].

Then he discusses the concept of the *interpretation* of an abstract theory. "A true interpretation of an abstract theory will be called a *conceptual model* of it just in case the primitive symbols are made to correspond to concepts existing in some theoretical context but having no real reference. In other words, a conceptual model is an interpretation of the given abstract theory in terms of concepts belonging to a nonabstract theory" (Bunge, 1967), p. 417). A conceptual model is conferred upon the primitives of a formalism. Thus we arrive at the following general schematization of scientific theories (Bunge, 1967):

Disregarding the presuppositions of theory, the basis of it consists of (i) a list of specific *primitives,* (ii) a list of *interpretation* (or correspondence) assumptions that confer a meaning to some of the primitives (partially interpreted theory) or to all of them (fully interpreted theory) and (iii) a list of *axioms* (unproved assumptions), i.e., of basic formulas interconnecting the primitives. Just as an abstract theory is a set of assumptions partially ordered by the relation $\vdash$ of deducibility, an interpreted theory is a set of assumptions ordered by $\vdash$ and with a content given by a set I_n of interpretation assumptions. In brief,

Theory $\begin{cases} \text{Structure S} = \langle \text{A}, \vdash \rangle \text{ Syntactical system or abstract theory} \\[1em] \text{Model } M_n \text{ (S)} = \langle \text{A, } I_n, \vdash \rangle \text{Semantical system or interpreted} \\ \qquad\qquad\qquad\qquad\qquad \text{theory.} \end{cases}$

There are as many theoretical models $M_n(S)$ of a given abstract structure S as sets I_n of rules of interpretation (or correspondence) of the primitive symbols. Thus, one and the same set of equations may recur in the most varied fields; i.e., one and the same structure may be endowed with a variety of contents—whence all scientists ought to learn roughly the same mathematics. . . .

To conclude. Every abstract theory, or structure, can be interpreted in a number of ways, either partially or fully. Conversely, if a theory is divested of the interpretation assumptions that confer a content upon it, a purely syntactic schema remains. The simplest interpretation an abstract theory can be given is to regard the theory's objects (the members of the universe of discourse *U*) as natural numbers; every syntactically consistent structure allows for such an interpretation, which yields what is miscalled a *denumerable model.* A factual model can be built instead of or above such a conceptual model if the appropriate interpretation clues (referitions and semantical hypotheses) are added. But not every interpretation is acceptable. In order for an interpretation to be adequate, hence acceptable, it must not be *ad hoc* (artificial), it must satisfy (if only approximately) the theory's initial assumptions, and it must satisfy the condition of semantic closure, which is necessary to avoid semantical inconsistencies (double-talk). Only under such conditions is a (partially) interpreted theory entitled to be subject to test; and, of course, only favorably tested theories are candidates to (partial) truth [pp. 430–434].

Note 10.2. Axiomatization has to do solely with formal consistency. Bunge (1967) defines that concept thusly: "A set of formulas is said to be *formally consistent* if and only if it contains no contradictions. Equivalently: a set of formulas is formally inconsistent if and only if it contains both a formula and its contradictory, and consequently the conjunction of the two, i.e., a self-contradiction [p. 436]." Axiomatization is one procedure that we can follow to ascertain whether or not a theory is formally consistent (Bunge, 1967):

In a completely axiomatized theory all the theorems can be derived from the initial assumptions alone by purely formal (logical or mathematical) means, i.e., by application of rules of deductive inference. In other words, given the axioms of the theory and the rules of inference presupposed by the theory (i.e., the underlying systems of logic and mathematics), all the theorems remain uniquely determined even if none of them has actually been derived. Logical predetermination is the only effective predetermination and it is peculiar to axiomatic theories.

In formal science an *axiom* or postulate is an unproved assumption the function of which is to help prove other formulas of the theory. In factual science, too, an axiom is unproved and helps in proving other statements, but its introduction is justified to the extent to which these other statements (the theorems) are somehow validated by experience. The most ambitious task a theoretician can set himself is to invent an axiom set to cover exhaustively a given field of knowledge [p. 401].

Note 10.3. The term "model" is not without ambiguity even when referring to models in science. Bunge provided a helpful classification of types of models in science, as evidenced by the following diagram.

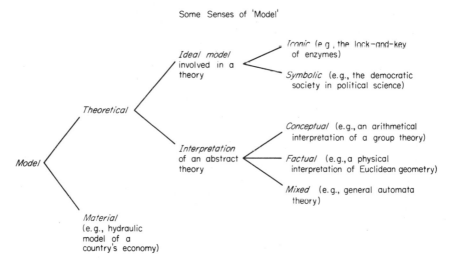

Some Senses of 'Model'

(From Bunge, 1967. Vol. 1, p. 42.).

Material models are real systems that instantiate the principles of a theory. The majority of models are theoretical rather than real, and Bunge divides theoretical models into two classes: *ideal* models and *interpretations*. We have been concerned with interpretations of abstract theories in the text. *Conceptual* models, as interpretations of abstract systems, were defined in

Note 10.1. *Factual* models result when an abstract system is given nonformal interpretation, i.e., (Bunge, 1967), when "every primitive becomes a nonformal predicate—e.g., a concept standing for some physical property or other [p. 418]." *Mixed* models occur in those theories "some predicates of which represent real (or presumably real) properties whereas the remaining properties are given no factual or empirical interpretation [p. 419]." These nonfactual, nonempirical variables are given a conceptual (i.e., mathematical) interpretation. Bunge (1967, Vol. 1) sees mixed-model theories as representing a rather advanced state of scientific development:

> A small but rapidly increasing set of factual theories are *mixed models* characterized by the definite predominance of conceptually interpreted variables over factually interpreted primitives. Among such semi-interpreted systems we recognize: (1) information theory, which can be applied to open systems of any kind, from radars to organisms; (2) the fundamental theory of servomechanisms, which is the same for electrical and for mechanical automatic control devices; (3) network theory, which can be applied to electric circuits and mechanical vibrating systems alike. All three theories can in turn be subsumed under a general black box theory in which the most general relation among an input function $I(t)$ and an output function $O(t)$ is hypothesized and worked out. In such a theory t is the only factually interpreted primitive: in fact, it stands for time. The input I and the output O are noncommittal symbols interpreted only as numerical variables (conceptual interpretation), but with no fixed factual meaning. The incomplete interpretation that characterizes mixed models is a source of their generality—as well as of their low testability. And the fact that they can be interpreted (applied) in so many different ways shows that law formulas belonging to different fields may be formally identical [pp. 419–420].

Ideal models, on the other hand, are part of the hypothesis of a theory and refer to idealized entities or processes or analogies. These are nonempirical models essentially contained in the theoretical statements. Ideal models are equally a problem for the meaning of theoretical terms if the upward seepage doctrine is accepted.

Turner (1967), referring primarily to interpretive models, distinguishes between *formal* and *structural* models. "The logician tends to defind a formal model as that by which any set of valid sentences of a theory are satisfied or represented by another set of entities which are the realization of the theory (Tarski, 1941; Suppes, 1957) [p. 237]." *Formal* models are representations, but they are not committed to any specific interpretability in the observation language. Structural models are those that "represent" in the observational language. According to Turner (1967), "A structural model, therefore, is taken to be one such that not only is it a realization of a theory, but the realization is such that some of its nonlogical terms are interpretable in an existential medium different from that of the thing modeled. By 'existential medium' I mean some uniquely classified domain of predicates in the observation language [p. 238]." The only formal models Turner finds in psychology are those formalizations of mathematical learning theory that have achieved systematic axiomatization. All other models, such as those in neurophysiological theory, are alleged to be structural.

Whether or not Turner's breakdown is helpful remains to be seen. Apparently, the basis for his distinction is Bunge's classification of general black box theorizing into phenomenological and representational types of theories. The "formal" models Turner distinguished pertain to phenomenological black box theories that do not make any ontological claims about the "contents" of the black box. These theories merely relate input and output variables without specifying the structural nature of the black box that actually does the relating. Representational theories, which employ structural models, do attempt to specify the internals of the black box, and thus these models have ontological implications. Turner thus seemed to follow the upward seepage doctrine of meaning, because he conflated ontological status with a representation in the "observation language." If this blunder is avoided (since existential status has nothing to do with observability), some distinction between models for phenomenological and representational theories may prove useful. But that distinction will have to be drawn very differently from Turner's.

Note 10.4.   We do need to pause long enough to mention Pierre Duhem's famous contention, later taken up by Quine, that the testing of a scientific proposition can never conclusively cause its rejection in the event that a falsification occurs. As a revolutionary conventionalist who opposes the cumulative record, growth-by-accumulation model of scientific progress, Duhem was well aware of the existence of scientific revolutions and the fact-correcting nature of theoretical science. As a skeptical justificationist, he used this to argue against positive justificationism. But he also advanced a skeptical argument against the received view account of testing and assessment, an argument that denied the possibility of instant rational assessment. Duhem's contention was that we can never prove that a theory is wrong on the basis of a falsification resulting from an experimental test. We can never conclusively reject a theory, because we can always make sufficient adjustments to the theory and to our background knowledge such that any experimental result will remain compatible with the theory. There can never be an *"experimentum crucis,"* a crucial experiment that decides once and for all that a theory is to be rejected. Thus Duhem argued against instant rational assessment procedures by contending that no test or experiment is sufficient to compel rejection of a theory. The reason that this is so stems *not* from the testing procedure per se, but rather from the fact that no hypothesis is tested *in isolation.* To test one hypothesis, one must presuppose many others; when a refutation occurs, all that can be concluded is that there is an *inconsistency*. According to Duhem (1954):

> In sum, the physicist can never subject an isolated hypothesis to experimental test, but only a whole group of hypotheses, when the experiment is in disagreement with his predictions, what he learns is that at least one of the hypotheses constituting this group is unacceptable and ought to be modified; but the experiment does not designate which one should be changed....
>
> People generally think that each one of the hypotheses employed in physics can be taken in isolation, checked by experiment, and then, when many varied tests have established its validity, given a definitive place in the system of physics. In reality, this is not the case. Physics is not a machine which lets itself be taken apart; we cannot try each piece in isolation and, in order to adjust it, wait until its solidity has been carefully checked. Physical science is a system that must be taken as a whole; it is an organism in which one part cannot be made to function except when the parts that are most remote from it are called into play, some more so than others, but all to some degree [pp. 187–188].

Duhem's argument is thus an argument against the justificationist goal of a theory of instant rational assessment. All that need be emphasized in this context is that many sophisticated logical empiricists are now willing to entertain Duhem's thesis as part of a "liberalized" empiricism (see Hempel, 1970, p. 161), yet they seem not to realize the implications this has for "confirmation theory."

Note 10.5.   There have been a few proposals made concerning how theories could gain "meaning." There are a number of theorists, critical of the "deductivist" account of theories, who wish to bolster it with one or another source of meaning. For example, Mary Hesse (1970) has argued that the standard account of theories can handle neither the inferences to prediction we normally find justifiable nor the meanings of theoretical terms. Her solution to both problems (which she sees as related) is found in *analogy*. With regard to the problem of analogical meaning in theories, Hesse (1970) reasoned that:

> It may be doubted whether we wish to identify a theoretical predicate such as "mass" of a molecule or electron with "mass" of a macroscopic particle. On the other hand I think it has been correct to say that "mass" cannot be simply equivocal without destroying the possibility of theoretical inference. What we need to reconstruct is a notion of analogical meaning of the word "mass" in the two domains, where "analogical" is used as a middle term between "univocal" and "equivocal," as in some Thomist philosophy. "Mass" is not always used "in the same sense" when predicated of different systems, but it is not on the other hand a pun when it is used of positrons, neutrons, quasars, and the like. The problem of determining how far the meaning of "mass" can be extended analogically and the problem of deciding what analogical inferences are

justifiable are closely related. Predicates can be stretched just as far as analogical argument remains justifiable, and conversely. How far this is would have to be decided by looking at the whole complex of evidence in all domains in which the predicate is applied [pp. 175-176].

This approach would provide a source of meaning for theoretical terms *provided* we had a theory of analogy that could indeed tell us how far "analogical arguments *do* remain 'justifiable.'" Unfortunately Hesse merely takes the existence of such analogical inference for granted in arguing against the adequacy of the standard account, and she provides no positive theory of analogy that will tell one how far analogies can be extended. Hence she has no theory of theoretical meaning at all, only a possible location of a source of meaning, in analogy.

Precisely the same argument is devastating to her earlier contention that "the deductive model of explanation should be *modified* and *supplemented* by a view of theoretical explanation as metaphoric redescription of the domain of the explanandum" (Hesse, 1966, p. 170-171). Although this may be true, no one—least of all Hesse—has a theory of metaphor adequate to the task of explicating how explanation could be "metaphoric redescription." The point remains: We need adequate theoretical accounts of the nature and function of metaphor and analogy before these concepts can be of use in pointing out and then supplementing (or replacing) the standard account of theories and explanations. Hesse's intent is laudable, but the achievements thus far are nil.

Note 10.6.   This contention was recently expressed in an enthusiastic, if slightly misleading, manner by Rescher (1970). After asking the rhetorical question of what sorts of things can be explained, he answered:

> "Any and all facts whatsoever." The conceivable subjects of explanation therefore exhibit an enormous, indeed a limitless variety. The properties and states of virtually anything, any and all occurrences and events, the behavior and doings of people, indeed every aspect of "what goes on in the world," can be regarded as appropriate objects of explanation. And here "the world" can be taken in the very widest sense, including not only the physical universe, but also the "world of mathematics" and so on [pp. 3-4].

This is, to say the least, an optimistic statement. Something it glosses over completely is that the covering-law model can only handle *singular* explananda. This was explicitly recognized by Hempel and Oppenheim in Hempel (1965):

> Our analysis will be restricted to the explanation of particular events, i.e., to the case where the explanandum, E, is a singular sentence. . . . that is not a matter of free choice: the precise rational reconstruction of explanation as applied to

general regularities presents peculiar problems for which we can offer no solution at present [p. 273].

One would expect that this rather severe limitation would have been acknowledged and that considerable effort would have been expended to overcome it. For this limitation means that the covering-law approach has no model of the explanation of *laws;* it is adequate for "low-level" explanation-by-instantiation only and cannot address the higher level explanation of theories or laws. Yet this drastic limitation has rarely been acknowledged at all and then only accorded passing mention (the quotation above [except for the first sentence] is footnote material!).

The examples that Hempel and his colleagues presented of paradigmatic covering-law explanations reflect this deficiency. They were all drawn from "everyday" physics such as instances of sticking lids and cracked radiator blocks, and *theoretical* physics is never discussed at all. The paradigms of explanation were drawn solely from common sense and *never* from genuine physical theory. This led Radnitzky (1970) to comment:

> That this particular piece of ice floats on water is "explained" by producing a syllogism whose major clause is the statement that all pieces of ice float on water. Of course the pattern produced in this way fits the D–N-model. The question is whether it is also an example of what one would consider an explanation if one is unbiased by LE's model. To us it appears that the example looks more like a logistic travesty of idle-running small-talks: A says "Look, this piece of ice floats on water" and B rejoins with a resigned shrug of the shoulders: "Sure, they all do." Like Monsieur Jourdain in Moliere's comedie-ballet Le Bourgeois Gentilhomme, who with the help of the philosophy master discovers that he had been talking in prose for all his life, the person who is impressed by the examples offered by LE will discover that, whenever he has rejoined the question why something behaved in a certain way with the comment that all entities of that kind behave this way, he had been producing an explanation sketch [p. 169].

Radnitzky also proposes the interesting hypothesis that the covering-law model, as an explanation of individual events, is really a theory of *historical* explanation.

Note 10.7.   Hempel illustrated this by reference to an ambiguity in the arguments constituting statistical systematizations. The problem, which is the ambiguity, is that for each explanatory argument with statistical premises (of the form shown in Fig. 10.3), one can construct an argument of parallel form, *with equally true or confirmed premises,* that will (statistically) explain the *nonoccurrence* of the explanandum. One can statistically "explain" both the occurrence and nonoccurrence of an event from arguments whose premises are equallly "true" (statistically speaking). For this (and similar) reasons,

Hempel in 1962 abandoned completely the earlier Hempel and Oppenheim adequacy requirement (R4) that the explanans must be *true* for an explanation to be valid. His reasoning was that:

> The vague idea of correctness can be construed in two different ways, both of which are of interest and importance for the logical analysis of science: namely, as truth in the semantical sense, which is independent of any reference to time or to evidence; or as confirmation by the available relevant evidence—a concept which is clearly time dependent. We will therefore distinguish between true explanations, which meet the requirement of truth for their explanans, and explanations that are more or less well confirmed by a given body of evidence (e.g., by the total evidence available). These two concepts can be introduced as follows:
>
> First, we define a potential explanation (of deductive–nomological form) as an argument of the form which meets all the requirements indicated earlier, except that the statements forming its explanans and explanandum need not be true. But the explanans must still contain a set of sentences, $L_1, L_2, \ldots, L_r$, which are lawlike, i.e., which are like laws except for possibly being false. Sentences of this kind will also be called nomic, or nomological, statements.
>
> Next, we say that a given potential explanation is more or less highly confirmed by the evidence in question. If the explanation is formulated in a formalized languaged for which an adequate quantitative concept of degree of confirmation or of inductive probability is available, we might identify the probability of the explanation relative to e with the probability of the explanans relative to e.
>
> Finally, by a true explanation we understand a potential explanation with true explanans—and hence also with true explanandum [pp. 102–103].

Thus the explicandum to which Hempel shifted his attention in this article is that of *potential explanation*, and this concept is inextricably intertwined with the further explicandum, *confirming evidence*. The problems of explanation merge directly into those of inductive logic.

Note 10.8.   In his title essay, Hempel (1965) distinguished three models of explanation. The first is the deductive–nomological pattern discussed in the text. The second is the inductive–statistical (I–S) pattern discussed in this section. Here the key feature is that the explanandum cannot be deduced from the explanans because of the statistical nature of the laws involved. The third model is deductive–statistical (D–S). This model received only brief discussion and occurs only infrequently in science. It is the case where a deductive conclusion follows from a statistical argument solely in virtue of the mathematics of probability. In Hempel's words (1965), these explanations

> involve the deduction of a statement in the form of a statistical law from an explanans that contains indispensably at least one law or theoretical principle of

statistical form. The deduction is effected by means of the mathematical theory of statistical probability, which makes it possible to calculate certain derivative probabilities (those referred to in the explanandum) on the basis of other probabilities (specified in the explanans) which have been empirically ascertained or hypothetically assumed. What a D–S explanation accounts for is thus always a general uniformity expressed by a presumptive law of statistical form [p. 381].

Because these cases are rather rare, the text ignores them entirely.

Note 10.9.   At this point, it becomes clear that the research program within logical empiricism concerned with the problem of explanation has become submerged by the rival program of constructing an inductive logic. That is, research on explanation has now become a by-product of research on inductive inference (confirmation theory). Research on explanation is no longer *internally* directed by refinements and developments within the D–N model of explanation but is instead *externally* directed by developments within the separate program of confirmation theory. The "maneuver space" (as Radnitzky used the term) of the research program for explanation has shrunk to zero; there is nowhere left to turn within the domain of explanation. At this point, everything in explanation awaits the successful development of confirmation theory; there is nothing else left to do.

This in a sense explains the tremendous boom in the research program of confirmation theory; virtually everything else in the neojustificationist program hinges upon a successful confirmation theory. All other research programs, empirical significance, explanations, unified science, and reductionism, etc. have gradually led to blind alleys—the maneuver space has successively shrunk to zero in each case—and the only thing left to do is work on confirmation theory. Indeed, the program in explanation stagnated, being reduced to covering only the deterministic explanation of singular statements, until Hempel in 1962 had the insight to apply to explanation the probabilistic approach aready well "established" in confirmation theory. But now, without a viable confirmation theory, the best that can be expected of the schema of probabilistic explanation is that it tells whether a given explanans constitutes a potential explanation. No stronger statement can be made unless confirmation theory can be developed. In the event that no confirmation theory is forthcoming, the covering-law model of explanation dead-ends at deterministic deductive accounts of singular explananda.

Note 10.10.   Rescher (1970) put his finger on one reason:

Some writers have felt that an explanation cannot possibly be satisfactory if the logical link between explanans and explanandum is not airtight, and so are not prepared to recognize probabilistic explanations as truly scientific. The considerations involved in this issue will presently be canvassed in considerable detail, and a justification will be provided for the position which has been taken rather dogmatically at this juncture [p. 21].

Somewhat later, discussing the downfall of causal explanations with the stochastic revolution in physics, he elaborated this contention (1970):

> So deep-rooted did this way of looking at explanation come to be, that the stochastic revolution of turn-of-the-century physics seemed for a long time to leave it to all appearances unaffected. Various important twentieth-century students of science, including Rudolf Carnap, Norman Campbell, Karl R. Popper, and Herbert Feigl gave continued and powerful support to the deductive view of explanation. Perhaps its most elaborate and painstaking formulation was given as late as 1948, in an important article by C. G. Hempel and P. Oppenheim, where however there is an explicit, although unemphatic, recognition of its limitations. Adherence to the deductive conception of explanation continued well into the present century.
>
> Only since the 1940's, with the fading influence of logical positivism, so heavily imbued with nineteenth-century conceptions, have statistical explanations come to be recognized as deserving not only a measure of acceptance but almost a place of prominence. At last a state of theoretical affairs was realized which developments in physics since the turn of the century rendered appropriate and indeed inevitable. (Not that die-hard support of the exclusivity of the deductive concept of explanation cannot be found at the present writing!) However, a dogmatic insistence that only deductive accounts are to qualify as explanations flies in the face of historical experience. At various junctures, scientists have been inclined to insist that explanations cannot transgress certain limits. The sphere of proscribed explanatory instrumentalities has included such items as action at a distance, creation *ex nihilo*, and noncausal processes. Because of the repeated failure of such limiting restrictions, there has been a marked decline of *a priorism* in regard to scientific explanation: in the face of modern developments in science, people are increasingly disinclined to say that an explanation cannot proceed this or that way. (Even in psychology there is now a notably lessened tendency to dismiss parapsychological findings out of hand as a matter of "general principles.") [pp. 127–128].

The position Rescher is arguing against, which claims that *all* explanation, even statistical explanation, is deductive in character is exemplified in the same volume in which Hempel presented the new "liberalization." Consider May Brodbeck's (1962) claim that "From statistical generalizations, we do not deduce 'with probability' that a certain event will occur, rather we deduce exactly the relative frequency or 'probability' with which an event will occur in a certain group." And earlier on the same page, "Either the explanation is deductive or else it does not justify what it is said to explain. [p. 239]."

Note 10.11.   Considering this loosening of the bonds between explanation and fact, it is not surprising that some theorists would go so far as to deny that explanations are (pace Hempel) *arguments* that marshal the weight of evidence in favor of a conclusion. In a detailed examination of the nature of statistical explanation, Wesley Salmon (1970) advanced a Reichenbachian interpretation of explanation "as a set of probability statements, qualified by certain provisos, plus a statement specifying the compartment to which the explanandum event belongs [p. 221]." This issue that divides Hempel and Salmon with regard to statistical explanation concerns whether the relation between explanans and explanandum is one of *probability* or of *statistical relevance*. Hempel chose the former, and Salmon, in opting for the latter, introduced yet another "type" of explanation: *statistical relevance* (or S–R) explanation. In S–R explanation one does not draw a conclusion from premises; rather, one partitions "reference classes" into subclasses having specifiable probabilities, and this knowledge is used for practical decision making. According to Salmon (1970):

> We may think of an explanation as an answer to a question of the form, "Why does this x which is a member of A have the property B?" The answer to such a question consists of a partition of the reference class A into a number of subclasses, all of which are homogeneous with respect to B, along with the probabilities of B within these subclasses. In addition, we must say which of the members of the partition contains our particular x. More formally, an explanation of the fact that x, a member of A, is a member of B would go as follows:
>
> $$P(A. C_1, B) = p_1$$
> $$P(A. C_2, B) = p_2$$
>
> .
>
> .
>
> .
>
> $$P(A. C_n, B) = p_n$$
> $A. C_1, A. C_2, \ldots, A. C_n$ is a homogeneous partition of
>   A with respect to B,
> $P_i = P_j$ only if $i = j$, and
> $x \epsilon A. C_k$.

With Hempel, I regard an explanation as a linguistic entity, namely, a set of statements, but unlike him, I do not regard it as an argument. On my view, an explanation is a set of probability statements, qualified by certain provisos, plus a statement specifying the compartment to which the explanandum event belongs. ...

In my view, we must establish by inductive inference probability statements, which I regard as statements about limiting frequencies. But, when we come to apply this probability knowledge to single events, we procure a weight which functions just as Carnap has indicated—as a fair betting quotient or as a value to be used in computing an expectation of utility. Consequently, I maintain, in the context of statistical explanation of individual events, we do not need to try to establish the explanandum as the conclusion of an inductive argument; instead, we need to establish the weights that would appropriately attach to such explanandum events for purposes of betting and other practical behavior. That is precisely what the partition of the reference class into homogeneous subclasses achieves: it establishes the correct weight to assign to *any* member of A with respect to its being a B [pp. 221–222].

Salmon's account is based upon an examination of Hempel's (1965) and the construction of counterexamples that are clear cases of "explanations" that violate one or another of the requirements that Hempel has specified. Carnap's *requirement of total evidence* (adopted by Hempel in 1962) and Hempel's later *requirement of maximal specificity* bear the brunt of Salmon's attack, and his counterexamples show that these "requirements" do not hold in certain situations. His positive program stems from inductive logic and can be summarized in the statement that "the relation between explanans and explanandum would seem to be a degree of confirmation statement, and not an argument with premises and conclusions in the usual sense" (Salmon, 1970, p. 181).

Salmon knew well that an interpretation of explanation in terms of statistical relevance and practical betting behavior does violence to the usual notion of explanation. This was his reply (1970):

One might ask on what grounds we can claim to have characterized explanation. The answer is this. When an explanation (as herein explicated) has been provided, we know exactly how to regard any A with respect to the property B. We know which ones to bet on, which to bet against, and at what odds. We know precisely what degree of expectation is rational. We know how to face uncertainty about an A's being a B in the most reasonable, practical, and efficient way. We know every factor that is relevant to an A having property B. We know exactly the weight that should have been attached to the prediction that this A will be a B. We know all of the regularities (universal or statistical) that are relevant to our original question. What more could one ask of an explanation [p. 222]?

Just how many theorists would be satisfied with modeling science after the racetrack is hard to tell, but I suspect that few would come so close to equating explaining with gambling as does Salmon.

Regardless of whether S–R explanation is or is not central to statistical explanation, two features of Salmon's account require comment. First, as he explicitly acknowledged, S–R systematization applies *only* to explanation by means of empirical laws. "For all that has been said in this paper, theoretical explanation—explanation that makes use of scientific theories in the fullest sense of the term—may have a logical structure entirely different from that of statistical explanation [p. 225]." Salmon hoped that his treatment of S–R explanation would "provide a point of departure" for the study of theoretical explanation. Whether one can gain any understanding of explanation by such a building-block approach is indeed a moot point. And considering the theoretical involvement of all "levels" of explanation, it is not at all clear that explanation by empirical laws can be treated independently of theoretical explanation. The problem of the nomic force of laws is relevant to this (see the discussion of causality and lawfulness in the text).

The second feature to notice concerns the abdication of the research program concerned with explanation in favor of the research program of confirmation theory. Problems of explanation are now transferred to the problem of confirmation theory. The maneuver space within explanation has shrunk to zero, and nothing remains for one to do in explanation until confirmation theory is developed. Like Hempel, Salmon must await developments in confirmation theory before any further headway can be made in the theory of explanation. With explanation as with the other substantive research programs of the logical "-isms," everything hinges, sooner or later, upon the success of the research program of confirmation theory. Should the latter program fail, almost everything in the received view account would fail with it. No wonder, then, that there has recently been an enormous increase in articles, conferences, monographs, and books devoted to inductive logic and confirmation theory.

Note 10.12. Rescher concluded, upon the basis of an examination of indeterministic discrete state systems (such as those that physical theory postulates at the subatomic particle level), that explanation has limitations that scientific understanding does not. That is, if explanation is assumed to be what the covering-law model explicates, then there are indeterministic discrete state systems in which one can "know" or "understand" all the relevant variables and parameters and yet be incapable of either explanation, prediction, or retrodiction. Consider the system described in Fig. 10.5, in which certain "states" follow each other according to the probabilities in the matrix. Even if we are given a *complete* history of this system except for one "unknown" state, we cannot (even probabilistically) fill in the blank with either state S_1 or S_2. That is, if we are given the series:

$$\ldots S_2S_1S_1S_2 \text{—} S_1S_2S_1S_1 \ldots$$

We cannot fill in the blank. If we are given that it was in fact S_2, we cannot "explain" this fact; and given the symmetry between explanation, prediction,

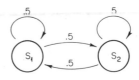

FIG. 10.5.

and retrodiction, we cannot predict or retrodict either. We can know or understand everything about the system, but we cannot explain it.

The interesting thing to note in this argument is that Rescher never stopped to consider the possibility that explanation might be something other than what Hempel has said it is. In good normal science manner, Rescher took the covering-law model of explanation for granted and assumed that because it has limitations, explanation in science also has limitations. Now this conclusion may hold, but it will require a defense that no one has yet given it. What one may conclude in the meantime is that Rescher has shown a limitation inherent in the covering-law model of explanation.

Note 10.13.   The classic conflict in the literature is between theorists who argue that laws are "nothing but" general statements and therefore are merely conventions and those who argue that they are "something more"— specifically, material mode *rules of inference.* The latter approach is gaining adherents among theorists who reject empiricism. Let us examine the conception of laws of nature as "season inference tickets" or as licenses sanctioning inferences.

Such a view considers universal, general statements as material mode rather than formal mode rules—as P-rules rather than L-rules, in Carnap's terminology. In its strongest form, this view claims that there are P-rules of inference, *more fundamental than the general statements derived from them,* that are implicit in both common sense and scientific discourse. The rules involved authorize what Sellars (1958) calls "intra-language" moves. Consider a lemon: *If* one knows that an object is a lemon, *then* one has a right to infer that it is yellowish, round, sour, and the appropriate size, etc. One is entitled to say, "*All* lemons have the following characteristics...." This example, although contrived, highlights the special character of these rules, which is to *sanction inferences.* On this view, there is a very important connection between *knowledge* and *rules;* one can determine whether a thing actually is an X-kind *only* by reference to the rules that specify the criteria for being an X. In this respect, the view under consideration acknowledges that as Körner (1966) makes clear, correspondence rules betweeen experience and empirical predicates are absolutely necessary. The striking claim of this view is that those correspondence rules are rules of inference.

The alleged problem with such a view is the following. Whether or not these P-rules are correct must somehow depend on 'empirical' facts. Presumably, a rule is correct if and only if the world is such that by following the rule we reach true conclusions about the world. Alexander (1958) puts the predicament this entails quite succinctly:

> Thus instead of saying that a general statement is universally true, we say that the corresponding rule of inference always enables us to reach true conclusions

> from true premises; instead of saying that most ϕ's are ψ's, we say that the rule of inference (x)(ϕx$\supset$$\psi$x) usually enables us to reach a true conclusion when we are given a true premise of the form ϕx. But if this is accepted, it becomes obvious that one of the advantages we had hoped for has been lost.... We now have the general statement that in all cases the use of the rule of inference enables us to arrive at true conclusions. So we are no better off [pp. 311–312].

The problem is that we still do not know whether or not the premises are true unless there are general statements that are *not* rules of inference. For if all general statements in science are rules of inference requiring empirical support, then we have no basis at all for saying, as we ordinarily do, that general statements are *true* (i.e., *proven*). Alexander continues (1958):

> But if this demand [of justification] is extended to *all* rules of inference, it makes nonsense of deduction. If it is applied only to nondeductive rules, it completely spoils the analogy that is being drawn between these so-called material rules of inference and the genuine (deductive) rules of inference. The one positive conclusion that one can draw from the statement of this impasse is that here also the introduction of the idea of material rules of inference raises more difficulties than it solves [p. 315].

Now there are at least two replies that "inference ticket" theorists can make to such a seemingly devastating attack upon their position. The first we mention but do not explore. Is there, as Alexander claims, so much sense to deduction to begin with? There are two things to note here: First, as we have seen, the logic of explanation has been liberalized to include inductive inference as well as deduction. This removes the centrality of deduction. Second, as we saw in Chapter 3, *strictly speaking,* deduction does not apply to the natural sciences *at all.* The H–D explanatory framework, as N. R. Hanson so constantly emphasized, is the logic of the finished science report, of the finished theory. But such a state of affairs never has been and never will be obtained. Insofar as the H–D framework is utilized in science, it requires lenient "misinterpretation" of its underlying assumptions, as Körner (1966) has shown. Indeed, he has shown more; not only are *general* statements inferences, but *singular* empirical statements are also. They are inferences from perceptual experiences to empirical "data."

Actually, what Alexander is requesting is an authoritative foundation for empirical knowledge. The argument is that since these intralanguage or P-rules "merely" *authorize* inferences, they cannot in themselves *justify* any basic premises. Without justified premises, we could never obtain justified (true) conclusions. Without true conclusions, we could never have knowledge of the real world. Once the justificationist metatheory that enshrines the foundation picture of knowledge is seen to be incorrect, the motivation for this argument disappears entirely.

The second reply to Alexander's argument concerns the role that law statements play in scientific explanation. The force of this reply is its claim that the received view theorist is not clear on what such statements do, or how they function, in theoretical 'explanation.' Specifically, general statements need not be true even though they allow one to arrive at factually true conclusions. Sellars wrote (1963):

> My contention, then, is that the widespread picture of theories which equates theoretical explanation with the derivation of empirical laws is a mistake which cannot be corrected by extending the term 'law' to include a spectrum of inductively established statistical uniformities ranging from 100 per cent to 50–50. Positively put, my contention is that theories explain laws by explaining why the objects of the domain in question obey the laws that they do to the extent that they do [p. 123].

Consider the function that inductive inference is alleged to perform in leading to scientific knowledge. The point of induction is to give us "a rational grip on *unobserved* or, better, in a suitably broad sense, *unexamined* cases. . ." (Sellars, 1958, p. 291). Later, Sellars wrote (1964):

> I have long defended the view that the law-like statements which it is the object of nomological induction to establish are principles of inference and that the problem of induction cannot be solved without this insight. In particular, I have rejected the view that law-like statements are to be construed as universally quantified material implications (with or without a pragmatic commentary) of the form, abstractly represented,
>
> $$(x)\ Ax \rightarrow Bx$$
>
> Rather I conceive them to have the form
>
> that x is A P-implies that x is B [p. 212].

In the same vein (1958):

> The point of this distinction is that while one does not inductively establish that A P-entails B by armchair reflection on the *antecedent* 'meanings' of 'A' and 'B', to establish by induction that A P-entails B is to *enrich* (and, perhaps, otherwise modify) the use of these terms in such wise that to 'understand' what one now 'means' by 'A' and 'B' *is* to know that A P-entails B.
>
> If to establish by induction that A causes B were to establish that (in all probability) (x) Ax $\supset$ Bx, perhaps as a member of a set of inductive conclusions, there would be little reason to say that to establish by induction that A causes B is to decide on empirical grounds to *give a new use* to 'A' and 'B'. If, however, it is, as I am arguing, a matter of deciding to adopt a new principle of inference, then there is every reason to say that to establish by induction that A causes B is to modify the use of 'A' and 'B' and, indeed, to modify it in such a way that these

terms can properly be said to have acquired a new 'meaning'.... The motto of the age of science might well be: *Natural philosophers have hitherto sought to understand 'meanings'; the task is to change them....* Instead of exploring implications within a *status quo* of 'meanings,' one is reasoning one's way into a decision to change the *status quo* [pp. 287–288].

In short, to accept a statement *as* a law of nature is *to be prepared to infer,* with respect to the indefinite number of cases that may conceivably arise, that the state of affairs described by that statement does obtain.

The logic of modalities is to be treated similarly (Sellars, 1958):

To make first hand use of these expressions is to be about the business of *explaining* a state of affairs, or *justifying* an assertion. Thus, even if to state that p entails q is, in a legitimate sense, to state that something is the case, the primary use of 'p entails q' is not to state that something is the case, but to explain *why q,* or justify the assertion *that q.* The idea that the world can, in principle, be so described that the description contains no modal expression is of a piece with the idea that the world can, in principle, be so described that the description contains no prescriptive expression [p. 283].

Sellars's conclusion on causality (1958) expresses this theme:

Once the development of human language left the stage when linguistic changes had *causes,* but not *reasons,* and man acquired the ability to reason about his reasons, then, and this is a logical point about having the ability to reason about reasons, his language came to permit the formulation of certain propositions which, incapable of proof or disproof by empirical methods, draw, in the heart of *language militant,* a picture of *language triumphant.* Kant's conception that reason is characterized by certain regulative ideals contains a profound truth which empiricism has tended to distort into the empirical psychology of the scientific enterprise [p. 307].

Thus the conception of laws of nature as rules of inference is intimately related to the logic of modalities, and the claim that the "inference ticket" theorist makes is that the thesis of extensionality and the doctrine of physicalism must be abandoned. The attempt to shave off the modal force of explanations utilizing laws of nature is as futile as the attempt to shave off the transempirical aspects of scientific theory via Ramsey or Craig procedures.

The compatibility of this conception of laws in science with the views argued for in Chapters 6 through 8 is obvious. It is, in effect, a nonjustificational approach to the nature and function of the laws of nature. It is thus ironic that this liberalized approach is accepted by some sophisticated neojustificationists. But once again we have a critical reformulation of a classic position that is a "necessary refinement" from an internal perspective and a devasting refutation from an external perspective.

Note 10.14.   There is a sleight-of-hand maneuver in Rescher's abandonment of causality that should not escape one's attention. The Humean
problem of causality has been and remains that of *avoiding* necessity; there
can be no modal force or necessary connection if all there is to causality is
constant conjunction or regular succession. Hume argued against any
necessity in nature; his contemporary advocates argue against necessity in the
language of science. Scientific explanations must not impute any necessity to
the occurrences they describe. The classic Kantian opposition to Humean
analysis countered with the claim that the human mind imposed causality
upon nature as a condition of human knowledge. For the Kantian, human
understanding requires the imputation of causality, not nature; causality is
mind dependent, the result of our imputation upon experience because of the
way the mind works.

Now Rescher's position is that causality is "nothing but" lawfulness.
However, in endorsing an "inference ticket" approach to the nature of laws,
with the thesis that lawfulness is a mind-dependent imputation of nomic
necessity, the overthrow of causality has done nothing but *relocate* the odious
necessity and modal force that Humeans abhor. Rescher followed Hume in
abandoning causality, but he has followed Kant in endorsing the inescapability of necessity in scientific understanding. Rescher's "advance" in
overthrowing causality is certainly no victory for the Humean position.

11 Historical Trends: Development of Nonjustificational Frameworks

Concern with metatheoretical foundations of philosophy and science is recent. Two decades ago one would have had difficulty finding an audience prepared to listen to the idea that *science* had such "disreputable" aspects lurking in its background. The first systematic study of metatheoretical concerns did not receive institutionally recognized and sanctioned form until the 1960s (Note 11.1). Indeed, metatheoretical inquiry is so new that we are as yet only dimly aware of areas and issues that may evolve sufficiently that we can construct normal science "puzzles" out of them. The four problem areas discussed in Chapter 1, around which this book is organized, merely look promising in that respect; they are by no means definitive of the area. *Systematic* inquiry into metatheoretical questions is quite recent, yet metatheoretical concerns have occupied philosophers since the dawn of reflective thought. The fascinating, probably unanswerable, question remains: Why has systematic study appeared only so recently?

Many answers suggest themselves. The relationship between metaphysics and metatheory is quite obscure, so it is possible that theorists assimilated the problems and issues of the latter domain to those of the former. Because metaphysics has had a bad press, metatheoretical questions could well have been ignored because of their assimilation to metaphysics. One significant factor that played a role in suppressing such inquiry is the all-pervasive character of the dominant justificationist metatheory. Having taken an explicit stand on some metatheoretical issues and having supplied implicit formulations on others, it created the impression that there is no need for such inquiry, as everybody presupposes the same (seemingly the only) framework. Through the years, justificationist terminology and convention have permeated ordinary language and thinking to such an extent that it is literally hard for one to conceive of nonjustificational conceptions of, e.g., knowledge and rationality. Western "common sense" appears thoroughly committed to justificationism. The considerations that lead one to reject justificationism thus also lead one to reject much of common sense reasoning.

Be that as it may, the dual issue of the origins of metatheoretical inquiry on a systematic basis and of the historical development of nonjustificational points of view remains. Can we say anything informative about either? We lack the historical data to even begin to tackle the matter of the origins of metatheoretical inquiry and the recency of systematic concern with such issues. This is an interesting issue, and I assume that it will be taken up in the future.

But the other matters, concerned with tracing the development of extant metatheoretical alternatives to justificationism, is far easier to come to grips with. Although he did not know it at the time, in developing the systematic philosophy presented in *The logic of scientific discovery*, Karl Popper was laying the groundwork for the first consistently nonjustificational metatheory. Popper's systematic position was developed in opposition to the philosophy of logical positivism, then a paradigm exemplar of justificationist philosophy. At first, Popper's position was also justificationist in nature. But as the system developed, and as the criticism of justificationist tenets improved, Popper and his students gradually abandoned major facets of justificational thought until a reasonably consistent nonjustificational philosophy of criticism remained.

Thus if we wish to trace the development of the first nonjustificational philosophy, we must trace the intellectual biography of Popper and his associates. Let us present one somewhat fictionalized historical reconstruction now.

THE DEVELOPMENT OF A NONJUSTIFICATIONAL APPROACH FROM SOPHISTICATED NEOJUSTIFICATIONISM: POPPER'S CRITICAL FALLIBILISM

The first metatheoretical alternative to justificationism is the sophisticated falsificationism or *critical fallibilism* of K. R. Popper. In order to understand the sophisticated variant of Popper's falsificationism, we must study two earlier versions of falsificationism that, although developed by Popper in opposition to the essentials of the justificationist metatheory, were still justificationist in nature.

There are several distinct stages in Popperian thought that, following Lakatos (1968b), we may distinguish by appending a subscript after Popper's name when reference is made to a particular one. (Although these subscripts are misleading in the sense that they imply distinct, compartmentalized stages where continuity and overlap undoubtedly prevailed, they are nonetheless helpful in understanding the development of Popper's ideas *if* one does not attach more significance to them than their role as didactic aids warrants.) There are two justificationist variants of Karl Popper—Popper$_0$ and Popper$_1$. Popper$_0$ is a transitional stage in the development of Popper$_1$, and Popper$_1$ (the author of the original edition of *The logic of scientific discovery* in 1934) constantly emphasizes that Popper$_0$'s philosophy is untenable. Popper$_0$ thought that although science cannot prove conclusively, it can *disprove conclusively*. That is, for Popper$_0$, the *dogmatic falsificationist*, science cannot confirm its propositions conclusively, but it can conclusively falsify or disprove them. He is thus a "negative" variant of classic justificationism, as opposed to the usually "positive" or confirming variant. Popper$_0$ never committed anything to print; He was, if anything, merely a stage in the development of a student at Vienna beginning to become seriously interested in philosophy in the early 1920s (Note 11.2).

Popper$_1$ is much more interesting. Instead of being "dogmatic" about falsification, he is much more sophisticated; yet according to Lakatos, he still is quite "naive." Popper$_1$ is a neojustificationist falsifier rather than a confirmer. Rather than *probable* confirmation, Popper$_1$ emphasizes *conventional falsification*. As the author of *The logic of scientific discovery,* Popper realized that when theories are refuted by the facts with which they are confronted, there are inevitably scare quotes around "refuted." We decide on a priori grounds that certain outcomes will count (conclusively) as disproof of our theory. The dogmatic falsificationism of Popper$_0$ has been replaced by the *methodological falsificationism* of Popper$_1$. We cannot understand the later, more sophisticated, nonjustificational Popper$_2$, who published, e.g., *Conjectures and refutations* in 1963, without understanding these two earlier variants. Lakatos makes it clear that the *sophisticated methodological falsificationist,* Popper$_2$, must be understood developmentally (1970):

> Popper began as a dogmatic falsificationist in the 1920's; but he soon realized the untenability of this position and published nothing before he invented methodological falsificationism. This was an entirely new idea in the philosophy of science and it clearly originates with Popper, who put it forward as a solution to the difficulties of dogmatic falsificationism. Indeed, the conflict between the theses that science is both critical and fallible is one of the central problems in Popperian philosophy. While Popper offered a coherent formulation and criticism of dogmatic falsificationism, he never made a sharp distinction between naive and sophisticated falsificationism. In an earlier paper, I distinguished three Poppers: *Popper$_0$*, *Popper$_1$*, and *Popper$_2$*. Popper$_0$ is the dogmatic falsificationist, Popper$_2$ the sophisticated falsificationist. The *real* Popper developed from dogmatic to a naive version of methodological

falsificationism in the twenties; he arrived at the *'acceptance rules' of sophisticated falsification* in the fifties.... But the real Popper never abandoned his earlier (naive) *falsification rules.* He has demanded, until this day, that *'criteria of refutation* have to be laid down beforehand: it must be agreed, which observable situations, if actually observed, mean that the theory is refuted'. He still construes 'falsification' as the result of a dual between theory and observation, without another, better theory necessarily being involved. The real Popper has never explained in detail the appeal procedure by which some 'accepted basic statements' may be eliminated. Thus the real Popper consists of $Popper_1$ together with some elements of $Popper_2$ [p. 181].

Both the philosophy of $Popper_0$ and $Popper_1$ exist in various forms on the contemporary neojustificationist scene. For example, $Popper_0$'s philosophy plays a role in the methodology of some scientists (Medawar, 1967), psychologists (Turner, 1967), and philosophers (Grünbaum, 1959, 1963). More sophisticated accounts along the lines of $Popper_1$ are likewise to be found; in science, J. C. Eccles (1964) is one example; in philosophy, Grünbaum (1969). But in the main, Popper's newer, nonjustificational position is not understood. To understand this latter version of Popper, one must be clear on the essential features of $Popper_1$'s philosophy.

The central feature of $Popper_1$'s philosophy, which is *most* at variance with the later $Popper_2$, is his implicit acceptance of the justificationist's monotheoretical model of theory testing. According the $Popper_1$ a theory— to be susceptible to criticism (and hence falsification)—must be thoroughly organized within the confines of the H–D model of theories. The theory, in order to be refutable, must *forbid* states of affairs. The set of protocol statements that describe the possible worlds that the theory forbids constitutes the 'empirical content' of the theory. (This stems from Popper's reasoning that a theory, to be scientific, must specify in advance the evidence that would overthrow it; that is, the theory is empirical if it forbids certain states of affairs. Thus, if an astronomical theory said that all planets move in circular orbits, there must be *no* planets observed to move in elliptical orbits. The "empiricalness" of a theory is thus defined negatively, in terms of what it does not allow to happen.) Within the totality of this empirical content, one must distinguish a set of 'basic statements' that will serve as the potential falsifiers of the theory. These 'basic statements' must be spatiotemporally singular existential statements, for only they can negate the logically and spatiotemporally universal statements that appear in scientific generalizations. To falsify a scientific generalization couched in universal terms—e.g., "all swans are white"—one must have (only) a spatiotemporally *singular* statement that contradicts it—e.g., "Here is a black swan from Australia." Thus even though $Popper_1$ recognized the theoretical nature of observation statements, according to his model of theory testing, it must be possible to maintain a distinction between the theory level of science (which is tested) and the observation level (which provides the 'facts' that do the testing). This separation entails a monotheoretical assessment model—i.e., one in which a *single* theory is tested in isolation—because everything 'theoretical' in nature is treated as part of the theory under test. A single theory confronted by the facts is the hallmark of naive falsificationism: "Only if *the asymmetry between verification and falsification* is taken into account—that asymmetry which results from the logical relation between theories and basic statements—is it possible to avoid the pitfalls of the problem of induction" (Popper, 1959, p. 265). Lakatos summed it up this way (1968b): "According to Popper$_1$'s logic of research, if there is a clash between a low-level, 'observational' hypothesis and a higher-level theory—shown in his 'deductive model'—the theory must be rejected, eliminated from the body of science [p. 154]."

Another crucial feature of Popper$_1$'s philosophy is its reliance upon *conventional* agreement of the scientists involved in testing their theories. There are two distinct conventional aspects of the test situation in Popper$_1$'s view: the conventional nature of the 'potential falsifiers' and the conventional nature of rejecting a "theory" when it confronts falsifying "facts." The 'potential falsifiers' are conventional, because Popper$_1$'s improvement over Popper$_0$ was his recognition that 'facts' cannot be known independently of theoretical involvement—that facts are *decided upon* rather than *given*. Thus the empirical basis must be based upon the conventional agreement of the theorists involved. Now when a theory is refuted, it is refuted by the logic of *modus tollens*. But *what* is refuted—the explanatory 'theory' or the 'theoretically determined' fact? As noted above, because he works at the within-theory level of analysis, Popper$_1$ rules that it is always the theory. He holds that we adopt a methodological convention that the "facts" are accepted as *unproblematic* for the purposes of testing the *problematic* theory.

A third ingredient, related to the two conventional aspects just discussed, is Popper$_1$'s methodological prescription that a theory, once falsified (even though this falsification is conventional in nature), must be abandoned once and for all. Falsification requires, as a matter of intellectual honesty, elimination of the theory in question. This methodological rule also reappears in the later Popper$_2$ who is the author of *Conjectures and refutation*.

As a fourth and final feature of Popper$_1$'s naive falsifiability, consider the corroboration a theory receives as a result of not having been falsified by a test, i.e., as a result of surviving an earnest attempt at refutation. Popper's concept of corroboration is an *analytical* appraisal of a theory. A theory is to be accorded a positive degree of corroboration if its consequences entail a nonempty set of 'basic statements.' He later proposed a metric for the assignment of numerical values to the concept (see Popper, 1959, Appendix *ix). But the crucial feature of Popper's concept of corroboration is that it is not directly concerned with logical probability or the probability calculus and thus has nothing to do with the inductivist's concept of confirmation. Degree of corroborability is related to the (empirical) *content* of a theory, rather than to its probability. On Popper's analysis, maximal probability is associated with minimal (zero) content.

Before criticizing naive falsifiability (obliquely, by developing Popper₂'s sophisticated falsificationism), let us note in conclusion Popper₁'s famous criterion of demarcation between the sciences and the nonsciences. According to Popper in 1934, the positivists' attempts to separate science from nonscience (which they mistakenly equated with metaphysics) via the verifiability theory of meaning were misguided. For Popper₁ (as well as his later forms), many metaphysical statements are meaningful, both in their own right and within empirical science. Indeed, many principles that the positivists would have labeled as 'metaphysical' are in fact *indispensable* (at least heuristically) to science (see Watkins, 1957, 1958, 1961, 1975). Popper was thus led to search for a criterion to demarcate science from nonscience with the foreknowledge that it could not be a principle of meaning. The solution he proposed centers around the concept of falsifiability: Those theories (or propositions) are 'scientific' which are susceptible to falsification; those which cannot, even in principle, be falsified are nonscientific. Falsifiability became the hallmark of the scientific enterprise. Scientific progress was to be maximized by attempting as sincerely as possible to refute theories rather than to confirm them. One must clearly specify *in advance* the conditions under which a theory is to be surrendered, i.e., when one will admit that it has been falsified. To search only for positive evidence that does not 'test' the theory is to be unscientific and dogmatic. It is an attempt to secure a theory from criticism, to make it eternally valid, exactly as speculative metaphysicians had attempted to do. What the positivists did in their attempts to develop an inductive logic (or a confirmation theory) was to enshrine their propositions in a dogmatic manner. Such an attitude is implicit in, e.g., Reichenbach's (1938) contention that science proceeds by the successive testing and *securing* of its propositions. Once secured, a proposition is no longer questionable. Thus the positivists, quite unwittingly, enshrined exactly what they wished to avoid (dogmatism and untestability), by combining inductive logic and the verifiability theory of meaning.

CRITICAL FALLIBILISM AS AN
ALTERNATIVE TO JUSTIFICATIONISM

If justificationism is on shaky grounds because of (among other things) the problems of inductive inference, it would be wise to see if science can be interpreted as a rational endeavor without assuming that "rationality" requires any theory of *instant* rationality. The essentials of such an approach were outlined by Popper in 1934 in his *Logik der Forschung*, translated in 1959 as *The logic of scientific discovery*. Popper's research program has been the elaboration of a methodology of science that shows how rational choices are possible between competing theories despite the absence of any theory of instant rationality (such as inductive inference). It is to the development of the matatheory of the "sophisticated" falsificationism of Popper₂, which I have labeled *critical fallibilism*, that we must now turn. Although the account will have a historical character and refer to the development of Sir Karl's ideas in their context, it is not exactly accurate historically. What follows is an idealized rational reconstruction; our present need is for critical exposition, which is not always served by strict historical exposition.

Critical fallibilism, however, transcends the work of Karl Popper alone. It is better characterized as a metatheory that has developed, at the hands of both Popper and his associates, from taking seriously Popper's famous slogan, "severely test your own theories," when applied to the basic position elaborated in *Logik der Forschung*. That is, the sophisticated falsificationism of Popper₂ in the 1960s is an amalgam of criticisms of and corrections to Popper₁ that stem from both Popper's own revisions and the critical revisions of his students and associates. Among the latter, mention must be made of J. Agassi (esp. 1966b, 1968), W. W. Bartley, III (esp. 1962, 1964, 1968), P. K. Feyerabend (1962, 1965a, 1965b), I. Lakatos (1963–1964, 1968a, 1968b,1970), and J. W. N. Watkins (1957, 1958, 1961). Popper₂ himself is the author of the additions written in the late 1950s, found in the English translation of *The logic of scientific discovery*, and also of *Conjectures and refutations* (1963). In the following overview, we often attribute to Popper₂—without sufficient elaboration or explanation—feature of critical fallibilism that are the results of other philosophers' work; "Popper₂" is an abstract theorist who incorporates the essentials of critical fallibilism regardless of their actual source.

Popper₂'s philosophy of science can only be understood as an outgrowth from, and as a decisive rejection of, Popper₁'s views. Thus we must reexamine the naive falsificationism of Popper₁ as presented in 1934. Popper₁ realized that the search for a theory of instant rationality as a theory of confirmation (inductive inference) was doomed and was led to add a new twist to justificationism. Popper₁'s emphasis in the search for a theory of rational inference was not directed, as have been all other justificationist attempts, toward the *propositions* of science per se; his attempt instead was directed at the empirical test conditions that a theorist would specify, a priori, as forcing one to abandon the theory under test. Thus was born the criterion of falsifiability, which held that a theory was scientific if it were capable of being falsified by empirical tests. According to Popper₁, science is a series of duels between theories and facts; when the theory's predictions fail to accord with the facts, then the theory is falsified via the logic of *modus tollens* and must be eliminated from the body of science. Popper₁'s philosophy is based upon bold (i.e., highly falsifiable) conjectures held in check by no longer certain but still conclusive refutations. Science does not prove, but under *certain conditions* it can disprove. Naive falsificationism was every bit as justificationist in nature as $Popper_0$'s dogmatic falsificationism, *even though* $Popper_1$ realized that theories cannot by logic alone be conclusively disproved. But he assumed that it was possible to *agree* that a theory was refuted when it was confronted with 'facts' inconsistent with its predictions. Thus $Popper_1$ is at heart a conventionalist much like Duhem, as we must now indicate.

To allow falsification to reject a theory, $Popper_1$ had to have *two* logically distinguishable classes of statements in the body of science. He required a set of observational statements or 'basic propositions' to serve as the potential falsifiers of a theory. (The other set consists of the 'theoretical' statements of science.) But $Popper_1$ knew that even the basic statements are contaminated by theory and that a scientist must decide, according to Popper solely upon the basis of some convention, what statements will be regarded as 'observational.' For this task, he chose spatiotemporally singular existential statements, and they constituted a "lower" level than the theoretical terms tested. With this was born the 'empirical basis' (in scare quotes, as opposed to the empirical basis of $Popper_0$) and the crucial 'empirical content' of a theory (the possible worlds *forbidden* by the theory). Popper denoted the *nonempirical* character of this basis and content by placing the terms in inverted commas. With this we have a new demarcation criterion: A theory is scientific for $Popper_1$ if it has an 'empirical basis.'

$Popper_1$ is clear that one must separate the rejection of a theory from its refutation *in the logical analysis of the test situation*, but he instituted a *methodological rule* (another convention) that required the elimination of a theory if one of its hypotheses was falsified. Although such 'empirical' refutation does not *prove* that the refuted theory is false, its elimination from science *must* be effected (Popper, 1959):

> In general we regard an inter-subjectively testable falsification as final (provided it is well tested): this is the way in which the asymmetry between verification and falsification of theories makes itself felt. . . . A corroborative appraisal made at a later date—that is, an appraisal made after new basic statements have been added to those already accepted—can replace a positive degree of corroboration by a negative one, but not *vice versa* [p. 268].

Thus "naive falsificationism *consists exactly of the conflation of refutation and rejection (or elimination)*, and it is the thesis which is at the heart of $Popper_1$'s methodology" (Lakatos, 1968b, p. 155).

It is the decisive if only implicit rejection of this conflation that is at the heart of $Popper_2$'s philosophy. $Popper_2$ is interested primarily in growth, not refutation. This shift in emphasis appears to have come about because "he" abandoned the monotheoretical model of theory assessment in favor of a pluralistic methodology when it became obvious that the former failed to account for many features of scientific practice. The early Popper₂'s contributions to the methodology of science, aside from stimulating Feyerabend's theoretical pluralism, were directed at the *acceptance* of scientific theories. If scientific theories (or propositions) cannot be either proved, probabilified, or disproved, then how can they be criticized and assessed? Popper₂'s answer is that *only* a competing plurality of theories can be assessed, rather than a single theory in isolation, and that assessment consists in the scrutiny of inconsistencies rather than in refutations. Indeed, confirmations (of a sort) seem to play a more crucial role than most refutations. According to Lakatos (1970):

> It is not difficult to see at least two crucial characteristics common to both dogmatic and our methodological (naive) falsificationism which are clearly dissonant with the actual history of science: that (1) *a test is—or must be made— a two-cornered fight between theory and experiment so that in the final confrontation only these two face each other; and* (2) *the only interesting outcome of such confrontation is* (*conclusive*) *falsification:* '(*the only genuine*) *discoveries are refutations of scientific hypotheses*'. However, history of science suggests that (*1'*) tests are—at least—three-cornered fights between rival theories and experiment and (*2'*) some of the most interesting experiments result, *prima facie*, in confirmation rather than falsification [p. 115].

Popper's solution to the problem of acceptance (which had then become the central problem of growth) is twofold: A theory is more acceptable than a rival: (a) if it has more empirical content, i.e., forbids more possible 'observable' states of affairs; and (b) if at least some excess empirical content is subsequently corroborated. The first condition (or perhaps 'desideratum') which we have designated following Lakatos as acceptability₁, requires a theory to have more content, to "go farther" than a rival. The second condition, acceptability₂, requires that it successfully predict *novel* observational outcomes. Thus we distinguish between 'empirical content' (for acceptability₁) and 'excess empirical content' (for acceptability₂). This twofold reformulation of acceptance is in effect a reformulation of Popper's demarcation criterion. A theory is 'acceptable' or 'scientific' for a naive falsificationist like Popper₁ if it is experimentally falsifiable. Popper₂ holds a theory to be truly 'scientific' only if it leads to the discovery of novel facts. Good, *progressive* science is now demarcated from nonscience by its successful prediction of novel occurrences (that is, novelty relative to the alternative and background theories).

Now, how is falsification construed by Popper₂? Recall that the naive falsificationist considers a theory falsified by an 'observational' statement that conflicts with it (i.e., that one interprets or *agrees* to interpret as conflicting with it). But (Lakatos, 1970):

The sophisticated falsificationist regards a scientific theory T as falsified if and only if another theory T' has been proposed with the following characteristics: (1) T' has excess empirical content over T: that is, it predicts *novel* facts, that is, facts improbable in the light of, or even forbidden, by T; (2) T' explains the previous success of T, that is, all the unrefuted content of T is contained (within the limits of observational error) in the content of T'; and (3) some of the excess content of T' is corroborated [p. 116].

Again, falsification is not the main concern of the critical fallibilist. All theories are or can be falsified with little if any effort. But how can we go about saving "good" theories (known to be false in advance) without lapsing into purely conventionalist and possibly solely irrational or authoritarian stratagems? Popper's approach is only subtly removed from the conventionalism of Duhem (Lakatos, 1970):

Popper agrees with the conventionalists that theories and factual propositions can always be harmonized with the help of auxiliary hypotheses: he agrees that the problem is how to demarcate between scientific and pseudoscientific *adjustments*, between rational and irrational changes of theory. According to Popper, saving a theory with the help of auxiliary hypotheses which satisfy certain well-defined conditions represents scientific progress; but saving a theory with the help of auxiliary hypotheses which do not, represents degeneration. Popper calls such inadmissible auxiliary hypothesis *ad hoc* hypotheses, mere linguistic devices, 'conventionalist stratagems'. But then any scientific theory has to be appraised together with its auxiliary hypotheses, initial conditions, etc., and, especially, together with its predecessors so that we may see by what sort of *change* it was brought about. Then, of course, what we appraise is a *series of theories* rather than isolated *theories* [pp. 117–118].

With this strategy, the *empirical* criterion for satisfactory theories is that they produce novel 'facts.' *Growth or scientific progress thus becomes wedded to the empirical character of theories.*

But even with this radical revision of methodology (monotheoretical assessment replaced by pluralistic evaluation) and the liberalized interpretation of falsification (such that it occurs only when a "better" theory is available) leading to the two notions of acceptance just discussed, Popper himself retained some features of Popper$_1$'s philosophy. Foremost among these is that Popper retains in unchanged form Popper$_1$'s rule for theory elimination: Once falsified (but now in the liberal sense), a theory must be discarded from the body of science. This prescription, however, is inconsistent with the positive aspects of Popper$_2$'s philosophy of proliferation, as Lakatos took pains to point out. The main improvement Lakatos offered in reconstructing Popper$_2$'s philosophy is to acknowledge that criticism must not kill a theory as quickly as Popper has claimed it must. The 'dogmatism' or "tenacity" of normal science is a necessary feature of the scientific endeavor, rather than the "danger" that Popper conceives it to be (see Popper, 1972, 1974).

Return to the problem of growth in its positive aspect of the appraisal of theories. In acknowledging the two notions of acceptance noted above, the problem has shifted from Popper$_1$'s concern with when a theory is refuted to Popper$_2$'s concern with when a theory is better than its rivals when all are known to be refuted. It must be that even a well-corroborated falsifying hypothesis is incapable, *by itself*, of eliminating a theory. A counterexample requires in addition the support of a well-corroborated rival theory. In this modification of the concept of falsification, which acknowledges a level of analysis above the theory under examination, Popper$_2$ implicitly rejects and replaces the philosophy of Popper$_1$. Rejection cannot be identified with the elimination of a theory; the injunction "make sincere attempts to refute your theories" falls flat when confronted by the fact that all theories are in effect born refuted. But Popper himself nowhere offered a decisive critique of Popper$_1$ in the manner in which Popper$_1$ criticized Popper$_0$ in 1934. Lakatos did reformulate a rejection rule consistent with Popper$_2$'s acceptance philosophy, with the introduction of new terminology. Lakatos added the notions of (progressive and degenerating) problem-shifts to Popper$_2$ in order to account for growth over time at the research program level of analysis. This enabled him to reformulate Popper's concept of demarcation as differentiating progressive and degenerating problem-shifts in research programs.

With the aid of the concept of a problem-shift, it is possible to introduce Lakatos's reformulated criterion of elimination. Addressing the issue of ascertaining which to reject in the event of inconsistency—the theory or the fact—Lakatos said (1968b):

> According to this new rule, if we have two conflicting theories, one explanatory and one interpretative, we do not know which is which—that is, we do not know which should prevail as the interpretative theory providing the *facts*—we have to try to replace first one, then the other, then possibly both, and opt for that new set-up which represents the most progressive problem-shift, with the biggest increase in corroborated content [p. 165].

Refutation without an alternative shows nothing except the poverty of our scientific creativity. The growth of science requires new theories *even more* than it requires falsifications. Rejection must be a slow, reasonably reluctant process, for otherwise the full import of a theory would never become known; we would abandon all theories before we had seen just how far they actually could go in accounting for their domains. By requiring elimination to wait upon the presence of a well-corroborated alternative, Lakatos ensured that science will not consist of purely revolutionary *change* that never becomes *progress* at all.

It is in this respect that confirming evidence (of a special sort) enters into (at least Lakatos's) sophisticated falsificationism; the corroborating instances that are the prediction of novelty *by the rival* are more important than refutations of the original theory. As Lakatos wrote (1970):

> Thus the crucial element in falsification is whether the *new theory* offers any novel, excess information compared with its predecessor and whether some of this excess information is corroborated. Justificationists valued 'confirming' instances of a theory; naive falsificationists stressed 'refuting' instances; in this approach the—rather rare—corroborating instances of the *excess* information are the crucial ones, these receive all the attention. We are no longer interested in the thousands of trivial verifying instances nor in the hundreds of the readily available anomalies: the few crucial *excess-verifying instances* are decisive. This consideration rehabilitates—and reinterprets—the old proverb: *Exemplum docet, exempla obscurant* [pp. 120–121].

At this juncture, it becomes obvious that science *can* perfectly well progress (i.e., a progressive problem-shift occur) in the absence of refutations altogether (recall Chapters 6 and 7). Science may, especially in a period of revolutionary fervor, proliferate theories at such a rapid rate that the refutation of theory *N* occurs only after theory *N + 1* has been accepted. Growth need no longer be linear in the sense that one theory is put forth, refuted, and then succeeded by another theory. Naive falsifiability stressed the urgency of replacing a falsified hypothesis or theory with a better one; sophisticated falsificationism stresses the need for constant replacement of *any* theory or hypothesis with a better alternative. In the process of proliferating alternatives, we may corroborate (accept₂) theory *N + 1* without ever having "bothered" to consciously attempt the refutation of theory *N*. Thus *growth is logically independent of refutation in a pluralistic methodology.*

Sophisticated falsificationism is also less conventional than its naive predecessor. Rather than conventionally deciding to replace a theory when it conflicts with an observational outcome, sophisticated falsificationism requires one to attempt to replace *both* and choose whichever combination yields a progressive problem-shift. According to Lakatos (1970):

> To show this we only have to realize that if a scientific theory, consisting of some 'laws of nature', initial conditions, auxiliary theories (but without a *ceteris paribus* clause), conflicts with some factual propositions we do not have to decide which—explicit or 'hidden'—part to replace. We may try to replace *any* part and only when we have hit on an explanation of the anomaly with the help of some content-increasing change (or auxiliary hypothesis), and nature corroborates it, do we move on to eliminate the 'refuted' complex. Thus

sophisticated falsificationism is a slower but possibly safer process than naive falsificationism [p. 125].

(Indeed, this procedure even allows for the appraisal of syntactically metaphysical theories [those which are couched in *all* or *some* statements, see Watkins, 1958]. Rather than automatically eliminating a metaphysical theory in a clash with a refutable theory, by convention—as the naive falsificationist does—one can assess it by asking whether or not it leads to a progressive shift.)

But the problematic, if not the conventional, nature of deciding the class of and the truth value of some of the 'observational' level propositions cannot be avoided. One can, following Agassi (1966b), acknowledge the problematic nature of the 'basic statements,' and allow under certain circumstances for an appeal to overrule a falsifying fact. This can be done by questioning the adequacy of the *interpretative theory* providing the basic statement in question. "The theoretician may demand that the experimentalist specify his 'interpretative theory,' and he may then replace it—to the experimentalist's annoyance—by a better one in the light of which his originally 'refuted' theory may receive positive appraisal" (Lakatos, 1970, p. 130). But the verdict of this appeal court is not infallible. We have postponed and hopefully improved the decision, but we have not avoided it (Lakatos, 1970):

> We cannot get rid of the problem of the 'empirical basis', if we want to learn from experience: but we can make our learning less dogmatic—but also less fast and less dramatic. By regarding some observational theories as problematic we may make our methodology more flexible: but we cannot articulate and include *all* 'background knowledge' (or 'background ignorance'?) into our critical deductive model. This process is bound to be piecemeal and some conventional line must be drawn at any given time [p. 131].

The problem of the continuity of science remains for Popper₂. Popper's account of science pictures it as Kuhnian revolutions *in permanence*; the philosophy of proliferation developed by Feyerabend demands the constant overthrow of all theories at all times. The reasoning is that because knowledge is fallible, criticism must always be critical and must strive to better our fallible, tentative conclusions. What Lakatos called a progressive problem-shift *could* result merely from the addition of totally unrelated low-level hypotheses to a theory, i.e., by simply conjoining them. But science does not progress in this manner; succeeding theories are *related* in many, often subtle ways. Attempting to specify how, Lakatos referred to the succeeding theories of a domain as constituting a *research program*. His additions to Popper₂'s philosophy are invariably concessions to Kuhn's arguments to the effect that the practice of normal science cannot be understood except within the framework of a "paradigm" (in Kuhn's earlier [prior to 1970] terminology).

Thus it is time to examine Kuhn's conception of science to see how and why the Popperians react so violently to it. We shall see that the major differences concern the levels of analysis necessary for the understanding of science and the nature of an "objective" approach to epistemology.

KUHN'S CONCEPTION OF SCIENCE

The model of science that Kuhn proposed in 1962 (1970c) is so familiar that it is more presupposed than discussed in previous chapters. This model rejects the justificationist picture of science as a cumulative record of factual discoveries and theoretical generalizations based upon them in favor of the conception of *mature* science as a series of alternating periods of relatively continuous puzzle-solving research (normal science) on one hand and occasional periods of extraordinary reconceptualization (revolutionary science) on the other. Beyond this broad outline, however, there is evidence of considerable misunderstanding. Thus we must overview Kuhn's major points, such as the nature of "paradigms" and "normal science," and the relationships between them and "revolutionary science."

Let us begin with the most characteristic feature of mature science: the activity of normal science puzzle solving. Kuhn's initial characterization (1970c) was that "'Normal science' means research firmly based upon one or more past scientific achievements, achievements that some particular scientific community acknowledges for a time as supplying the foundation for its further practice [p. 10]." Note immediately that community structure becomes the key to understanding the practice of science; Kuhn's account is sociological rather than philosophical. Indeed normal science holds philosophical considerations, such as theory and metaphysics, at arm's length in order to get its work done. The exemplary past achievements are paradigms, and paradigms are the locus of the cognitive content of the science.

Kuhn has been systematically ambigious in his usage of 'paradigm.' Masterman (1970) isolated at least twenty-one ways in which the term occured in *The structure of scientific revolutions*. In general, these divide into sociological–metaphysical usages on one hand and the paradigm–as–exemplar on the other. Kuhn now (1970c, 1974) prefers to restrict the term to its original usage as an exemplary puzzle, and it is the exemplar as the source of knowledge in this fashion that is discussed in Chapter 8. The sociological sense of paradigm Kuhn would prefer to refer to as a *disciplinary matrix*, the major components of which are symbolic generalizations, models, shared values, and exemplars. As yet Kuhn has said virtually nothing about any of these components except exemplars. The metaphysical aspects of a paradigm (disciplinary matrix) would seem to involve primarily the deep commitments of a research community to shared values and the preferred analogies (and perhaps ontological claims) of particular models. No one has yet explored this in sufficient depth to flesh out the intuitive notions in *The structure of scientific revolutions.*

Achievement of a paradigm, in the exemplary puzzle sense, enables the practitioners of a specialty to do research that substantially increases their knowledge of nature. With such a paradigm, both fact collection and theory articulation become highly directed activities; the paradigm suggests which experiments are primary and which secondary, thus enabling the researchers to undertake very precise, time-consuming, and esoteric research without bothering to reestablish their discipline with each experiment. Normal research is simultaneously "an attempt to force nature into the preformed and relatively inflexible box that the paradigm supplies" (Kuhn, 1970c, p. 24) and also a period in which innovation is neither expected nor desired. "Normal science does not aim at novelties of fact or theory and, when successful, finds none [p. 52]."

Possession of exemplars promises success. Normal science research attempts to actualize that promise, "achieved by extending the knowledge of these facts that the paradigm displays as particularly revealing, by increasing the extent of the match between those facts and the paradigm's predictions, and by further articulations of the paradigm itself (Kuhn, 1970c, p. 24)." *Failure* in a normal science period is not likely to reflect badly upon the theory and paradigm exemplars; instead, it will discredit the experimental ability of the researcher. Failure reflects upon personal competence rather than the adequacy of the paradigm.

Success in normal science is a result of the care with which problems are selected; it accepts only those problems that can be turned into puzzles modeled upon exemplars and therfore solved. Kuhn wrote (1970c): "To a great extent these are the only problems that the community will admit as scientific or encourage its members to undertake. Other problems, including many that had previously been standard, are rejected as metaphysical, as the concern of another discipline, or sometimes as just too problematic to be worth the time [p. 37]." One reason for the rapid rate of progress is that normal science researchers limit themselves to tackling those problems that only their own lack of ingenuity would prevent solving. Such normal science research falls into three classes: determination of significant facts, matching of facts and theory, and articulation of theory. The paradigm is the touchstone for all three. For example, "What is factually significant with respect to what?" admits only one answer: "With respect to the paradigm."

Normal science research, although often successful, contains within itself the mechanism of its own overthrow: the collection of anomalous research findings. Normal science always swims in an ocean of anomalous results (some of which are falsifications of accepted theories). Usually researchers ignore them or consign them to the class of puzzles that the paradigm will in the future be able to resolve in satisfactory fashion. Since what is perceived by one researcher as a normal puzzle to solve may be perceived by another as an intolerable anomaly, the genesis of a revolutionary reconceptualization becomes a largely psychological affair, a matter of coming to perceive the domain in one or another novel manner. When a number of researchers see anomalies in abundance, a state of crisis may be said to exist in the research community. But Kuhn has been careful to state that a crisis, although usual, need not be an inevitable precursor to revolution. A revolution can occur if a single researcher reacts to anomaly in a manner that brings about a new way of conceptualizing the domain (i.e., succeeds in supplying a new disciplinary matrix).

Characterizing an incident as normal or revolutionary returns one to the community structure of science; it is necessary to specify normal or revolutionary *for whom*. The unit of analysis is the research group rather than the scientific subject matter or institutionalized academic discipline. As Kuhn (1970b) said:

> The analytic unit would be the practitioners of a given speciality, men bound together by common elements in their education and apprenticeship, aware of each other's work, and characterized by the relative fullness of their professional judgment ....
> Typical communities, at least on the contemporary scientific scene, may consist of a hundred members, sometimes significantly fewer. Individuals, particularly the ablest, may belong to several such groups, either simultaneously or in succession, and they will change or at least adjust their thinking caps as they go from one to another....
> It is, therefore, with respect to groups like these that the question 'normal or revolutionary?' should be asked. Many episodes will then be revolutionary for no communities, many others for only a single small group, still others for several communites together, a few for all of science [p. 253].

What is a scientific revolution? Kuhn's (1970c) answer is deceptively simple: "scientific revolutions are here taken to be those noncumulative developmental episodes in which an older paradigm is replaced in whole or in part by an incompatible new one [p. 92]." (Paradigm here refers to both sociological and exemplary senses.) Thus a revolution involves a new conceptual framework (a change in "world view") and the substitution of one exemplar or set of exemplars for another. What is really involved in such episodes is a matter for detailed historical, sociological, and psychological analysis to disclose; and Kuhn's account, although both pioneering and informative, is obviously going to be changed by the addition of more adequate data.

Kuhn's account of revolutions has been violently attacked by two classes of critics: residual justificationists, whose metatheory prohibits them from acknowledging that noncumulative growth can occur in science; and other nonjustificationists, such as the Popperians, who agree that revolutions occur but wish to reconstruct them in such fashion that science is rational from a purely philosophical point of view. The text discusses how Popperians working within the research program as a level of analysis have argued against Kuhn. Imre Lakatos was the most capable of such critics, elaborating the distinctions between $Popper_1$ and $Popper_2$, championing his approach (as the real $Popper_2$ or, perhaps $Popper_{2.5}$) until his death.

But there is another variant of the Popperian position that—to proliferate the number game—may be dubbed $Popper_3$. $Popper_3$ was not discussed in the text, primarily because "he" is a retrograde version of Popper that exists only to combat what Popper perceives to be the "horror" of subjectivism in quantum physics and scientific methodology. In physics the problem to be overcome is the Copenhagen interpretation of quantum mechanics, in which Niels Bohr's principle of complementarity often became an ad hoc prohibition against challenging the orthodox theory. Popper's approach to this problem has been to elaborate a new version of probability, the propensity interpretation, in combination with an epistemology that attempts to dispense with the human observer as either a human or an observer. In methodology, the problem is posed by Kuhn's conception of science, which is now considerably more popular than Popper's views and which the Popperians see as rendering science and its growth merely psychological and *therefore* irrational. If $Popper_1$ is the author of *Logik der Forschung* and $Popper_2$ of *Conjectures and refutations*, then $Popper_3$ is best portrayed as the author of *Objective knowledge* and as defending *neutral epistemology* rather than critical fallibilism. Since the mid-1960s the Kuhn–Popper clash has shifted from Kuhn versus $Popper_1$ to Kuhn versus $Popper_3$ by way of Kuhn versus Lakatos as $Popper_2$ in the transition.

POPPER₃, NEUTRAL EPISTEMOLOGY, AND OBJECTIVITY

Popper has fought for the objectivity of science since the 1930s. He has consistently identified objectivity with intersubjectivity. Testing, as the hallmark of science, "is merely a very important aspect of the more general idea of intersubjective *criticism*, or in other words, of the idea of mutual rational control by critical discussion" (Popper 1959, p. 44). Such criticism, on Popper's account, is the essence of rationality; the scientific endeavor is a rational one to the extent that it is critical. That rationality, seemingly so threatened by Kuhn and Lakatos, can be reinstated if we regard science as an autonomous "third world" similar to that inhabited by Plato's eternal forms. "We may distinguish the following three worlds or universes: first, the world of physical objects or of physical states; secondly, the world of states of consciousness, or of mental states, or perhaps of behavioral dispositions to act; and thirdly, the world of *objective contents of thought*, especially of scientific and poetic thoughts and of works of art" (Popper, 1972, p. 106).

As a resident of the third world, scientific knowledge is independent of all subjective beliefs: "Knowledge in this objective sense is totally independent of anybody's claim to know; also it is independent of anybody's belief, or disposition to assent; or to assert, or to act. Knowledge in the objective sense is *knowledge without a knower*: it is *knowledge without a knowing subject*" (Popper, 1972, p. 109). Scientific knowledge retains its objectivity by being divorced from subjectivity. Popper perceives justificationist epistemologists, as well as Kuhn, as *belief epistemologists* (1972):

> *Traditional epistemology* is interested in the second world: in knowledge as a certain kind of belief—justifiable belief, such as belief based upon perception. As a consequence, this kind of belief philosophy cannot explain (and does not even try to explain) the decisive phenomenon that scientists criticize their theories and so kill them. *Scientists try to eliminate their false theories, they try to let them die in their stead. The believer—whether animal or man—perishes with his false beliefs [p. 122]*.

Thus we can see the motivation for a retreat to the third world. In arguing against subjective or belief epistemologies, Popper identifies his *critical* epistemology with *objective* epistemology. And because he believes (1972) that "logic may be regarded as *the organon of criticism* [p. 121]," it is not surprising that Popper₃ talks of a logic of discovery in the third world of "objective knowledge."

But what is the logic of discovery that Popper₃ finally proposes? It is nothing more, nothing less, than "the schema of the growth of knowledge through error elimination by way of systematic *rational criticism* [p. 121]." This is the schema (1972):

$$P_1 \rightarrow TT \rightarrow EE \rightarrow P_2;$$

That is: problem P_1—tentative theory—evaluative elimination—problem P_2.
The evaluation is always *critical*, and its aim is the discovery and *elimination of error*. The growth of knowledge—and thus the learning process—is not a repetitive or a cumulative process but one of error elimination. It is Darwinian selection, rather than Lamarckean instruction [p. 144].

Thus when Popper₃ talks of the logic of discovery, he actually means the *theory* according to which scientific growth is rendered explicable. He does not mean to use the word 'logic' in the "deductive-transmissibility-of-truth" sense found in logic and mathematics, nor does he mean the notion to refer to what have been called heuristics of discovery. All Popper means by 'logic of discovery' is that scientific growth can, in a rational manner, be *explained* as following a consistent pattern. The pattern Popper proposes is captured by his 'growth schema':

$$P_1 \rightarrow TT \rightarrow EE \rightarrow P_2;$$

One who understands this schema and the Popperian notion of the third world understands how "neutral epistemology" can rationally reconstruct the growth of science only ex post facto.

THE INADEQUACY OF NEUTRAL EPISTEMOLOGY

One may criticize Popper's recent views in several ways. The third world, for example, is a tenuous notion; and Feyerabend (1970a, 1970b) ridiculed its philosophical utility by pointing out that all artifacts, such as birds' nests, are denizens of the third world on Popper's criteria because of their functional specification: "everything that is noticed by some organism. . . will be found in the third world which will therefore contain the whole material world and all the mistakes mankind has made. It will also contain 'mob psychology'" (Feyerabend, 1970b, p. 219).

But one may grant the existence of a 'third world' and still question Popper's account of the rationality of science within it. Here the alleged logic of discovery is hard to find. All Popper proposes is the idea that growth is a matter of error elimination via *modus tollens*. But this conception of "logical growth" cannot account for science, as Lakatos and Kuhn have both pointed out. The growth of science simply is not explainable *solely* in terms of error elimination; progress can occur in the absence of critical testing and refutation. Thus Popper$_3$'s logic of discovery is neither logical in the strict sense (because it involves more than the theory of deducibility, which is what logic is), nor is it adequate to the task of understanding the rationality of the scientific endeavor. The only way to employ this conception of science is in conjunction with an internal–external history distinction that rules out vast stretches of history simply because it is not rational or logical according to this model. Popper (1970, 1974) appears willing to do this, and Lakatos (1971) retreated to the third world when pressed. But little historical research has been done from this framework; a historian would have to ignore too much of history in order to employ it.

We can dismiss neutral epistemology entirely if there is a satisfactory manner in which to reconstruct science as both psychological (and sociological) and objective. Recall that Popper's dismay at belief epistemologies is that they are subjective; the third world became inviting because it promised to avoid subjectivism and belief. Thus we need to know if we can reconstruct scientific knowledge as other than subjective belief without abandoning reality for the third-world science museum. Such an account has already been proposed in earlier chapters. Within a nonjustificational framework, knowledge (or the propositions in the third world that are its appropriate reconstructions) is a matter of warranted assertions. Regardless of whether one talks of assertions as psychological phenomena or propositions as third-world entities, it is their *warrantability* that renders knowledge claims both as knowledge *and* objective. Subjective belief is irrelevant to determination of the warrant of an assertion. One can recognize that human knowledge is embodied in a system of beliefs within the heads of individuals; but one must also recognize that the objectivity of claims, necessary for them to be *knowledge* claims, transcends subjective belief. Construing knowledge as a matter of warranted assertions thus acknowledges both the psychological nature of human knowledge and its objectivity. There simply is no need to retreat to commitment in the third world.

Thus I am inclined to dismiss neutral epistemology as a viable alternative to either critical fallibilism (even in the conventional guise advocated by Lakatos) or psychological fallibilism. This is why the position is mentioned only in this appendix rather than in the text.

DIRECTIONS FOR FUTURE RESEARCH

We began in Chapter 1 by presenting four problems that have been central to attempts to understand the scientific endeavor. What we have done in the chapters just past was to switch from one to the next as it has become clearer that satisfactory resolution to any of them is not presently possible. So long as we abandon justificationism, there is neither the need to work nor the hope of success in tackling instant rationality and assessment. Thus we followed Popper's lead, attempting to explain growth without recourse to instant rational assessment. Both the history of science and the critical arguments of neo-Popperians have made the prospects for a philosophical theory of growth look slim indeed. Examination of history and historical approaches such as Kuhn's led us to the problems of pragmatic action. It appears at this point that an adequate understanding of growth will wait upon an adequate psychology of inference and sociology of research communities—which will then become intrinsic to an adequate theory of science and its history. If the arguments in Chapter 8 are correct, we also require an account of science as a rhetorical transaction to unite psychology, sociology, and history. Thus if these problems of pragmatic action are as central as our analysis makes them, intellectual honesty now demands that they become the major focus of subsequent research.

CHAPTER NOTES

Note 11.1.   The university of Göteborg, Sweden, established a department of metascience in 1963 (see Radnitzky, 1970). This was, as far as I am aware, the first institutionalization of such a program. Under the direction of Håken Törnebohn, a conception of metascience as the study of scientific enterprises developed. There is now at the same university an interdisciplinary *Institute for the Theory of Science*, which has projected a series of publications in the area of metascience so defined (Radnitzky, 1970, is an example), conducts seminars and research meetings on relevant topics, etc. Törnebohm and Radnitzky take as their general orienting strategy a systems–theory approach to the study of science and "research about research." Radnitzky's book is an undertaking of monumental scope, comparing the metascience of logical empiricism with that of the continental hermeneutic–dialectic approach to philosophy. Radnitzky favors the H–D approach and argues strenuously for it. Unfortunately, it appears to be a sophisticated variant of skeptical justificationism, but defense of that claim requires another book.

Note 11.2. $Popper_0$, although he never actually published a word, has been attacked and defended in both philosophical and psychological literature as though he had published, especially a book entitled *Logik der Forschung*. Lakatos attributed the invention (for the purpose of criticism) of a published $Popper_0$ to A. J. Ayer in the original edition of his *Language, truth and logic* (1936). Ayer has continued to criticize this interpretation of Popper: see, for example, his 1959 citation. Recent expository commentary of $Popper_0$, in an approving vein, is found in Medawar (1967, esp. p. 144). Nagel, reviewing Medawar's book, criticizes him for endorsing Popper's claims (1967, p. 70). Were such commentary restricted to the philosophical literature, it would be bad enough; however, Turner (1967) has commented on $Popper_0$ for psychologists. In a section on the hypothetico–deductive method, Turner criticizes the H–D approach to scientific explanation (which, somewhat strangely, he calls "deductivism") and refers to $Popper_0$ as an exponent of it (1967):

> If deductivism, or the hypothetico–deductive method, is inconclusive as concerns positive assertions about evidential support of its presumptive hypotheses, it proves inconclusive also in the region of decision wherein presumably lies its strength. Namely, this is the region of disconfirmation. *According to Popper, falsification and the criterion of falsifiability are to be defended on the grounds that they are more conclusive than verification and the criterion of verifiability* (italics added) [p. 223].

It is clear that the italicized sentence refers to $Popper_0$ rather than $Popper_1$, the author of *The logic of scientific discovery*. Also in an earlier explication of Popper's views in a section on falsifiability (pp. 147–152), Turner conflates $Popper_0$ and $Popper_1$ in such a manner that it it unclear which 'theorist' is being commented upon.

Turner *is* correct on one point, however; because he understands (at best) only $Popper_1$, it is correct for him to lump together $Popper_1$ and logical empiricism in one chapter heading. This is because both positions are variants of neojustificationism.

12 Justificationism in Psychology

This chapter continues to overview justificationism, but here our concern shifts to the manner in which that metatheory pervades a particular discipline. Largely upon the basis of my familiarity with it, psychology (at least in America) has been selected for brief overview. One need not look far for evidences of justificationist thought in psychology. Indeed, because it is so pervasive, the problem becomes how to selectively overview it in limited space. Strategically, it appears better to ignore justificationist principles in substantive theory to concentrate upon the justificationist conception of methodology that permeates the discipline. This can be overviewed by selecting examples in philosophy–methodology of science writings of psychologists for consumption by colleagues, by focusing upon the assumptions of statistical methodology, and by overviewing how the history of psychology is presented.

PHILOSOPHICAL PRIMERS IN PSYCHOLOGY

The standard histories of psychology (which we examine later) uniformly exhibit variations on the building-block, history-must-be-the-accumulation-of-certified-propositions model overviewed in Chapter 5; this is one reason why psychologists have usually thought that nonjustificational models of science such as Kuhn's or Popper's are inappropriate for the "immature" discipline (see Weimer, 1974a, 1974b). Psychologists trained in the logical empiricist tradition with regard to methodology take the same attitude, so it is worth a brief overview of obvious justificationist traits in their philosophy of science primers. Since there has never been a nonjustificational methodology made available to psychologists, it follows that all the standard accounts exhort practitioners to do science according to a conception that is the blackest of available metatheoretical lies.

A decade or so ago, it would have sufficed to examine Mandler and Kessen (1959), a relatively straightforward incorporation of 1950s logical empiricism; now there is a plethora of possibilities. Two more recent books have had a decade's currency and seem to have been influential: Turner (1967) and Rychlak (1968). Let us consider them in turn.

Turner's text is a compendious survey of "hard-headed" literature, with incursions into "soft-headed" positions only when necessary to criticize them in defense of his overriding concern—advancement of the thesis of reductionism. "The questions of alternative theoretical conceptions will be resolved by reducing the terms of one science to those of a more basic science. In some such sense there is a real convergence in scientific endeavor. It is in the reduction that one finds whatever sense of scientific realism is philosophically defensible"(Turner, 1967, p. x). Turner defends reductionism to the bitter end for one reason: He sees it as the only way to stave off Hume's skeptical sensationalist conclusion that we have no genuine theoretical knowledge at all. "For the empiricist, the alternative to absolute skepticism is the wistful embrace of a principle of convergence" [p. 7].

But because convergence can only be justified by evidence supporting it, and because evidence is itself fallible, Turner retreats to conventionalism. As a justificationist, Turner wants proof in science, but he is well aware that it is not available (1967):

> We should like to be treated to strong confirmation. The discovery of neptune... is part of the confirmational lore of science, as was the verification that light rays are subject to the effects of gravitational fields. We should like to think that as our own scientific theories become more formally sophisticated, we should be able to derive incisive hypotheses reducing to explicit sets of data expectations [pp. 378–379].

At this point Turner endorses the neojustificationist quest for probabilifying hypotheses rather than proving them (1967):

> Typically, our defense of induction is based upon statistical methodology. We make assumptions concerning the nature of our data, we adopt a statistical model based upon some theory of probability, and then, on the premises of the data and the models, we propose some decision procedure for evaluating the plausibility of an experimental hypothesis. ... The support for our decision rests in our stipulating what is probable or improbable on the basis of some hypothesis. The overall strategy is hypothetico–deductive in character. ... Such a decision is straighforward. It coincides with the deductive strategy of

disconfirmation (Popper, 1959) and with all the semantic advantages appertaining thereto [pp. 377–378].

But as disconfirmation is just as conventional as confirmation, Turner has nothing to fall back on except conventional agreement (determined by the sophistry of statistical methodology) that a hypothesis is "plausible." "Even though our decision procedure commands us to accept the hypothesis, we do so only with misgivings that other hypotheses may also be plausible. At most, the hypothesis we test and find acceptable may itself be judged plausible; yet plausibility may not be the substance we empiricists should like to take as the foundations of positive knowledge" (Turner, 1967, p. 378).

(Not surprisingly, Turner does not understand Popper's position on "disconfirmation." He stated (1967) that "according to Popper, falsification and the criterion of falsifiability are to be defended on the grounds that they are more conclusive than verification and the criterion of verifiability [p. 223]." This makes Popper out to be a dogmatic falsificationist who thinks that science advances by disproof rather than proof.)

But how does Turner avoid "absolute" skepticism? By providing a "justification" (albeit conventional rather than genuine) of induction in statistical methodology (Note 12.1). Turner's version of confirmation theory is formulated in terms of statistical decision procedures borrowing from Neyman–Pearson and the Bayesians. Instead of justifying induction, Turner substitutes the never-ending task of *justifying particular inductions*. For Turner (1967), "the problem of justifying induction is the problem of formulating criteria of evidential support [p. 472]." Thus to justify induction he must continue, forever, to support particular applications of inductive inference. Somehow he has lulled himself into believing that toiling upon a never-ending task avoids "absolute" skepticism (1967): "The fact that every inductive inference involves presuppositions, is not fatal to the possibility of inductive inference. Nor is it fatal to our efforts to justify inductive inference. Such, I think, becomes apparent in the examination of statistical induction [p. 473]." This is an identical stategy to Ayer's attempt to make the skeptic's acknowledged victory as bloodless as possible. A retreat to commitment, in a wistful embrace of the "principle" of convergence within the confines of critical rationalism, is all this text has to offer.

Since its inception, psychology has been divided into opposing camps that are variously tough- or tender-minded, experimentalists or naturalistic demonstrators, behavioral or phenomenological, nomothetic rat runners or ideographic people interviewers, etc. This split has produced characteristically different conceptions of psychology and philosophy relevant to psychology; and if Turner's views are represetntative of the mild conventionalism that is all that remains of the hard-headed logical empiricist tradition, then Rychlak's (1968) text may be taken as representative of the "loyal opposition"—presenting a philosophy of science for the human and personal side of the discipline. Rychlak's stated goal (1968) is: "we hope to leave the reader with a viable alternative to the view of science he must now so often reluctantly accept in the name of rigorous psychology [p. 6]." Not surprisingly, the "revolutionary liberation" rests upon an all-too-familiar ploy: substitution of one justificationist philosophy for another.

To see this, we need only look at the justificationist nature of the scientific enterprise that Rychlak provides, often in explicit definitions. Consider knowledge: "*Knowledge* is the understanding of why a given theoretical construct or proposition is true *or* false *after* that proposition has been submitted to the test of method [p. 43]." Knowledge is thus either proven truth or proven falsity; the epistemological authority is "method." Method is the procedures of proof; and here Rychlak—having heard of the fallacy of affirming the consequent—states that although science cannot prove, it can conclusively disprove (1968): "All validating evidence can establish convincingly is the *negation* of the theoretical proposition. Having postulated an *If A, then B*, sequence, when our researchers *fail* to confirm this sequence, we can logically reject the theoretical relation originally postulated [p. 81]." But now Rychlak is faced with gaining "positive" knowledge, or his definition will be inconsistent with his authoritative proof procedure. This he does by retreating to conventionalism in distinguishing two types of method: "the cognitive, which makes use of procedural evidence, and the *research* method, which uses validating evidence in addition [p. 43]." All *positive* evidence must be procedural; this means that *self-evidence* is the "cognitive" method of proof (Rychlak, 1968):

> ...to begin a line of reasoning one must make certain assumptions, accept certain plausibilities, and accede to the weight of certain self-evidences. Philosophical argument, the weight of logic, and even the immediate personal significance of a psychological insight proffered by one's psychotherapist, all carry great impact and stimulate a sense of conviction if it we take these as proofs [pp. 74–75].

This, of course, means that conventionalism follows inevitably; consider how he moves from theory to coherence as the sole criterion of method:

> ...when a decision must be made concerning the truth or falsity, plausibility or implausibility of a theoretical proposition, we are no longer dealing with theory, we are dealing with method. This method bases its decision—true or false plausible or implausible—on the consistency with which the entire body of knowledge—the "common sense"—hangs together [p. 76].

But conventionalism in one location spreads everywhere; and if Rychlak had looked at his "system," he would have noticed there is now no difference between positive and negative evidence: Both must rest upon convention and nothing else. This follows because the negative evidence of *modus tollens*—being logical—is now based upon self-evidence, or "cognitive" proof! Rychlak is now in exactly the same boat as Descartes; from his peculiar version of the "cogito," Rychlak must now erect the entire edifice of science. It goes without saying that the failure of this task is foreordained, but one can now see the sense in which this text, although full of (then) current references, strikes many as being unbelievably out of date.

STATISTICAL "INFERENCE" AND RESEARCH METHODOLOGY

The three most familiar "schools" of statistical methodology found in psychology (and social science) are represented by the classic or "significance testing" approach pioneered by R. A. Fisher (e.g., 1935, 1956), the "decision theory" approach of Jerzy Neyman and Egon Pearson (e.g., Neyman, 1937, 1938), and the loosely bound position known as Bayesian inference (e.g., Edwards, Lindman, & Savage, 1963). We can compare and contrast the justificational underpinnings of these statistical inference procedures by examining the theories of "instant rational assessment" that they manifest.

Consider first the significance testing approach stemming from Fisher. These theorists represent the classic justificationist approach to methodology. If one asks the Fisherian the question, "What is the probability that can be assigned to a scientific hypothesis, and how is it to be interpreted?", the result is a statement of classic justificationism. Fisherians reply that the probability can only be zero or one and that the hypothesis can either be true or false—and nothing else. Significance testing as a methodological procedure is utilized by the Fisherian for tentatively accepting or decisively rejecting the hypothesis as scientifically established, i.e., as "true." If the result obtained is deemed a significant deviation from expectation, it is falsified; otherwise it is "not falsified."

Thus it is not surprising that there has been widespread dissatisfaction with the rationale underlying Fisher's approach: For example, a book of readings (Morrison & Henkel, 1970) critically surveying the significance test controversy argued that the procedure is simply not applicable in the social sciences. But in all cases, the reasoning utilized failed to take account of the "philosophical" refutation of classic justificationism stemming from Fries (recall Chapter 1). Indeed, if this criticism has been understood, significance testing would never have gotten off the ground.

Skipping decision theory for a moment, let us consider the neojustificationist theory of inference: the Bayesian approach. It is somewhat surprising that this approach is so recent in the social sciences, because it is almost a word–for–word substitution for the "confirmation theory" of the inductive logicians. This approach is very sophisticated, in that it recognizes the impossibility of the classic justificationist quest and retreats to a probabilistic conventionalism. To the question, "What is the probability of a scientific hypothesis, and how is it interpreted?", the Bayesian gives a neo-justificationist answer: The probability ranges from zero to one, and it is to be interpreted *subjectively* in terms of the personal probability of its truth. Both of these answers are taken to be strong points of the position. "Bayesian procedures can strengthen a null hypothesis, not only weaken it, whereas classical theory is curiously asymmetric. If the null hypothesis is classically rejected, the alternative hypothesis is willingly embraced, but if the null hypothesis is not rejected, it remains in a kind of limbo of suspended disbelief" (Edwards, Lindman, & Savage, 1963, p. 235). These authors also refer to the "key ideas" of Bayesian statistics (1963): "...that probability is orderly opinion, and that inference from data is nothing other than the revision of such opinion in the light of relevant new information [p. 194]." Thus the position attempts to combine sophisticated inductivism (in the form of statistics mirroring the mathematics of confirmation) with a retreat to conventionalism; the acceptance of a probabilified hypothesis is a matter of personal *decision*. This is exactly analogous to the confirmation theorist going subjective with talk about, e.g., "rational betting quotients." Thus hypotheses are true or false only in terms of our degrees of belief in them—which means, of course, that truth is now a matter of convention and that no *informative* theoretical knowledge is possible (see Agassi, 1966b).

Defenses of Bayesian inference often take on the tone of the "sadder but wiser" neojustificationist who knows that his Titanic of rationality is sinking after encountering the iceberg. Turner (1967) provides numerous examples of this:

> Being well-bred to skepticism, yet still prone to dogmatism, the empiricist welcomes the opportunity to ritualize his decision. He never forgets that he operates in a world of uncertainty. Yet the ritual of a calculation and a rule enables him to make decisions—sometimes to make optimal decisions wherein he might maximize his gain, but more often simply to distinguish what is significant, and perhaps worthy of publication, from that which is not significant. He adopts policy positions, with all the comfort and cares of optimality. *And if he is encouraged ever so slightly, he may speak boastfully of the return of the rational man.* And yet, if our contemporary empiricist is pressed, he will soon let you know that all is not quite well (italics added) [p. 433].

The problems so ever-present behind the statistical empiricist's "ritual of calculation" concern *decision procedures* rather than *justification* of inference; Turner and the Bayesians have simply ignored (literally aban-doned) the justification of inference as a source of knowledge in favor of the more manageable problem of "justifying" decision procedures in statistical methodology. Empirical proof has been willingly sacrificed for conventional acceptance. The boast of a return of rational man results from an irrational retreat to commitment. Both Turner and the Bayesians (albeit for different reasons; see Turner's Chapter 14) have simply shouted *tu quoque*.

The decision theory approach begins quite differently from either previous model. For Neyman, probability is applicable only to classes of statements each equally representing an hypothesis but not to the hypothesis per se; "the probability of a hypothesis" is thus not meaningful. Further, it is asserted that inductive *inference* reduces (in the long run) to inductive *behavior*. Thus application of statistical procedures results in a behavioral decision; we decide to act as if the hypothesis is true (if not disconfirmed) or false (if it is falsified). Prior to 1938, all statistical methodology was concerned with justifying propositions on the basis of data; it was Neyman who turned from justifying inference to codifying conventional rules for behavior. Within decision theory, there is no such thing as *inferential* statistics, where that refers to statistical "methods" for proving or probabilifying propositions; probability statements are descriptive of our behavior in making inferences, not a truth property of a parameter, nor of an explicit hypothesis about that parameter. Statistical decision (decisions based upon statistical procedures) demands that one reject or accept a hypothesis; it is addressed specifically to the problems of the guidance of scientific life.

The decision theorist is thus a conventionalist from the outset. Unlike classical and Bayesian theorists, decision theory never attempts inductive certification and thus faces no loss of integrity when its procedures end in conventional decision. Decision theory simply says nothing about knowledge—only about the behavior that is appropriate for the "knowledge gatherer." Attempts to incorporate epistemic issues into the decision theory framework are illegitimate —even though decision theorists themselves often make them. No doubt they make such attempts because they want to assess the "scientific merit" or propositions, but that assessment is simply not permitted by the framework in which they operate. But since this is rarely recognized, the frustrated decision theorist often slips over into the Bayesian approach, no doubt assuming that talking about prior and posterior probabilities provides more basis for making decisions. But even if such talk aids decisions, no decision in the framework of conventionalism will justify a putative knowledge claim. What is most problematic for the justificationist use of decision theory is why one should use it at all.

Parenthetically we may ask what "probability" is assignable to. Primarily five notions have been advanced by one or another philosopher, scientist, or statistician: events, statements, beliefs, hypotheses, theories. Fisher spoke of the probability of events, but it is obvious that he was thinking in terms of hypotheses about events (see also his concept of fiducial probability).

Neyman spoke of statements. Bayesians and many inductive logicians speak of beliefs (or some cognate). Philosophers, but never statisticians, have spoken of the probability of theories. And in all cases, probability has been interpreted either "objectively" in terms of relative frequency in the (totally undefined) long run or "subjectively" in terms of degrees of belief or credence. Recently, a third conception of probability has been advanced that does purport to range over events: Popper's propensity interpretation, which was intended to clear up "subjectivism" in quantum physics. Whether it does or not is debatable; all we need note is that no statistical methodology has yet utilized it. In any case, the moral is clear: What it is that "has" probability is highly problematic.

One might ask what the nature and role of statistics would be in a nonjustificational methodological framework. No exhaustive account can be given, but a few obvious points bear mention. Foremost is that the distinction between inferential and decriptive statistics simply cannot be made; if methodology is unfused from the attempt to certify knowledge claims (as either proven, disproven, or probable), then *all statistics are descriptive.* Thus, there is no such thing as a "test" of "significance," because one can never infer that something is or is not significant by an algorithmic procedure. The only significance test in science was aptly characterized by J. Berkson as the "interocular traumatic test"—if it leaps out and hits you, it is significant. If it does not, no amount of computation or number of asterisks can "add" significance. Second, if something like Popper's concept of corroboration is to be "staticized," or some other notion of acceptability, then the Neyman–Pearson decision theoretic approach (which is purely conventional and can be divorced from the attempt to justify) is worthy of development. Third, if the justificationist overtones were removed, many Bayesian "liberations" and "flexible approaches" could no doubt be utilized, especially because the Bayesian approach is already oriented toward description of data rather than toward justification. Fourth, and no doubt hardest to effect, researchers would have to be reeducated in the use and role of statistical tools, and journal editors would have to find other criteria for publication decisions.

HISTORY AS A CUMULATIVE RECORD

There have been two major approaches utilized by historians of psychology. One emphasizes the dominant role of the intellectual climate of the times. On this view, science progresses because the tenor of the times, the intellectual *zeitgeist*, directs the research of the individual. Scientific creativity is subordinate to the zeitgeist; were the general ideas not present in the zeitgeist, the specific contributions of individual scientists would not have taken the form that they in fact did. If a particular scientist had not made a particular discovery or put forth a particular theoretical formulation, then someone in the same area would have made a similar contribution, due to the common effects of the zeitgeist upon the researchers in a domain. The role of the individual scientist is subservient to that of the intellectual climate.

The other major viewpoint is the "great man" philosophy. This approach emphasizes the originality of particular individuals in historical development. Although the zeitgeist—as commonly shared opinion and factual know-ledge–is of central importance, it must share the spotlight with the individual great man. On this view, history is the dynamic interplay between the zeitgeist and the great man: The great man determines the zeitgeist of his era, and is given the basic materials of his creativity from a earlier zeitgeist. Great men become agents of the zeitgeist as well as determiners of it. Although the intellectual climate may be ripe for innovation, it is the particular makeup of the individual that gives innovation its concrete shape and direction. On the "great man" view, the zeitgeist account is not incorrect, but it *is* incomplete.

Our concern is not psychological history per se but the professed (and, of course, implicit) philosophy of history of the historians who have attempted to chronicle the discipline. Our task is to unmask and lay bare the justificationist conception of historiography behind the prominent received view histories of psychology. My claim is that the 'surface structure' controversy between "zeitgeist" and "great man" interpretations of the *agency* of historical change merely masks the 'deep structure' agreement that historians share with regard to the *nature* of scientific change. The justificationist historiography underlying both themes is a building-block, "growth by gradual accumulation" model that pictures scientific progress in psychology as analogous to gradual trial–and–error learning in a Skinner box. There is no place in such a scheme for insightful and rapid learning. The zeitgeist historian denies the "insight" and creativity of the great man by emphasizing his role within the zeitgeist. The proponent of the "great man," although emphasizing the ideographic factors in history, likewise builds historical progress out of the accumulation of insights of "great men." In either case, the history of psychology that is offered to psychologists *by* psychologists is a cumulative record; there is as yet no "insight" into the revolutionary nature of scientific change within psychology.

THE ZEITGEIST INTERPRETATION OF THE
CUMULATIVE RECORD

For many, E. G. Boring's monumental *A history of experimental psychology* (1950) is the *only* history of psychology. It is the most widely known publication in the history of psychology (and perhaps in psychology proper) and remains the definitive treatise. Because this is so, it requires no explanation beyond mention of the fact that Boring advocated the zeitgeist interpretation of history to substantiate the claim that the majority of psychologists know of no alternative to the zeitgeist interpretation. To understand Boring's philosophy of history and scientific progress is to understand what the vast majority of psychologists have been trained to accept.

Boring began, in the preface to the first edition, with a theme that is at the heart of all historical inquiry today: that the historian is reconstructing his or her domain rather than just making additions to older accounts. Boring wrote (1950):

> The modern history of psychology cannot, however, be written merely by adding chapters to the older history. Strange as it may seem, the present changes the past; and, as the focus and range of psychology shift in the present, new parts of the past enter into its history and other parts drop out. Experimental psychology of today has its own history, even though that history is not all an account of experimentation. The systematic problems persistently enter into it, but they appear in a different way [p. ix].

His second preface (1950) echoed that theme:

> Can history be revised? Yes. As time goes on, there come to be second thoughts about the interpretation of it. There are also new discoveries. And, as the once recent past moves back into a more balanced perspective, its delineator must discard his preliminary sketches in order to preserve the now clearer view in more permanent colors [p. xiii].

Having admitted that historical inquiry is revisionary or reconstructive in nature, there remains the task of specifying the point of view from which to carry out the reconstruction.

As to his point of view, Boring admitted to having changed in the 20 years between the first and second editions. Once an out-and-out zeitgeist theorist, he later saw *both* the zeitgeist and the "great man" as *both* causes *and* effects of historical development. That is, the individual was admitted as a causative factor in shaping the zeitgeist of the times, and vice versa. According to Boring (1950):

> I wanted to say something about why, as well as how, science emerged, to speak of the role of the Zeitgeist and of the great man in determining progress in science, and to show that these two views of the development and emergence of thought are not mutually exclusive but obverse and reverse of every historical process. I have tried to echo that thought throughout the book [p. xiii].

Speaking in a retrospective chapter on the nature of progress, he strengthened that theme (1950):

What is the function of the great man in science or, for that matter, in history? Are these great men the *causes* of progress or are they merely its symptoms? The answer is: they are neither; they are the *agents* of progress. The tiniest element of scientific progress—the all-or-nothing step-phenomenon that takes science further on toward whither it is going—is a human event in a man's thought and brain, the insight that creates something new by relating two old items that had never before been put together in just that way. That man is counted great whose insights are crucial and lead to long continued important progress in new directions [p. 744].

What Boring was attempting to "take back" is the stronger theme of a younger self (Boring, 1927)—that originality in science is a product of the zeitgeist and that the zeitgeist renders scientific discovery *all but* inevitable. That younger Boring inserted this commentary on theories of history into his first chapter (1950):

There are two theories of history, the *personalistic* and the *naturalistic*. The personalistic theory, which is also the theory of common sense, says that astronomy forged ahead because Copernicus had the insight to see and the courage to say that the heliocentric view of the solar system is more plausible than the geocentric. The naturalistic theory, on the other hand, holds that it was almost inevitable that the heliocentric view should be realized in the Age of Enlightenment, that it should then, as men's attitudes toward themselves shifted, come to seem plausible, and that Copernicus was, therefore, only the agent or perhaps the symptom of inexorable cultural change [p. 3–4].

Boring implicitly equated the impersonal, naturalistic causative agency—the zeitgeist—with a *scientific* explanation in opposition to the personalistic, seemingly *super*natural causative agent—the great individual. A note at the end of the first chapter indicates that Boring assimilated the zeitgeist-"great man" controversy to the issue of naturalistic versus personalistic determination in history. He wrote (1950):

The suggestion that historical determination is naturalistic rather than personalistic is not new. Count Leo Tolstoy saw the dilemma and wrote about it in his *War and Peace*. ...His thesis was that war transcends the wills and decisions of the men who make the war, that they are but agents of greater natural forces. Many others have held this view, including Herbert Spencer. William James took, in a limited pragmatic way, the other side of the argument defending "the great-man theory of history" on the grounds that a belief in human decision as a proximal yet efficient cause is necessary since only omniscience can pass beyond relatively proximal causation and view the entire determining system [p. 11].

Thus an initial motivation for Boring's thesis may have been the desire to have (what he conceived to be) a scientific account of history utilizing only naturalistic determinism. In his retrospective chapter, the more mature Boring showed very explicitly that the bias of the younger Boring continued to guide his thought (1950):

> To think of the man whose brilliant novel thought heads an important development as the originator is to abandon scientific psychology and suppose that among all orderly lawful mental phenomena the insights of genius constitute an exception in that they occur without causes. That view of nature makes the great man, if not a *deus*, at least an *homunculus ex machina* [p. 745].

It is clear from these passages that one factor determining Boring's continued allegiance to the zeitgeist (despite his professed reservations) was his belief that only if the zeitgeist approach were maintained could scientific principles be applied to history. In order to remain a scientist (as all "hard-headed" psychologists constantly strive to do), Boring advocated a position that he felt exemplified good scientific principles.

This led to a discrepancy between the mature Boring's moderate preachment on the issue of historical causation and his actual practice as indicated by the text of the revised edition. The text remains biased in favor of the zeitgeist interpretation. (Friedman [1967] documents this continuity in Boring's historiography.) The stage for the zeitgeist interpretation was set in the same note after the first chapter quoted above. Consider this passage for both the role of the zeitgeist *and* the cumulative, inevitable effect of 'building-block' progress (Boring, 1950):

> Someone else could have made the decision, perhaps under these conditions would have made it, thus becoming the means by which the *Zeitgeist* prevails. Thus decisions are important historical events, and if one man does not make a decision which has been readied by the times, then another may. Similarly in science the crucial insights are the events that make the steps in progress. The great man has the crucial insight, becoming great because he had it. If he dies before he has the insight, then another may have it, since the times are ready for it, and greatness will go not to the first man who died too soon, but to this second who lived to show in his own wise choice for what the times were ready [p. 23].

In overview, these are the dominant themes in Boring's approach: First, the zeitgeist prevails as the major determinant of scientific (and indeed *all* historical) change; second, progress within a domain is inexorably determined by the nature of the zeitgeist; individual creativity is not important *as such*.

But regardless of the question of the agency of historical change, one can also examine a theorist's conception of the *nature* of such change. It is here that it becomes clear that the zeitgeist–great man controversy is only an epiphenomenal clash at a relatively superficial level in the presentation of theorists who otherwise agree upon a justificationist cumulative record or building-block approach to historiography. Both Boring as a zeitgeist theorist and proponents of the "great man" share the same justificationist historiography. Let us further document the cumulative record approach to the nature of progress subtly interwoven with Boring's zeitgeist approach to the agency of historical progress. Boring's preachment on the issue of the *rate* of scientific progress is clear: The zeitgeist takes only small steps (1950):

> Does science run along on a plateau and then suddenly shoot ahead because of an important discovery, or does it move steadily, inevitably, onward, always by small increments? Is its course discrete and step-wise or is it gradual and continuous? Mature opinion favors many small steps as the general rule. Nearly all great discoveries have had their anticipations which the historian digs up afterward. Disproved theories hang on indefinitely, often for a century or more, until displaced by some positive substitute. Again and again it seems as if the crucial insight either does not come until the *Zeitgeist* has prepared for its reception, or if it comes too soon for the *Zeitgeist*, then it does not register and is lost until it is unearthed later when the culture is ready to accept it [p. 4].

Aside from studying a theorist's explicit preachment and reconstruction of an ideal instance of scientific progress, the question to ask to best see whether or not a historical account is really justificationist with regard to the nature of progress is quite simple: Can the account countenance genuine scientific revolutions—i.e., changes that are incompatible with both prior theory and fact? It is obvious that Boring's account cannot countenance such changes.

Yet when approached from a nonjustificational historiographic point of view, there are many occurrences in the history of psychology that can easily be reconstructed as revolutionary in nature. One way to see the inherently evolutionary or building-block character of Boring's account is to examine his treatment of such occurrences. One of the most obvious potentially revolutionary features of the development of contemporary psychology is the rise to prominence of behaviorism. An examination of Boring's treatment of behaviorism from its prehistory before J. B. Watson to the time of his revised publication thus becomes informative.

With regard to behaviorism, it appears that Boring weighed carefully the possibility of its revolutionary nature. His answer revealed his evolutionary approach quite clearly (1950):

> Behaviorism seems to have been a movement in the *Zeitgeist*, not a simple revolution. Instead of giving it a chapter to itself, I have turned Chapter 24 to behavioristics, have picked up the threads of animal psychology and of objective psychology from the earlier chapters, and have then passed on through behaviorism proper to the newer positivism and what has sometimes been called operationism [p. xiv].

Boring's chapter on behavioristics has as its chief task the reconstruction of a long and honorable tradition for *objective* psychology, the generic name under which animal and comparative psychology, behaviorism, and operational analysis are all subsumed. Boring felt that the "objective" approach to psychology (as opposed to the "subjective," which dealt with consciousness as a subject matter) can be traced to Descartes and the French materialists such as La Mettrie. By choosing to emphasize the long developmental history of the "objective" approach to psychology, Boring was able to ignore the revolutionary aspects of the revolt of behaviorism; by showing that objective psychology has a long and honorable past and by subsuming behaviorism to the "objective" tradition, it automatically follows that behaviorism can be treated as a movement in the zeitgeist that has shown consistent development, a trend that has flourished for centuries. And surely one would not want to call a movement that exemplified trends that had existed for hundreds of years "revolutionary." This is his strategy (1950):

> Comparative psychology led directly into behaviorism, which was also, of course, an objective psychology. To that development we shall come presently. The purpose of the present section is to review the history of psychological objectivism prior to behaviorism—before 1913. ... This history does not properly begin until Descartes' dualism [pp. 631-632] (Note 12.2).

Cumulative record theorists write history backward rather than forward; they refer only to that part of prior theory and the work of past scientists that can readily be viewed as contributions to present problems and positions of the theorists' own substantive points of view, as determined by the research tradition in which they operate (Boring admitted that he did this: "[this book] selects that part of the past whose lineal descendants are today important [1950, p. 31].") Science is seen as cumulative and directed to the present, simply because it is written to seem continuous and cumulative. This contributes to the invisibility of scientific revolutions; occurrences that are inherently revolutionary in nature are customarily viewed by the scientist and historian alike not as revolutions but merely as additions to scientific knowledge. Both the historical remarks of practicing scientists and the accounts of historians are geared to portray past achievement as continuous with the ongoing normal science puzzle-solving tradition.

Kuhn captured this state of affairs well when he wrote (1970c):

> Both scientists and laymen take much of their image of creative scientific activity from an authoritative source that systematically disguises—partly for important functional reasons—the existence and significance of scientific revolutions. Only when the nature of that authority is recognized and analyzed can one hope to make historical example fully effective. ... As the source of authority, I have in mind principally textbooks of science together with both the popularizations and the philosophical works modeled on them. ... For reasons that are both

obvious and highly functional, science textbooks (and too many of the older histories of science) refer only to that part of the work of past scientists that can easily be viewed as contributions to the statement and solution of the texts' paradigm problems. Partly by selection and partly by distortion, the scientists of earlier ages are implicitly represented as having worked upon the same set of fixed problems and in accordance with the same set of fixed canons that the most recent revolution in scientific theory and method has made seem scientific. No wonder that textbooks and the historical tradition they imply have to be rewritten after each scientific revolution. And no wonder that, as they are rewritten, science once again comes to seem largely cumulative [pp. 136, 138].

THE "GREAT MAN" APPROACH

Two manifestations of the "great man" approach are current in the psychological literature: the analysis in terms of *individual* great men, and the analysis in terms of *schools* of thought. Let us consider these approaches in turn.

The foremost proponent of the "great man" theme within psychological history is R. I. Watson, and *The great psychologists* (1963) has already become something of a classic. The structure of this book is quite different from Boring's. Watson's 20 chapters deal primarily with individual thinkers—such as Plato, Aristotle, James, Freud, etc.—and his presentation attempts to focus upon the *originality* of these contributors within their historical frames of reference.

Watson said this of history in his preface (1963):

> As in any science, a slow, steady advance is illuminated from time to time by a brilliant step forward. Great men—not science as a reified impersonal force—contribute to these advances. Great men in psychology live on in the work for which they are the inspiration in the field. Without these men, advances would have proceeded less rapidly. The lives; occupations; motives; families; views on fields of knowledge related to psychology; social, political and economic circumstances of each of these men have to be considered if we are to understand them and their contributions to psychology [p. vii].

Thus it is clear that Watson acknowledged the role great men have in determining the zeitgeist and in the origination of scientific discovery. And he was clearly aware of the role of personal and social idiosyncrasies in the originality and creativity of particular men of science.

In subsequent work Watson even evidenced some familiarity with Kuhn's *The structure of scientific revolutions* and some of his other work. Indeed, Watson consciously attempted to apply Kuhnian notions to the history of psychology. But an examination of psychology led Watson to conclude that it has not as yet had anything as "dominant" and as "universally agreed upon" as what Kuhn in 1962 called a "paradigm." Watson wrote (1967):

Psychology has not experienced anything comparable to what atomic theory has done for chemistry, what the principle of organic evolution has done for biology, what laws of motion have done for physics. Either psychology's first paradigm has not been discovered or it has not yet been recognized for what it is. Although the presence of an unrecognized paradigm is not ruled out completely, it would seem plausible to proceed on the assumption that psychology has not yet had its initial paradigmatic revolution [p. 436].

Watson then set himself the task of asking what, if not a Kuhnian paradigm, serves to take its place within psychology.

His answer is that it is a series of contrasting *prescriptions*, of which he has isolated 18 pairs. But what is a prescription, and how does it function? There are two defining characteristics that Watson mentioned (1967):

The overall function of these themes is orientative or attitudinal; they tell us how the psychologist–scientist must or should behave. In short, they have a directive function. . . . The other essential characteristic is that of being capable of being traced historically over some appreciable period of time. On both counts, the term *prescription* seems to have these connotations [p. 437].

Watson presents his prescriptions in one of the ways they function—as contrasting or opposing trends. This is central to their directive–orientative function; they are "habits of thought, methodological and contentual, which [have been] taken from the past" (Watson, 1967, p. 438). On the same page, he also noted that they "are acted upon without examination,... are taken for granted." A further characteristic of Watson's prescriptions is that they endure over time (1967):

In choosing the particular prescriptions with which I deal the presence of historical continuity over at least most of the modern period was a major decisive factor. If an instance of some conception serving a directive function was of relatively short temporal dimension, it was not considered a prescription. It is for this reason that some prominent trends in psychology today do not appear as prescriptions [p. 438].

But he quickly pointed out that "prescriptions are by no means simple, dominant, isolated themes moving monolithically through history [p. 439]."

On the face of it, Watson's analysis of psychological history as the interplay of a complex of polarly opposed prescriptions appears quite removed from Boring's *zeitgeist* interpretation. But one may ask first, "How far removed?" and second, "Are they not *equally* 'cumulative record' or 'building-block' interpretations at an underlying level?" It becomes clear that Watson's approach is a *refinement* within Boring's zeitgeist theoretical framework and that it is equally as "cumulative record" in nature as Boring's account. Let us examine these contentions in turn.

Our first contention would seem to be invalidated by Watson's own reservations about the zeitgeist approach (1967): "One of the puzzling facets of the Zeitgeist theory is just how to account for differential reaction to the same climate of opinion. The prescriptive approach may be helpful in this connection [p. 442]." This passage suggests that Watson was offering prescriptions as a *substitute* for the *zeitgeist* theory. But is that substitution a refinement within the "global" zeitgeist framework, or is it antagonistic to it? Watson leaves little doubt that his position is a refinement within the zeitgeist approach and is perfectly compatible with it (1967):

> When we wish to emphasize the then current intertwined pattern of dominant prescriptions as having a massive cumulative effect, we refer to the *Zeitgeist*. The *Zeitgeist* in itself is empty of content until we describe that which we assign to a particular *Zeitgeist*. The strands that enter into the *Zeitgeist* include the dominant prescriptions of that times. So the *Zeitgeist* and prescriptive concepts are considered complementary [p. 442].

A hint of this interpretation may be found by returning to Watson's *The great psychologists*. There he said in his preface (1963) that:

> In emphasizing the "brilliant steps forward" of a few great psychologists, therefore, I have had to neglect the work of many others who contributed to the steady advance of the field. A chapter on the work of one man in comparison to a hundred years dismissed in a few pages, serves as an inevitable, but necessary distortion of history [p. vii–viii].

We need do little to substantiate our second contention: If the "prescription" approach is a development within the zeitgeist framework, it is the same *kind* of approach. Consider Watson's prefatory remark just quoted that "I have had to neglect the work of many others who contributed to the steady advance of the field." It seems that Watson was merely selecting those "masons" who have cemented more than a few bricks into the edifice of knowledge or those who have done an exceptionally good job with a few bricks and called them "great men." He thus followed in Boring's (1963) footsteps in considering "great men" to be *eponymic* of the era, or zeitgeist, in which they occur. Focusing upon the outstanding individual in history is for Watson no less than for Boring merely one way of studying the zeitgeist. The notion of contrastive prescriptions as the dominant forces in psychological history is merely an attempt to unpack the concept of the zeitgeist in a satisfactory manner (Note 12.3). Watson's attempt to bolster the zeitgeist conception (by supplementing it with the "great man" approach) in no way changes his conception of history as a cumulative endeavor. Regardless of whether the *vehicle* of change is the zeitgeist or the human being, the *nature* of historical change remains the same—the evolutionary accretion of facts and generalizations based upon them and theories based in turn upon the generalizations. This is justificationist historiography no matter what vehicle of change is postulated.

One final feature in Watson's veiwpoint provides a transition to our next topic. That feature is his emphasis on the role of *schools* of psychological thought in the overall integration of the discipline. Watson (1967) felt that "the highest level of integration in psychology is still that of the schools [p. 442]." Watson saw schools of psychological thought as composed of characteristic combinations of prescriptions or, as he called them, *interlocking* prescriptions. Salience or nonsalience of particular prescriptions and of their combination characterizes the "school." He wrote (1967):

> In the preparadigmatic stage of a science, a scientist may also become an adherent to a school, that is to say, he may accept a set of interlocking prescriptions espoused by a group of scientists generally with an acknowledged leader. Functionalism, behaviorism, Gestalt psychology, and psychoanalysis are representative [p. 441].

Let us look briefly at the concept of 'schools' in psychological history to see how it relates to the "great man" and zeitgeist concepts of history.

What was yesterday an excellent contemporary introduction to a field is often today an excellent historical account of that field. This is certainly the case with Edna Heidbreder's *Seven psychologies* (1933). Written when psychology perceived itself to be in an even greater state of flux than it is now, when a very conscious desire to get down to the business of normal science abounded, Heidbreder depicted seven "schools" of psychological inquiry as potential means to that desired normal science. In doing so, Heidbreder acknowledged much more complexity in psychological growth (as is perhaps to be expected of a practicing scientist rather than an historian) than do the majority of building-block theorists. And still more important, Heidbreder explicityly discussed philosophy of science issues related to the practice of psychology. For these and other reasons, *Seven psychologies* is as worthy of study today as in the 1930s.

What does Heidbreder mean by a "school" or a "system" of psychology? Essentially, what she was referring to as a school or system is any attempt to survey the field from a definite point of view in order to organize the discipline's "facts" from that standpoint (1933):

> A system of psychology is an envisagement of the total field of psychology as a consistent and unified whole. It assumes that the apparently chaotic particulars which lie within its domain can, if properly understood, be brought into order and clarity: that the subject-matter can be defined, the central problem stated, the methods of investigation agreed upon, the relations to other bodies of knowledge determined, the elements or basic processes identified, the

distinctive features brought into relief, the general outline or characteristic movement indicated. ... For the essential fact about a system of psychology is the position from which it surveys its field, the vantage-point from which it examines the concrete data of the science and from which it discerns a coherent pattern running through them and giving them unity [pp. 18–19].

Schools as *points of view* lead to research programs in scientific *practice*; as a program for action, the "school" exerts its greatest force upon psychology. Schools, when brought into the laboratory, are *tools* of scientific inquiry (Heidbreder, 1933):

> Systems of psychology are to be regarded not as statements of scientific knowledge, but as tools by which scientific knowledge is produced; not as accounts of scientific fact, but as means of acquiring scientific fact.... They are the tools by which knowledge is extracted, but as different from knowledge as are the instruments from the ore that they expose. They provide zeal for the work, but are as different from work as inspiration is from production. They offer a specific and sometimes glamorous program of action, but the program is not to be confused with accomplishment [pp. 13–14].

She sees in the problem of factual relativity the justification for "schools" as tools of inquiry (1933):

> Why does not psychology turn from its systems and devote itself to collecting the facts it so sorely needs? The answer to this question is the justification of systems: that without the systems few facts would be forthcoming. For scientific knowledge does not merely accumulate; it is far more likely to grow about hypotheses that put definite questions and which act as centers of organization in the quest of knowledge. As a matter of historical fact, science has not grown by following the method Bacon described—that is, by the steady amassing of data and the emergence of generalizations [p. 15].

Heidbreder was well aware that the sensationalist picture of science cannot account for actual scientific growth. She took a seemingly Popperian attitude that science is a matter of *conjectures and refutations* (1933):

> Frequently the victories of science are won through the use of conjectures not yet established by fact, conjectures that become the basis of active and ingenious research especially directed toward that particular body of evidence which will prove or disprove the point at issue. Guesses on the basis of inadequate evidence have proved to be powerful and, in actual practice, indispensable tools, which science regularly employs [p. 15].

And another Popperian theme, learning from trial and error, received prominent mention (Heidbreder, 1933):

> A system may fulfill its function by proving itself either right or wrong, or as is far more likely to be the case, by proving itself partly right and partly wrong. The very errors of systems, especially if they are clear-cut and decisive, may further the cause of science by revealing mistakes that need not be repeated [pp. 15–16].

Further, a familiar Kuhnian theme—that of the social nature of the scientific enterprise—is wedded to the thesis of learning from mistakes. "For the development of science is a vast social enterprise in which an individual's most valuable contributions may be his brilliant mistakes" (Heidbreder, 1933, p. 16).

Thus Heidbreder, like Watson, appears to be far removed from the building-block theory of history and the underlying substratum of justificationist thought. At first blush, there is little in her conception of science that belies any justificational underpinnings or a cumulative record approach to history. Her denial of sensationalism and naive Baconian inductivism, the conception of science as a matter of conjectures and attempted refutations, and the acknowledgment of factual relativity combine to make her philosophy of science far more contemporary than Watson's, despite the 30 years' difference in their publications.

But this appearance of unrelatedness to the received view conception of science is just that—an appearance. Although Heidbreder saw some points that are crucial in a nonjustificaitonal context, her understanding of them was marred by an explicitly justificationist picture of knowlege and scientific inquiry.

Consider first the justificationist conception of scientific knowledge that permeates Heidbreder's account. Recall the concern evidenced in the foregoing "Popperian" quotation for "conjectures not yet *established* [italics added] by fact." The idea that scientific knowledge is established or founded or *proven* is at the heart of justificationism. Nor is this an isolated instance in Heidbreder's account—an incautious formulation for a more truly Popperian conception of "conjectural" knowledge. For although Heidbreder recognized very clearly the difficulties of finding suitable "facts," she accepts them completely with no further questioning once found. After having tested a proposition severely, it is accepted and as Reichenbach and Feigl emphasized, *secured*. Consider this passage (Heidbreder, 1933):

> A person does not look with immediate credulity upon every large nugget of possible knowledge that a fellow-worker offers as a fact. He accepts it only when he has thoroughly assayed it by submitting it to all the critical tests he knows. All this is a tremendously good thing for the young science of psychology. For anything that emerges from this treatment as a fact, making its way against the opposition of very earnest, very belligerent, very persistent criticism must have at its core the streak of stubbornness that makes a fact a fact [p. 6].

Thus not only is knowledge proven assertion for Heidbreder, but it also has a building-block foundation; for once severely tested, it is secured. Once secured, scientific "facts" *must* invariably accumulate.

And the conscious desire of the times, which Heidbreder echoed, that psychology should cease speculating and become a Kuhnian normal science, led her to stress the building-block nature of science. Although Baconian inductivism does not work, it still remains as an implicit ideal in her picture of psychology as a science. As she wrote (1933):

> Psychology can point to no imposing storehouse of facts; it knows that its greatest virtue is its determination to follow the scientific method, and that at its best, it attempts to push that method into a region which hitherto the inquiries of science have not penetrated. Above all, psychology is aware of a great need for the factual substance of which a science is so largely made, and it has learned to look with disapproval, almost with dread, on speculation that is not steadied by the ballast of fact [pp. 7–8].

This quest for building-block, factual normal science goes hand in hand with a distrust fro the proliferation of rival research programs that accompanies each new "school" (Heidbreder, 1933):

> System after system announces its principles, each imposes its order on the facts that arrest its attention, and each puts its case with a degree of plausibility. The difficulty is that they all do so and that they are all more or less at odds with each other. It is significant, too, that the more definitely a system draws the lines of its pattern, the more rigidly it selects its facts; that the clearest and most consistent systems are those most given to denials and exclusions [p. 413].

At this point Heidbreder's concern for cumulative progress overrides the analysis of psychology in terms of schools. The seeming "concilience of inductions" of the disparate schools was seen as pointing to the "true" psychological body of knowledge that ultimately will accumulate *independently* of the schools that produce it. Heidbreder (1933) elaborated:

> The view of psychology as seen through its divergent systems is only one aspect of the whole, and as such, it is partial and to that extent unjust. For there is more in psychology than systems, more even then scattered facts. Running through its factual content, even as seen through the eyes of rival systems, are converging lines of evidence that point to the same conclusions. The most impressive are those marked out by workers who, starting from very different theoretical bases, meet on common ground in the discovery of common facts—or rather, of facts that call for a common interpretation. There is nothing in psychology more promising than the trends of agreement in independent pieces of research that different systems have inspired, trends which may be the beginning of a solid groundwork on which a factual science of psychology will be founded. Systems

may thus serve as the basis of operations which reveal facts that are independent of systems [p. 414].

It is from this consilience of inductively established facts that the truly cumulative science of psychology will hopefully emerge. And it is in that sense that Heidbreder (1933) hoped that the dynamic interplay of the competing schools "is a useful and practical necessary step in the process of bringing objective knowledge into existence [p. vii]" (Note 12.4).

Thus the overall picture of Heidbreder's historiography remains a building-block one despite momentary lapses to acknowledge points that are seemingly incompatible with that approach. Indeed, her entire analysis in terms of schools led her to almost apologize for the sadly unscientific state of psychology. She conveys the impression that were psychology *truly* scientific rather than merely an aspirant to the title, that one all-encompassing normal science research program would render discussion of schools superfluous, a bit of 'prescientific' history. She put it thusly (1933):

> For psychology is a science that has not yet made its great discovery. It has found nothing that does for it what the atomic theory had done for chemistry, the principle of organic evolution for biology, the laws of motion for physics. Nothing that gives it a unifying principle has yet been discovered or recognized. As a rule, a science is presented, from the standpoint of both subject-matter and development, in the light of its great successes. Its verified hypotheses form the established lines about which it sets its facts in order, and about which it organizes its research. But psychology has not yet won its great unifying victory [pp. 425-426].

For Heidbreder, the significant fact about psychology is that it is in "the very midst of the struggle for that command of tools and materials which is characteristic of a mature science [p. 425]," *not* that it is not as yet a "factual" science.

This is coupled to a very 'building-block' conception of the nature of the disagreement between competing schools. Heidbreder felt that although they disagree definitionally and theoretically, the various schools do not deny (or correct) each others' facts. "The disagreements between systems are neither so profound nor so disorganizing as they seem. For the most part, differences in definition involve differences in the selection of facts; they do not imply denial of the facts themselves" (1933, p. 421).

Perhaps our conclusion, that the analysis of psychological history in terms of schools is as equally justificationist and 'building-block' in nature as the others reviewed in this chapter, will seem less startling when the relationship between the "schools" and the "great men" approaches is pointed out. For schools in psychological history appear to be nothing more, nothing less, than extensions to a larger population of the individuality of "great men." This being so, it is not at all surprising that the "schools" approach to the agency of progress in psychology is no more in conflict with the zeitgeist interpretation than is the "great man" approach. As the differences are presently articulated, there is no essential conflict *at all* between these *prima facie* different accounts of history. They *all* manifest the same underlying approach to historiography: the justificationist building-block theory that pictures psychological history as a cumulative record.

CHAPTER NOTES

Note 12.1.   Neojustificationists became so preoccupied with saving the rationality of science (by putting inductive inference on a firm foundation) that they in effect substituted a new idol—that of (statistical) exactness—for the classic justificationist's idol of certainty. With regard to the symbolic and logistic tenor of the logical "-isms," this led Popper to the following comment (1959):

> In this post-rationalist age of ours, more and more books are written in symbolic languages, and it becomes more and more difficult to see why: what it is all about, and why it should be necessary, or advantageous, to allow oneself to be bored by volumes of symbolic trivialities. It almost seems as if the symbolism were becoming a value in itself, to be revered for its sublime 'exactness': a new expression of the old quest for certainty, a new symbolic ritual, a new substitute for religion [p. 394].

Exactly this sort of pseudocertainty is evident on almost every page of the journals of the nascent social sciences and particularly in the "hard-headed" areas of experimental psychology!

Another stifling effect of the preoccupation with symbolic exactitude that Popper (1959) rightly condemns concerns the right to employ "natural" languages and "occult" concepts if the scientist so desires:

> I do not believe in hampering scientific language by preventing the scientist from using freely, whenever it is convenient, new ideas, predicates, 'occult' concepts, or anything else. For this reason, I cannot support the various recent attempts to introduce into the philosophy of science the method of artificial calculi or 'language systems'—systems supposed to be models of a simplified 'language of science'. I believe that these attempts have not only been useless so far, but that they have even contributed to the obscurity and confusion prevalent in the philosophy of science [p. 378].

Note 12.2.   Boring then developed the zeitgeist from which the behaviorist movement arose as an instance of objective psychology. He discussed eight categories of "objective thought" that influenced this zeitgeist, ranging from

Cartesian materialism and French positivism (stemming from Comte), through the Russian "reflexological" and physiological school, the tropism of Loeb, American functionalism, the emphasis on the unconscious, and even the Würzburg School work on the unconsciousness of the contents of thought. After summarizing these movements, Boring said that (1950):

> Objective psychology became *behaviorism* (with the *ism*) in 1913 when John B. Watson initiated his vigorous propaganda against introspection and for an objective psychology. The event provides an excellent example of the way in which movements start, for behaviorism had both positive and negative conscious reasons for being brought forward and supported and there was also operative the unconscious positive influence of the *Zeitgeist*. All three of these factors seem to have been necessary causes of behaviorism, though no one would have been sufficient in itself [p. 641].

The three factors Boring cited are: (a) the inherent interest of the study of behavior per se; (b) the protest against introspectionism; and (c) the zeitgeist.

It is in the now familiar *deus* of the zeitgeist that Boring buried any possibility of a revolutionary interpretation of Watson and his movement (Boring, 1950):

> The unconscious positive influence was, of course, the *Zeitgeist*. Psychology was all ready for behaviorism. America had reacted against its German parentage and gone functional, for reasons which we have already discussed (pp. 505–508). Behaviorism simply took from functionalism part but not all of the parental tradition. Meanwhile objectivism, as we have just been seeing, was growing to include, not only much of functional psychology, but most of psychopathology and all of the mental testing and applied psychology. Behaviorism could simply take over all these fields, and that is what it did more or less—or else it was they which took over behaviorism. At any rate, the times were ripe for more objectivity in psychology, and Watson was the agent of the times [p. 642].

Thus it should be clear that as long as Boring utilized the concept of the zeitgeist as a primary causative agency of historical change, he could not countenance an actual scientific revolution. This is so, because the zeitgeist— as he developed the concept—must be both the common possession of an entire research community (thus effectively excluding *individual* innovation and creativity) and the product of an extended era (the temporal *inertia* of the concept). As long as this conception of the agency of progress is combined with the justificationist conception of knowledge, a building-block interpretation of the nature of scientific progress *must* result. For Boring, the history of psychology *must* be written so that all developments seem to be inevitable way stations toward the goal of the development of contemporary behaviorism (no matter what the state of "contemporary" behaviorism). The problem facing Boring was more to account for why it took so long for

Watson to propagandize behaviorism than to account for the genesis of behaviorism itself. History becomes all but inevitable for a consistent cumulative record theorist (see Agassi, 1963). Such theorists tend to account for lapses from the true path of progress in terms of the individual idiosyncrasies of the individuals who are agents of the zeitgeist. These and other "baffling" aspects of historical development become assimilated to the "personal" nature of history (Boring, 1950):

> Perhaps I should say also why there is so much biographical material in this book, why I have centered the exposition more upon the personalities of men than upon the genesis of the traditional chapters of psychology. My reason is that the history of experimental psychology seems to me to have been so intensely personal. Men have mattered much. Authority has again and again carried the day. What Johannes Müller or Wundt said was nearly always important, quite independently of the weight of experimental evidence for the view of either. Moreover, personalities have been reflected in schools, and the systematic traditions of the schools have colored the research [p. x].

Note 12.3.   It is clear that Watson actually *sees* continuity and cumulative change in history. Considering Kurt Lewin's (1931) discussion of the conflict of Aristotelian and Galilean modes of thought, Watson said (1967):

> They are, in my opinion, not so much a matter of qualitative leaps as they are gradual changes with the older views still very much operative. Lewin's conceptualizing in relation to the historic facts seems similar in spirit to Piaget's brilliant strokes on the process of development. I suspect that if we were to take Lewin as seriously, as did the American investigators who followed the leads of Piaget into painstaking detailed research, we would find that there was much blurring and overlap of these Lewinian shifts, as there seems to be at the Piagetian levels [p. 437].

Note 12.4.   And it is clear that on Heidbreder's account, proponents of different schools have no trouble communicating with one another, for they share a common language with the meanings of its terms specified in advance. On her account, they can and do make their disagreements *perfectly clear* to one another. According to Heidbreder (1933):

> It is interesting to consider how much extra systematic psychology is left standing after the attacks of opposing schools have done their worst; how much groundwork is implied in the fact that they can make their criticisms significant to each other. Not the least enlightening aspect of such controversies is the fact that the antagonists, when pointing a difference, use terms and refer to facts that imply admissions on both sides. They meet on common ground to make their disagreements clear [p. 424].

References

Achinstein, P. *Concepts of science*. Baltimore: Johns Hopkins Press, 1968.

Alexander, H. G. General statements as rules of inference. In H. Feigl, M. Scriven, & G. Maxwell (Eds.), *Minnesota studies in the philosophy of science* (Vol. II). Minneapolis: University of Minnesota press, 1958.

Agassi, J. Towards a historiography of science. *History and theory*, Beiheft 2, Wesleyan University Press, 1963.

Agassi, J. The confusion between science and technology in standard philosophies of science. *Technology and Culture*, 1966, *7*, 348–366. (a)

Agassi, J. Sensationalism. *Mind*, 1966, N. S. Vol. *75*, 1–24. (b)

Agassi, J. The novelty of Popper's philosophy of science. *International Philosophical Quarterly*, 1968, *8*, 442–463.

Arnold, C. C. Reflections on the Wingspread conference. In L. F. Bitzer & E. Black (Eds.), *The Prospect of rhetoric*. Englewood Cliffs, N. J.: Prentice-Hall, 1971.

Arnold, C. C. *Criticism of oral rhetoric*. Columbus, Ohio: Charles E. Merrill, 1974.

Ayer, A. J. Demonstration of the impossibility of metaphysics. *Mind*, 1934, *43*, 335–345.

Ayer, A. J. *Language, truth, and logic*. New York: Dover Publications, 1936; 2nd ed., 1946.

Ayer, A. J. *The foundations of empirical knowledge*. London: Macmillan, 1940.

Ayer, A. J. *Philosophical essays*. London: Macmillan, 1954.

Ayer, A. J. *The problem of Knowledge*. Baltimore: Penguin Books, 1956.

Ayer, A. J. Editor's introduction. In A. J. Ayer (Ed.), *Logical positivism*. Glencoe, Ill.: The Free Press, 1959.

Bartley, W. W., III. *The retreat to commitment*. New York: A. A. Knopf, 1962.

Bartley, W. W., III. Rationality versus the theory of rationality. In M. Bunge (Ed.), *The critical approach*. New York: The Free Press, 1964.

Bartley, W. W., III. Theories of demarcation between science and metaphysics. In I. Lakatos & A. Musgrave (Eds.), *Problems in the philosophy of science*. Amsterdam: North-Holland Publishing Co., 1968.

Bitzer, L. F., & Black, E. (Eds.). *The prospect of rhetoric*. Englewood Cliffs, N. J.: Prentice-Hall, 1971.

Black, M. *Problems of analysis*. London: Routledge, 1954.

Black, M. *Models and metaphors*. Ithaca: Cornell University Press, 1962.

Bohm, D. *The special theory of relativity*. New York: Benjamin, 1965.

Bohm, D. Science as perception–communication. In F. Suppe (Ed.), *The structure of scientific theories*. Urbana: University of Illinois Press, 1974.

Boring, E. G. The problem fo originality in science. *American Journal of Psychology*, 1927, *39*, 70–90.

Boring, E. G. *A history of experimental psychology* (2nd ed.), N. Y.: Appleton–Century-Crofts, 1950.

Boring, E.G. *History, psychology and science: Selected papers*. R. I. Watson & D. T. Campbell (Eds.). New York: John Wiley & Sons, 1963.

Brodbeck, M. Explanation, prediction, and 'imperfect knowledge.' In H. Feigl & G. Maxwell (Eds.), *Minnesota Studies in the Philosophy of Science* (Vol. III). Minneapolis: University of Minnesota Press, 1962.

Bunge, M. *Scientific research (Vols. I, II)*. New York: Springer–Verlag, 1967.

Burke, K. *A grammar of motives*. Englewood Cliffs, N. J.: Prentice–Hall, 1945.

Burke, K. *Counter-statement* (2nd ed.). Englewood Cliffs, N. J.: Prentice–Hall, 1953.

Burke, K. *A rhetoric of motives* (revised edition). Cleveland, Ohio: The World Publishing Co., 1962.

Burke, K. *Language as symbolic action*. Berkeley: University of California Press, 1966.

Burke, K. *The philosophy of literary form*. Baton Rouge: Louisiana State University Press, 1967.

Campbell, N. R. *Physics, the elements*. Cambridge: Cambridge University Press, 1920.

Campbell, N. R. *What is science?* Cambridge: Cambridge University Press, 1921.

Capra, F. *The Tao of physics*. Berkeley: Shambhala, 1975.

Carnap, R. *Der Logische Aufbau der Welt*. Berlin: Weltkris–Verlag, 1928. [*The logical structure of the world*] (Rolf A. George, trans.). Berkeley: University of California Press, 1967.

Carnap, R. [Truth and confirmation]. Original in German as "Wahrheit and Bewahrung," Actes du Congres International de Philosophie Scientifique, 1936. Translated in H. Feigl & W. Sellars (Eds.), *Readings in philosophical analysis*. New York: Appleton–Century–Crofts, 1949.

Carnap, R. *Logical syntax of language*. London: Kegan Paul, 1937.

Carnap, R. Testability and meaning. *Philosophy of Science*, 1936, *3*, 419–471; 1937, *4*, 1–40.

Carnap, R. *Logical foundations of probability*. Chicago: University of Chicago Press, 1950.

Carnap, R. The continuum of inductive methods. Chicago: University of Chicago Press, 1952.

Carnap, R. Psychology in physical language. In A. J. Ayer (Ed.), *Logical positivism*. Glencoe, Ill.: The Free Press, 1959.

Cassirer, E. *The philosophy of symbolic forms* (Vols. I, II, III). New Haven: Yale University Press, 1953, 1955, 1957.

Cavell, S. *Must we mean what we say?* New York: Scribner's, 1969.

Copi, I. M. *Symbolic logic*. New York: Macmillan, 1954.

Craig, W. Replacement of auxiliary expressions. *Philosophical Review*, 1956, *65*, 38–55.

Duhem, P. [*The aim and structure of physical theory*]. Original in French as *La Theorie Physique: Son Objet, Sa Structure*, 1906. Translation of 2nd ed by Princeton University Press, 1954. Reprinted by Atheneum Press, New York, 1962.

Eccles, J. C. The neurophysiological basis of experience. In M. Bunge (Ed.), *The critical approach to science and philosophy*. New York: The Free Press, 1964.

Edwards, W., Lindman, H., & Savage, L. J. Bayesian statistical inference for psychological research. *Psychological Review*, 1963, *70*, 193–242.

Feigl, H. The logical character of the principle of induction. Philosophy of science, 1934, *1*, 20–29. Also in H. Feigl & W. Sellars (Eds.), *Readings in the philosophy of science*. New York: Appleton–Century–Crofts, 1949.

Feigl, H. Operationism and scientific method. *Psychological Review*, 1945, *52*, 250–259.

Feigl, H. Beyond peaceful coexistence. In R. H. Stuewer (Ed.), *Minnesota Studies in the Philosophy of Science* (Vol. V). Minneapolis: University of Minnesota Press, 1970. (a)

Feigl, H. The "orthodox" view of theories: Remarks in defense as well as critique. In M. Radner & S. Winokur (Eds.), *Minnesota studies in the philosophy of science* (Vol. IV). Minneapolis: University of Minnesota press, 1970. (b)

Feyerabend, P. K. Explanation, reduction, and empiricism. In H. Feigl & G. Maxwell (Eds.), *Minnesota studies in the philosophy of science* (Vol. III). Minneapolis: University of Minnesota Press, 1962.

Feyerabend, P. Problems of empiricism. In R. Colodny (Ed.), *Beyond the edge of certainty*. Englewood Cliffs, N. J.: Prentice–Hall, 1965. (a)

Feyerabend, P. Reply to criticism. In R. S. Cohen & M. W. Wartofsky (Eds.) *Boston studies in the philosophy of science*. New York: Humanities, 1965. (b)

Feyerabend, P. Against method. In M. Radner & S. Winokur (Eds.), *Analyses of theories and methods of physics and psychology*. Minneapolis: University of Minnesota Press, 1970. (a)

Feyerabend, P. Consolations for the specialist. In I. Lakatos & A. Musgrave (Eds.), *Criticism and the growth of knowledge*. Cambridge: Cambridge University Press, 1970. (b)

Feyerabend, P. Problems of empiricism, Part II. In R. Colodny (Ed.), *The nature and function of scientific theories*. Pittsburgh: University of Pittsburgh Press, 1970. (c)

Finocchiaro, M. Logic and rhetoric in Lavoisier's sealed note: Toward a rhetoric of science. *Philosophy and Rhetoric*, 1977, *10*, 111–122.

Fisher, R. A. The logic of inductive inference. *Journal of the Royal Statistical Society*, 1935, *98*, 39–54.

Fisher, R. A. *Statistical methods and scientific inference*. Edinburgh: Oliver and Boyd, 1956.

Friedman, R. A. Edwin G. Boring's "mature" view of the science of science in relation to a deterministic personal and intellectual motif. *Journal of the History of the Behavioral Sciences*, 1967, *III*, 17–26.

Gombrich, E. H. *Art and illusion*. London: Phaidon, 1960.

Goodman, N. *The structure of appearance*. Cambridge, Mass.: Harvard University Press, 1951.

Goodman, N. *Fact, fiction, and forecast*. Cambridge, Mass.: Harvard University Press, 1955.

Goodman, N. *Language of art*. New York: Bobbs–Merrill, 1968.

Grünbaum, A. The falsifiability of the Lorenz Fitzgerald contraction hypothesis. *British Journal for the Philosophy of Science*, 1959, *10*, 48–50.

Grünbaum, A. *The philosophy of space and time*. New York: A. A. Knopf, 1963.

Grünbaum, A. Can we ascertain the falsity of a scientific hypothesis? *Studium Generale*, 1969, *22*, 1061–1093.

Grünbaum, A. Is the method of bold conjectures and attempted refutations *justifiably* the method of science? *British Journal for the Philosophy of Science*, 1976, *27*, 105–136.

Hagstrom, W. O. *The scientific community*. New York: Basic Books, 1965.

Hanson, N. R. *Patterns of discovery*. Cambridge: Cambridge University Press, 1958.

Hanson, N. R. A picture theory of theory meaning. In R. Colodny (Ed.), *The nature and function of scientific theories*. Pittsburgh: University of Pittsburgh Press, 1970.

Hayek, F. A. *Individualism and economic order*. Chicago: University of Chicago Press, 1948.

Hayek, F. A. *The counter-revolution of science*. Glencoe, Ill.: The Free Press, 1952. (a)

Hayek, F. A. *The sensory order*. Chicago: University of Chicago Press, 1952. (b)

Hayek, F. A. The primacy of the abstract. In A. Koestler & J. R. Smythies (Eds.), *Beyond reductionism*. New York: Macmillan, 1969.

Hayek, F. A. *Studies in philosophy, politics and economics*. New York: Simon & Schuster, 1967. (Reprinted from University of Chicago Press)

Heidbreder, E. *Seven psychologies*. New York: Appleton-Century-Crofts, 1933.

Hempel, C. G. Studies in the logic of confirmation, I and II. *Mind*, 1945, *54*, 1–26 and 97–121.

Hempel, C. G. The empiricist criterion of meaning. In A. J. Ayer (Ed.), *Logical positivism*. New York: The Free Press, 1959.

Hempel, C. G. Deductive-nomological versus statistical explanations. In H. Feigl & G. Maxwell (Eds.), *Minnesota studies in the philosophy of science* (Vol. III). Minneapolis: University of Minnesota Press, 1962.

Hempel, C. G. *Aspects of scientific explanation and other essays in the philosophy of science*. New York: The Free Press, 1965.

Hempel, C. G. *Philosophy of natural science*. Englewood Cliffs, N. J.: Prentice-Hall, 1966.

Hempel, C. G. On the "standard conception" of scientific theories. In M. Radner & S. Winokur (Eds.), *Minnesota studies in the philosophy of science* (Vol. IV). Minneapolis: University of Minnesota Press, 1970.

Hempel, C. G. Formulation and formalization of scientific theories. In F. Suppe (Ed.), *The structure of scientific theories*. Urbana: University of Illinois Press, 1974.

Hempel, C. G., & Oppenheim, P. Studies in the logic of explanation. *Philosophy of Science*, 1948, *15*, 135–175.

Hesse, M. B. *Models and analogies in science*. Notre Dame: University of Notre Dame Press, 1966.

Hesse, M. B. An inductive logic of theories. In M. Radner & S. Winokur (Eds.), *Minnesota studies in the philosophy of science* (Vol. IV). Minneapolis: University of Minnesota Press, 1970.

Hesse, M. B. Bayesian methods and the initial probabilities of theories. In G. Maxwell & R. M. Anderson, Jr. (Eds.), *Minnesota studies in the philosophy of science* (Vol. VI). Minneapolis: University of Minnesota Press, 1975.

Hintikka, J. The possibility of rules of acceptance. In I. Lakatos (Ed.), *The problem of inductive logic*. Amsterdam: North-Holland, 1968.

Johnstone, H. W., Jr. Some trends in rhetorical theory. In L. F. Bitzer & E. Black (Eds.), *The prospect of rhetoric*. Englewood Cliffs, N. J.: Prentice-Hall, 1971.

Keynes, J. M. *A treatise on probability*. London: Macmillan, 1952. (Originally published, 1921.)

Körner, S. *Experience and theory*. New York: Humanities Press, 1966.

Kuhn, T. S. The essential tension: Tradition and innovation in scientific research. In C. W. Taylor & F. Barron (Eds.), *Scientific creativity: Its recognition and development*. New York: Wiley, 1963.

Kuhn, T. S. Logic of discovery or psychology of research? In I. Lakatos & A. Musgrave (Eds.), *Criticism and the growth of knowledge*. Cambridge: Cambridge University Press, 1970. (a)

Kuhn, T. S. Reflections on my critics. In I. Lakatos & A. Musgrave (Eds.), *Criticism and the growth of knowledge*. Cambridge: Cambridge University Press, 1970. (b)

Kuhn, T. S. *The structure of scientific revolutions* (2nd ed.). Chicago: University of Chicago Press, 1970. (Originally published, 1962). (c)

Kuhn, T. S. Second thoughts on paradigms. In F. Suppe (Ed.), *The structure of scientific theories*. Urbana: University of Illinois Press, 1974.

Kyburg, H. Recent work in inductive logic. *American Philosophical Quarterly*, 1966, *1*, 249–287.

Lakatos, I. Proofs and refutations. *British Journal for the Philosophy of Science*, 1963, *14*, 1–25; 120–139; 221–243; 1964, *15*, 296–342.

Lakatos, I. Changes in the problem of inductive logic. In I. Lakatos (Ed.), *The problem of inductive logic*, Amsterdam: North-Holland Pub. Co. 1968. (a)

Lakatos, I. II—Criticism and the methodology of scientific research programmes. *Proceedings of the Aristotelian Society*, 1968, *69*, 149–186. (b)

Lakatos, I. Falsification and the methodology of scientific research programmes. In I. Lakatos & A. Musgrave (Eds.), *Criticism and the growth of knowledge*. Cambridge: Cambridge University Press, 1970.

Lakatos, I. History of science and its rational reconstructions. In R. Buck & R. S. Cohen (Eds.), *Boston studies in the philosophy of science* (Vol. 8). Dordrecht, Netherlands: D. Reidel Publishing Company, 1971.

Lakatos, I. Popper on demarcation and induction. In P. A. Schilpp (Ed.), *The philosophy of Sir Karl Popper*. La Salle, Ill.: Open Court, 1974.

Laudan, L. *Progress and its problems*. Berkeley: University of California Press, 1977.

Lewin, K. The conflict between Aristotelian and Galilean modes of thought in contemporary psychology. *Journal of Genetic Psychology*, 1931, 5, 141–177.

Lewis, C. I. *Mind and the world order*. Harvard: Harvard University press, 1929. (Reprinted by Dover, 1956.)

Lewis, C. I. *An analysis of knowledge and valuation*. La Salle, Ill.: Open Court, 1946.

Mahoney, M. J. *Scientist as subject: The psychological imperative*. Cambridge, Mass.: Ballinger, 1976.

Mandler, G., & Kessen, W. *The language of psychology*. New York: Wiley, 1959.

Masterman, M. The nature of a paradigm. In I. Lakatos & A. Musgrave (Eds.), *Criticism and the growth of knowledge*. Cambridge: Cambridge University Press, 1970.

Maxwell, G. Induction and empiricism: A Bayesian–frequentist alternative. In G. Maxwell & R. M. Anderson, Jr. (Eds.), *Minnesota studies in the philosophy of science* (Vol. VI). Minneapolis: University of Minnesota Press, 1975.

McKeon, R. Communication, truth, and society. *Ethics*, 1957, 67, 89–99.

McKeon, R. Discourse, demonstration, verification, and justification. *Logique et Analyse*, 1968, 11, 37–92.

Medawar, P. *The art of the soluble*. London: Methueun, 1967.

Merton, R. K. *Social theory and social structure*. Glencoe, Ill. The Free Press, 1968.

Merton, R. K. *The sociology of science: Theoretical and empirical investigations*. Chicago: University of Chicago Press, 1973.

Mitroff, I. I. *The subjective side of science*. New York: Elsevier, 1974.

Morrison, D. E. & Henkel, R. E. *The significance test controversy*. Chicago: Aldine, 1970.

Mulkay, M. J. *The social process of innovation*. London: Macmillan, 1972.

Nagel, E. *The structure of science*. New York: Harcourt and Brace, 1961.

Nagel, E. What is true and false in science: Medawar and the anatomy of research. *Encounter*, 1967, 20, 68–70.

Neyman, J. Outline of a theory of statistical estimation based on the classical theory of probability. *Philosophical Transactions of the Royal Society*, (A), 1937, 236, 333–380.

Neyman, J. L'estimation statistique traitee comme un probleme classique de probabilite. *Actualities Scientifiques et Industrielles*, 1938, 739, 54–57.

Pap, A. *Semantics and necessary truth*. New Haven: Yale University Press, 1958.

Pap, A. *An introduction to the philosophy of science*. Glencoe, Ill.: The Free Press, 1962.

Passmore, J. *A hundred years of philosophy*. Baltimore: Penguin, 1966.

Pepper, S. C. *World hypotheses*. Berkeley: University of California Press, 1942.

Perelman, C. The new rhetoric. *In L. F. Bitzer & E. Black (Eds.), The prospect of rhetoric*. Englewood Cliffs, N. J.: Prentice–Hall, 1971.

Plato. *Gorgias*. (Translated by W. C. Helmbold), The library of liberal arts. Indianapolis: Bobbs-Merrill, 1952.

Plato. *Republic*. (Translated by Benjamin Jowett) in *The dialogues of Plato* (Vol. II). New York: Chas. Scribner's, 1907.

Polanyi, M. *Personal knowledge*. New York: Harper, 1958.

Polanyi, M. *The tacit dimension*. Garden City, N. Y.: Doubleday, 1966.

Popper, K. R. *The logic of scientific discovery*. New York: Harper, 1959. (Originally published as *Logik der Forschung*, Vienna, 1935).

Popper, K. R. *Conjectures and refutations*. New York: Harper, 1963.

Popper, K. R. Normal science and its dangers. In I. Lakatos & A. Musgrave (Eds.), *Criticism and the growth of knowledge.* Cambridge: Cambridge University Press, 1970.

Popper, K. R. *Objective knowledge.* Oxford: Oxford University Press, 1972.

Popper, K. R. Intellectual autobiography and replies to my critics. In P. A. Schilpp (Ed.), *The philosophy of Karl Popper.* (The library of living philosophers, Vols. 14.I, 14.II.) La Salle, Ill.: Open Court, 1974, 3–181; 961–1297.

Radnitzky, G. *Contemporary schools of metascience* (Vols. I and II). New York: Humanities Press, 1970.

Ramsey, F. P. *The foundations of mathematics and other logical essays.* London: Kegan Paul, 1931.

Ravetz, J. R. *Scientific knowledge and its social problems.* Oxford: Oxford University Press, 1971.

Reichenbach, H. *Experience and prediction.* Chicago: University of Chicago Press, 1938.

Reichenbach, H. *The rise of scientific philosophy.* Berkeley and Los Angeles: University of California Press, 1951.

Rescher, N. *Introduction to logic.* New York: St. Martin's, 1964.

Rescher, N. *Scientific explanation.* New York: The Free Press, 1970.

Russell, B. *Problems of philosophy.* London: Oxford University Press, 1912.

Russell, B. *Philosophy.* New York: W. W. Norton, 1927.

Russell, B. *A history of western philosophy.* New York: Simon and Schuster, 1945.

Russell, B. *Human knowledge: Its scope and limits.* New York: Simon and Schuster, 1948.

Rychlak, J. F. *A philosophy of science for personality theory.* New York: Houghton Mifflin, 1968.

Salmon, W. *The foundations of scientific inference.* Pittsburgh: University of Pittsburgh Press, 1967.

Salmon, W. Statistical explanation. In R. Colodny (Ed.), *The nature and function of scientific theories.* Pittsburgh: University of Pittsburgh Press, 1970.

Salmon, W. Confirmation and relevance. In G. Maxwell & R. M. Anderson, Jr. (Eds.), *Minnesota studies in the philosophy of science* (Vol. VI). Minneapolis: University of Minnesota Press, 1975.

Scheffler, I. *Science and subjectivity.* Indianapolis: Bobbs–Merril, 1967.

Schlick, M. The foundations of knowledge. *Erkenntnis,* Vol. IV, 1934. (Translated by D. Rynin in A. J. Ayer [Ed.], *Logical positivism.*) Glencoe, Ill.: The Free Press, 1959.

Schlick, M. Facts and propositions. *Analysis,* 1935, *2,* 65–70.

Schlick, M. Meaning and verification. *Philosophical Review,* 1936, *45,* 449–469. Reprinted in H. Feigl & W. Sellars (Eds.), *Readings in philosophical analysis.* New York: Appleton–Century–Crofts, 1949.

Schlick, M. Positivism and realism. In A. J. Ayer (Ed.), *Logical positivism.* Glencoe, Ill.: The Free Press, 1959.

Scott, R. L., & Brock, B. L. *Methods of rhetorical criticism.* New York: Harper and Row, 1972.

Sellars, W. S. Counterfactuals, dispositions, and the causal modalities. In H. Feigl, M. Scriven, & G. Maxwell (Eds.), *Minnesota studies in the philosophy of science* (Vol. II). Minneapolis: University of Minnesota Press, 1958.

Sellars, W. S. *Science, perception, and reality.* New York: Humanities Press, 1963.

Sellars, W. S. Induction as vindication. *Philosophy of Science,* 1964, *31,* 197–231.

Sellars, W. S. *Science and metaphysics.* New York: Humanities Press, 1968.

Sesonske, A., & Fleming, N. *Plato's Meno: Text and criticism.* Belmont, Calif.: Wadsworth, 1965.

Settle, T. W. The point of positive evidence—Reply to Professor Feyerabend. *British Journal for the Philosophy of Science,* 1969, *20,* 352–355.

Settle, T. W. Induction and probability unfused. In P. A. Schilpp (Ed.), *The philosophy of Karl Popper.* La Salle, Ill.: Open Court, 1974.

Shapere, D. Meaning and scientific change. In R. Colodny (Ed.), *Mind and cosmos: Explorations in the philosophy of science*. Pittsburgh: University of Pittsburgh Press, 1966.

Siu, R. G. H. *The tao of science*. Cambridge, Mass.: M. I. T. Press, 1957.

Spencer Brown, G. *Laws of form*. New York: Julian Press, 1972.

Suppe, F. Editor's introduction. In F. Suppe (Ed.), *The structure of scientific theories*. Urbana: University of Illinois Press, 1974.

Suppes, P. *Introduction to logic*. Princeton: Van Nostrand, 1957.

Tarski, A. *Introduction to logic*. New York: Oxford University Press, 1941.

Tarski, A. The semantic conception of truth and the foundations of semantics. *Philosophy and phenomenological research*, Vol. IV, 1944. Reprinted in H. Feigl & W. Sellars (Eds.), *Readings in philosophical analysis*. New York: Appleton–Century–Crofts, 1949.

Tarski, A. *Logic, semantics, and metamathematics*. Oxford: Clarendon Press, 1956.

Toulmin, S. E. *The uses of argument*. Cambridge: Cambridge University Press, 1958.

Trigg, R. *Reason and commitment*. Cambridge: Cambridge University Press, 1973.

Turner, M. B. *Philosophy and the science of behavior*. New York: Appleton–Century–Crofts, 1967.

Turner, M. B. *Realism and the explanation of behavior*. New York: Appleton–Century–Crofts, 1971.

Turvey, M. T. Construction theory, perceptual systems, and tacit knowledge. In W. B. Weimer & D. S. Palermo (Eds.), *Cognition and the symbolic processes*. Hillsdale, N. J.: Lawrence Erlbaum Associates, 1974.

Wartofsky, M. W. *Conceptual foundations of scientific thought*. New York: Macmillan, 1968.

Watkins, J. W. N. Between analytic and empirical. *Philosophy*, 1957, *32*, 112–131.

Watkins, J. W. N. Confirmable and influential metaphysics. *Mind*, 1958, *67*, 344–365.

Watkins, J. W. N. When are statements empirical? *British Journal for the Philosophy of Science*, 1961, *90*, 287–308.

Watkins, J. W. N. Against normal science. In I. Lakatos & A. Musgrave (Eds.), *Criticism and the growth of knowledge*. Cambridge: Cambridge University Press, 1970.

Watkins, J. W. N. Metaphysics and the advancement of science. *British Journal for the Philosophy of Science*, 1975, *26*, 91–121.

Watson, R. I. *The great psychologists*. Philadelphia: Lippincott, 1963.

Watson, R. I. Psychology: A prescriptive science. *American psychologist*, 1967, *22*, 435–443.

Weimer, W. B. The history of psychology and its retrieval from historiography: I. The problematic nature of history. *Science Studies*, 1974, *4*, 235–258. (a)

Weimer, W. B. The history of psychology and its retrieval from histeriography: II. Some lessons for the methodology of scientific research. *Science Studies*, 1974, *4*, 367–396. (b)

Weimer, W. B. The psychology of inference and expectation. In G. Maxwell & R. M. Anderson, Jr. (Eds.), *Induction, probability, and confirmation*. Minneapolis: University of Minnesota Press, 1975.

Wittgenstein, L. *Tractatus logico-philosophicus*. London: Routledge, 1922.

Ziman, J. *Public knowledge*. Cambridge: Cambridge University Press, 1968.

Author Index

Subject Index

MY JOURNEY

FROM AN IOWA FARM TO A CATHEDRAL OF DREAMS

Faith!
Hope!
Love!

made my
journey unbelievable
See it! and
seize it for
yourself too!

Rev Schuller

Nov. 2001

ROBERT H. SCHULLER